SCOTTISH COMPANY LAW

Cavendish
Publishing
Limited

London • Sydney

SCOTTISH COMPANY LAW

Professor Nicholas Bourne, LLB, LLM (Wales), LLM (Cantab), Barrister
Dean and Professor
Swansea Law School

Brian Pillans, LLB, Diploma in Legal Practice
Lecturer in Law
Glasgow Caledonian University

Cavendish
Publishing
Limited

London • Sydney

First published in Great Britain 1996 by Cavendish Publishing Limited, The Glass House, Wharton Street, London WC1X 9PX, United Kingdom.

Telephone: +44 (0) 171 278 8000   Facsimile: +44 (0) 171 278 8080

E-mail: info@cavendishpublishing.com

Visit our Home Page on http://www.cavendishpublishing.com

Bourne, Nicholas

Scottish Company Law

I Title II Pillans, Brian

344.110666

ISBN 1 85941 204 1

Printed and bound in Great Britain

TO
MY DAUGHTER INEZ

Preface

Two's company but three's a crowd. Too many cooks spoil the broth. You've heard it all before – the more persons involved in an affair, the more likely it is to go wrong. But what has all this to do with company law?

Say you have an 'infallible' business idea but you are broke. What do you do? Do you borrow the necessary resources from someone else, but retain control. If so, and it all goes wrong, you still have to repay the lender, even if it means losing everything you've ever worked for.

Or do you get someone else to join as a partner. Then you'll get some financial input that you won't have to repay if it all goes wrong. But you'll also lose total control and if it does all go wrong, your partner (as well as you) stands to lose everything. Not an incentive for investment!

What about forming a company? With a company you and all of the other investors can measure how much to invest (how much each can afford to lose?). No matter what happens to the business the investors' private pockets are protected – or so it would appear since investors enjoy limited liability. Not only, but also – with a company control does not need to be surrendered to investors. Company law distinguishes between investors (shareholders and debentureholders) and managers (directors). Investors as such enjoy no right to manage the enterprise. This all sounds great – however there is the possibility of exploitation – I set up a company, trade for a period creaming off all of the income for myself, and then the company goes bust – meanwhile I've made a few quid at the expense of other investors and creditors. Is this fair?

There is an inherent tension in company law. It is supposed to facilitate an environment which encourages entrepreneurs to take (calculated) risks by cushioning against the possible negative effects. At the same time, company law needs to regulate the environment to reduce the possibility of exploitation and fraud. Since it did not get it right first time, company law can be regarded as reactionary – it creates an environment within which enterprising individuals find loopholes to exploit. The government closes these loopholes, and so those who can no longer exploit them set off in search of new ones – and so it goes on.

This perhaps begins to explain the bewildering array of rules governing the corporation and the relationships between those involved. This book attempts to explore at least some of these rules and the reasons for their existence. It is designed to give a snapshot depicting how in general the law regulates and deals with the various problems and practicalities confronting companies and those concerned with their finance and management.

This book is designed for all students studying company law in Scotland. It examines the major Scottish statutory and common law rules regulating companies. Although company law is at first sight very similar both north and south of the border, the book considers the effect of the differing backgrounds of the respective legal systems on the contemporary law in each jurisdiction. Although it looks at company law from a Scottish perspective, it attempts to draw the reader's attention to those areas where English law is different.

I am immensely grateful to my colleagues at Glasgow Caledonian University, particularly Aidian O'Donnell, Con McMahon and Tom McDonnell, whose constructive criticism has been invaluable, and to the staff at Cavendish for their patience!

Brian Pillans
January 1996

Contents

Table of Cases

Table of Statutes

Chapter 1

Introduction

When a group of businessmen get together and decide to start a business, one decision that they will need to make early on is whether to operate as a company or as a partnership. There are certain advantages, and indeed certain disadvantages, that attach to incorporation. The following are therefore matters which businessmen will need to consider. The essence of the company is that it is a completely separate person in law, see *Salomon v A Salomon & Co Ltd* (1897) (see para 2.1). Although a Scottish partnership, unlike its English counterpart, does have a personality of its own, its personality is limited. Thus, unlike a company, a partnership cannot own heritable property (land and buildings) in its own name and a court decree obtained against a firm can be enforced against the individual partners personally. From this very basic difference between the company and the partnership flow many of the advantages and disadvantages of incorporation.

The most obvious advantage in incorporation is the access to limited liability. Not all companies are limited companies. Unlimited companies do not need to file accounts so sometimes this is an attraction for businessmen. However, the possibility of limiting the liability of the participators to the amount of the issued shares is an attractive one. Sometimes this advantage is, of course, more apparent than real. If a small private company goes to a bank and asks to borrow a large sum of money, the bank is unlikely to be satisfied with the possibility of recourse against the company's assets. In practice the bank manager will require some collateral security from the company's directors. In a partnership, however, all the partners will have unlimited liability for the business's debts and liabilities. This is the case except in a limited partnership governed by the Limited Partnerships Act 1907. In a limited partnership, however, only sleeping partners may have limited liability and it is not possible to form a partnership made up entirely of limited partners. There must always be somebody who is 'picking up the tab' with no limitation of liability.

A further advantage of the company is the possibility of separating ownership from control. In a partnership all of the partners are agents for the firm. In a company, and this is particularly the case in public companies, the ownership and the control are separated. Those people owning the share capital will not generally be the people who are running the

1.1   A company or a partnership

business (however, in private companies, the owners and the managers may well be the same).

An attraction of incorporation is what is sometimes termed perpetual succession. This means that the company need never die. Companies do go into liquidation but they need not do so. There is no theoretical reason why a company cannot go on for ever. The Hudson's Bay Company has been running for well over 300 years, for example. A company will retain its personality, regardless of any changes made to its name, membership or board of directors – see *Vic Spence Associates v Balchin* (1990). In the case of partnerships, however, wherever there is a change of partners, there has to be a drawing up of partnership accounts and, in principle, a reformation of the partnership.

Incorporation is an attractive business medium where the participators wish to be able to transfer their shares at some later stage. In a company, shares are freely transferable, subject to the terms of the articles of association and the memorandum of association (Chapters 5 and 6). In a partnership, by contrast, a partner's share is not so transferable unless the agreement so provides. The advantage of transferability is seen at its clearest where a company is quoted on the Stock Exchange or the Alternative Investment Market. At this stage, there will be a market mechanism for disposing of and purchasing shares.

It is said to be easier to raise finance where a company is formed as opposed to a partnership. Clearly, if a company is quoted, it has access to the Stock Exchange to raise finance by issuing its shares and debentures (collectively called securities) to the public (Chapter 4). In the case of debentures, these may be secured by a floating charge over all of the company's assets and undertaking (Chapter 18). The device of the floating charge is unique to the company and thus a partnership cannot take advantage of this means of raising finance.

It is probably the case that there is more prestige attached to the company than to the partnership. There is no reason that this should be the case but probably the trading and investing public sees a company in a more favourable light than a partnership.

A further consideration, although it might not be an advantage for companies, is taxation. Companies will pay corporation tax on their profits. These profits may then be distributed as dividends to members who may be liable to pay tax on the dividend less any ACT (advance corporation tax) that has already been paid by the company. In the case of partnerships, the profits of the partnership business are attributable to the partners of the firm who will pay schedular income tax on those profits. It is not possible to say in isolation from factors concerning the circumstances of the participators and their other sources of income whether this is an advantage or not. It will depend on the circumstances.

The disadvantages that attach to incorporation are not numerous. There are clearly formalities to be complied with. A partnership agreement need not even be written. Clearly it is desirable to have a written agreement for evidential purposes but there is no legal reason why the agreement should be in writing. Companies are subject to a comprehensive code of rules contained in the Companies Act 1985 and elsewhere, the partnership is not subject to a detailed statutory regime although the Partnership Act 1890 does set out some rules.

In the case of a company, there are various formalities to be complied with. A constitution has to be drafted, made up of a memorandum of association and articles of association (Chapters 4 and 5). These documents have to be delivered to the registrar of companies at Companies House in Edinburgh (Cardiff in the case of English and Welsh companies) together with a statement of capital and a declaration of compliance. A certificate of incorporation will then be issued to the company. There are various ongoing formalities for a company including the filing of an annual return, the filing of annual accounts (unless the company is unlimited) and the filing of various forms connected with changes of directors, issue of shares, issue of debentures, change of company secretary etc. Companies also have to comply with formalities regarding the holding of meetings which is not the case in a partnership. Private companies may dispense with the need to hold an annual general meeting by unanimous resolution (see para 15.5.9).

Together with these formalities, there is the disadvantage of publicity in the case of the company. This is generally seen as a disadvantage as a company has no option but to make certain of its affairs public. These would include the company's directors, company secretary, the accounts of the company (unless unlimited), the annual return of the company, the company's constitution and various registers that have to be kept at the company's registered office.

Together with formalities and publicity, one may add expense as a disadvantage. However, the expense of setting up a company is not great. There is a charge for the issue of a certificate of incorporation and an annual fee for filing the company's annual return but few other charges are made by the company's registry. The cost of the annual audit may well be a deterrent, however, in the case of a limited company, although small private companies may be exempt from this requirement (see para 16.1).

Two other disadvantages of incorporation may be mentioned here. These are the rules on the maintenance of capital that apply to companies and which are much stricter than in relation to partnerships and the remaining rules on *ultra vires* that limit a company's freedom of manoeuvre. Partnerships by contrast are free to do what is legal within the law of the land.

1.2   Types of companies

There are various classifications of companies that may be made.

1.2.1   Chartered company

A company may be chartered, ie set up by a charter from the Crown, and may then derive its powers from the charter. The very first companies were of this variety, for example, the East India Company, the Massachusetts Bay Company, the Hudson's Bay Company. Today chartered companies are not of economic significance but they still exist. Generally they are not trading concerns. They may be professional organisations – the Institute of Chartered Accountants in Scotland is an example. Perhaps the most famous chartered company of them all is the British Broadcasting Corporation.

1.2.2   Statutory company

A further type of company is the statutory company. In Victorian England there was a great plethora of incorporations. Each company had to be set up by a separate act of parliament. During this period of industrial revolution, the great mass of companies involved public utilities such as gas and water, or transportation such as canal companies and railway companies. Today there are few statutory companies. The process is too cumbersome for periods of massive economic activity, as each company is incorporated by a separate act of parliament. However, the remaining nationalised industries are statutory companies, for example British Coal.

1.2.3   Registered company

The third type of company in this classification is the most common of all. This is the registered company. Registered companies originated with the Joint Stock Companies Act of 1844 when Gladstone was President of the Board of Trade. The current Companies Act under which registration may be sought by companies is the Companies Act of 1985. Provided a company complies with the formalities set out in the Act, it will be registered ie its name will be added to the list of registered companies and a file will be opened in its name at Companies House in Edinburgh. In fact today clearly a manual register is not opened, the company's registered details are kept on microfiche which is available for inspection at Edinburgh (or in Cardiff and London for English companies).

Another form of classification of companies is the distinction between a company limited by shares, a company limited by guarantee, a company limited by guarantee with share capital and an unlimited company.

> **1.2.4 Limited and unlimited company**

Most companies are limited by shares. Trading companies will need to raise share capital with which to purchase assets which they need for running their businesses. Companies limited by guarantee are the media, usually utilised by charities including educational institutions such as the London School of Economics. Such companies do not need capital with which to trade but may wish to have some of the other advantages of incorporation such as the ability to hold property in their own name. Since the Companies Act 1980, it has not been possible to create new companies limited by guarantee with a share capital but there are some companies falling into this category which existed in 1980 and remain registered companies. If the company is an unlimited one, as has already been mentioned, there will be no obligation to file annual accounts. However, this advantage must be balanced against the disadvantage that the members of the unlimited company will have unlimited liability and may be called upon to contribute to the company's assets if the company goes into liquidation.

A fundamental distinction which pervades the whole of company law is the distinction between public and private companies. Most companies are private but the more important larger companies are public companies. The basic distinction is that a public company may offer its shares and debentures to the public whilst it is a criminal offence for a private company to do so. See the Financial Services Act 1986, ss 143(3), 170 and 171(3). A further distinction is the capital requirement first introduced in the Companies Act 1980 which requires that a public company must have a minimum subscribed share capital of £50,000 (s 11 of the Companies Act 1985). This must be paid up to at least 25% so at least £12,500 must already have been raised by the issue of shares. A public company must furthermore have a trading certificate before it begins trading in addition to its certificate of incorporation (s 117 of the Companies Act 1985). This trading certificate will only be issued once the registrar of companies is satisfied that the company has satisfied the formalities of the Act and raised the required minimum capital.

> **1.2.5 Public and private company**

The name of the company will indicate whether the company is public or private. The description 'public limited company' or as abbreviated 'plc' (or Welsh equivalent 'ccc' and 'cwmni cyhoeddus cyfyngedig') will indicate that the company is a public one. By contrast if the company is expressed to be 'limited' or as abbreviated 'ltd' or 'cyfyngedig' or as abbreviated 'cyf', the company is a private company. If a company is registered as a public company this fact must be stated in its memorandum (s 25(1) of the Companies Act 1985). A private company need not state what kind of company it is in its memorandum. There are various other distinctions between public and private companies. It suffices to mention a few at this stage. The company secretary of a public company needs to have a relevant qualification as set out in s 286 of the Companies Act 1985 (see para 17.4). There is no such requirement for the company secretary of a private company. A public company needs to have at least two members and two directors, by contrast a private company now only needs one member and one director. There are various other distinctions which will be examined in this exposition of company law.

Introduction

A company is a completely separate entity in law and certain advantages flow from this:

A company or a partnership

- access to limited liability;

- separation of ownership from control;

- perpetual succession;

- transferability of shares;

- raising finance.

A partnership may be set up without formalities, without publicity and without expense, although a Scottish partnership has an incomplete legal personality.

The profits of a company are subject to corporation tax, the profits of a partnership are subject to schedular income tax in the hands of the partners.

There are various classifications of companies:

Types of company

- companies may be chartered, statutory or registered. The vast majority are registered;

- companies may be limited by shares, limited by guarantee or unlimited. A few are limited by guarantee with a share capital. Unlimited companies do not need to file annual accounts;

- an important distinction is between private companies and public companies. Most companies are private, but only public companies can offer their shares or debentures to the public. All companies quoted on the Stock Exchange are public.

Chapter 2

The *Salomon* Principle and the Corporate Veil

Aron Salomon and his boot and shoe business have done for company law what Mrs Carlill and her smoke ball did for the law of contract and what Mrs Donoghue and her allegedly adulterated ginger beer did for the law of delict.

Mr Salomon transferred his business to a limited company and he and six other members of his family subscribed the company's memorandum: the purchase price was £38,782. Salomon took 20,001 shares and the six other family members took one share each. Debentures (loan stock) of £10,000 and £8,782 cash were paid to Salomon as the balance of the purchase price. The business floundered and was wound up with liabilities in excess of its assets by £7,733. The company's liquidator claimed that the company's business was still Salomon's in that the company was merely a sham to limit Salomon's liability for debts incurred in carrying it on and the repayment of Salomon's debenture should be postponed until the company's other creditors were satisfied. At first instance Vaughan Williams J agreed with the liquidator. He held that Salomon's sole purpose in forming the company was to use it as an agent to run his business for him.

The Court of Appeal reached the same conclusion but for different reasons. It took the view that the principle of limited liability was a privilege conferred by the Companies Acts only on genuinely independent shareholders and not on 'one substantial person and six mere dummies'.

The House of Lords unanimously reversed the Court of Appeal. Lord Halsbury LC in *Salomon v A Salomon & Co Ltd* (1897) said:

> I must pause here, to point out that the statute enacts nothing as to the extent or degree of interest which may be held by each of the seven (subscribers) or as to the proportion of influence possessed by one or the majority of the shareholders over the others. One share is enough. Still less is it possible to contend that the motive of becoming shareholders or of making them shareholders is a field of enquiry which the statute itself recognises as legitimate, if there are shareholders, they are shareholders for all purposes; and even if the statute was silent as to the recognition of trust, I should be prepared to hold that if six of them were the *cestuis que* trust of the seventh, whatever might be their rights *inter se*, the statute would have made

2.1   Introduction

them shareholders to all intents and purposes with their respective rights and liabilities, and dealing with them in their relation to the company, the only relations which I believe the law would sanction would be that they were corporators of the body corporate.

This case thus established one of the basic articles of faith of British company law, indeed of company law of all common law systems, that a company is a legal person independent and distinct from its shareholders and its managers.

Salomon has long been accepted as the leading authority on separate personality in Scotland, although the Scottish courts were independently reaching similar decisions in contemporary cases – see, for example, *Grierson, Oldham & Co Ltd v Forbes, Maxwell & Co Ltd* (1895) where after contracting with the defenders, a company transferred its undertaking to another company formed specifically for that purpose. It was held that the successor company had an independent personality from that of its predecessor and therefore had no title to sue the defenders.

The principle of separate identity has been consistently applied.

In Scotland, for example, it has been held that the members of a company could not challenge a firm of solicitor's fees in respect of advice given by the firm to the company – *Davidson & Syme WS v Kaye* (1970). An action against the solicitors was only available to the company – in this situation represented by its liquidator. Likewise, in *P Boyes Contracts Ltd v Marden Investment Co* (1994), the Outer House held that a company could not sue in respect of poor advice it had obtained on directors' pension schemes, since the schemes were for the exclusive benefit of directors and therefore the company could not suffer any loss.

In *FJ Neale (Glasgow) Ltd v Vickery* (1973), the Sheriff Court declared that where a company in financial difficulties changed its name, and those in control of the company formed a new company using the original name of the pre-existing company, the two companies retained separate personas. Therefore a contract entered into in the common name prior to the incorporation of the new company could not be enforced against the new company.

In the New Zealand case of *Lee v Lee's Air Farming Ltd* (1961), which went to the Privy Council, Lee owned all the shares but one in the company that he founded. His wife held the other share. Lee was governing director of the company whose business was spraying crops from the air. When he was killed in a flying accident while on company business, his widow was held to be entitled to recover compensation from the company for his estate as the company was quite separate and distinct from her husband its employee.

In *Macaura v Northern Insurance Company* (1925), where the owner of a timber business incorporated the business but continued to insure the property in his own name, it was held when the property was destroyed that he had no insurable interest and so could not claim on the policy. The property was no longer his, it now belonged to the company. Interestingly on similar facts the Supreme Court of Canada reached a different decision in *Constitution Insurance Co of Canada v Kosmopoulos* (1987).

In *Adams v Cape Industries plc* (1990), the Court of Appeal held that an English company whose business was mining asbestos in South Africa was not present in the United States through another member of the corporate group. The Court of Appeal was restrictive in its approach to lifting the veil confining it to cases of agency, cases of interpretation of a statute or document and cases where the company is a mere sham.

The principle of separate identity was restated by Lightman J in *Acatos & Hutcheson plc v Watson* (1995). He considered that the principle of separate identity should be upheld unless there was a specific statutory provision or some other contractual term or established common law principle to the contrary. He said at p 223 'outside these exceptions [the company] is entitled to organise and conduct its affairs in the expectation that the court will apply the principle of *Salomon v A Salomon & Co Ltd* in the ordinary way'. The case concerned the company acquiring all the issued share capital of a company called Acatos Ltd and Acatos & Hutcheson plc sought a declaration that the proposal did not fall foul of s 143 of the Companies Act 1985 prohibiting a company from purchasing its own shares (see para 9.2).

However, the principle in *Salomon's* case does give way to exceptions. These are of two types: statutory and judicial.

Under s 24 of the Companies Act 1985 (except in the case of one member private companies which have been possible since July 1992), if a company carries on business without at least two members and does so for more than six months, any person who is a member of the company during any period thereafter and who knows that the company is carrying on

2.2   Exceptions to the *Salomon* principle

2.2.1   Statutory exceptions

business with one member is liable jointly and severally with the company for its debts contracted during that period.

If a company seal is used or if a letter, notice, bill of exchange, order for goods or money etc is issued on behalf of a company and it does not bear the correct company name, the officer or agent who took or authorised this action becomes liable to the holder of the document bearing the incorrect name unless the company honours the obligation. He is also liable to a fine (s 349(4) of the Companies Act 1985).

Perhaps the most obvious incidence of this would be where the word 'limited' is omitted from the company's name when the company is a limited one. Thus, in *British Airways Board v Parish* (1979), a director signed a company cheque and failed to put the word 'limited' at the end of the company name. The cheque was dishonoured and the payee agreed with the company that it should pay the due amount by instalments. It was held that this did not absolve the director from his statutory liability.

However, it was held in *Jenice Ltd v Dan* (1993) that the omission of the first 'e' in 'Primekeen' did not result in personal liability since it was unrealistic to say that 'Primkeen Ltd' did not represent the company name.

This issue also arose in *John Wilkes (Footwear) Ltd v Lee International (Footwear) Ltd* (1985) where the Court of Appeal held that a director was not liable where there was no evidence that he had authorised his fellow director to sign without using the company's proper name.

It is immaterial that the other party to the agreement has not been misled by the misdescription of the company.

Certain abbreviations are accepted. These are as follows:

ltd = limited or cyf = cyfyngedig (Welsh equivalent)

plc = public limited company, or

ccc = cwmni cyhoeddus cyfyngedig (Welsh equivalent)

It has also been held that it is acceptable to abbreviate the word 'company' to 'co' (*Banque de l'Indochine et de Suez SA v Euroseas Finance Company Limited* (1981)).

If the company's business has been carried on with intent to defraud creditors or for any fraudulent purposes, the court, on the application of the liquidator, may declare that the persons who were knowingly parties to the fraud are liable to make such contributions (if any) to the company's assets as the court thinks proper (s 213 of the Insolvency Act 1986). This section has a criminal counterpart in s 458 of the Companies

Act 1985. The section is applicable not merely to directors but to other persons who are trading through the medium of the company. By contrast, s 214 of the Insolvency Act 1986 which deals with wrongful trading empowers the court to make a declaration in the situation of insolvent liquidation against a person who was a director or shadow director who knew or ought to have known that there was no reasonable prospect of the company avoiding insolvent liquidation. See *Re Produce Marketing Consortium Limited (No 2)* (1989).

There are some other situations in respect of insolvency where the veil is lifted. Section 216 of the Insolvency Act makes it an offence for a person who is a director or shadow director of a company that has gone into insolvent liquidation to be in any way concerned in the next five years in the formation or management of a company with a name similar to that of the original company. Section 217 makes such persons personally liable in such a situation.

A further provision applicable in situations of insolvency is s 15 of the Company Directors Disqualification Act 1986 which provides that a person who has been disqualified from acting in the management of a company is personally liable for the company debts if he acts in contravention of this order.

In the case of a public limited company, if it acts before it has obtained its trading certificate, then the company and its officers are liable to fines. Furthermore, if the company fails to comply with its obligations within 21 days, the directors of the company are liable to a third party in respect of any loss or damage suffered (s 117(8) of the Companies Act 1985).

Group accounts have to be filed where companies are in a group. This is in addition to the separate sets of accounts that have to be filed for each of the constituent companies. In order to determine if a company is part of a group, clearly the veil is being lifted. To determine if a holding/subsidiary relationship exists, it is necessary to examine ownership of the shares, membership of the board of directors, or control of the board or company in general meeting (s 227 of the Companies Act 1985 and Sched 4a).

There are many other statutory examples. For example, s 414 of the Income and Corporation Taxes Act 1988 defines 'close companies' in terms of the number of people exercising control over the company.

It is difficult to identify a consistent thread running through the decided cases indicating when the veil will be lifted. It seems to be as the American Realists (commenting on the nature of legal decisions) indicate, dependent on the particular judge and what the judge has had for breakfast!

2.2.2   Judicial lifting of the veil

However, it is possible to identify certain consistent themes.

<table>
<tr><td>2.2.3</td><td>Fraud situations</td></tr>
</table>

The court will lift the veil to prevent fraud or sharp practice. In *Jones v Lipman* (1962), a vendor of land sought to evade a decree of specific performance of a contract for the sale of a piece of land by conveying the land to a company which he had purchased for the purpose of sidestepping the obligation.

The court held that the acquisition of the company and the conveyance of the land to it was a mere 'cloak or sham' to evade the contract of sale. The veil was lifted.

In *Gilford Motor Co v Horne* (1933), an employee who was subject to a restraint of trade clause set up a company to circumvent the restriction. He claimed that the company was not bound by the restrictive covenant as it was a separate legal person distinct from himself and was not a party to the contract between him and his former employer. He proceeded to operate a garage in Highgate, London through the company in competition with his former employer. The company's shares were allotted to his wife and an employee of the company who were appointed directors. The court held that since the defendant in reality controlled the company, its formation was a sham. An injunction was therefore issued against him restraining him from competing through the medium of the company. Likewise, in *Creasey v Breachwood Motors* (1992), where Company A (with a contingent liability to X) transferred all of its business and assets to Company B, it was held appropriate to lift the veil to determine whether Company B should replace Company A as defendant in proceedings brought by X (for unfair dismissal). A similar desire to prevent abuse is evident in *Re Bugle Press Ltd* (1960). The issued capital of Bugle Press Ltd was £10,000. £4,500 each was held by two directors Jackson and Shaw. The applicant Treby held the other £1,000 of shares. Jackson and Shaw formed another company of which they were the only two members and this company offered to acquire all the shares of Bugle Press Ltd. The intention of Jackson and Shaw was to compulsorily acquire the shares of Treby under the ss 428–430F procedures of the Companies Act 1985. In short, they were using the takeover provisions to rid themselves of a difficult dissentient member. The court held that Treby was entitled to a declaration that Jackson and Shaw could not acquire his shares as the offeror and the holders of 90% of the acquired company were the same and the section was being used to expropriate a minority shareholder.

Fraud was also at issue in *Wallersteiner v Moir* (1974). In this case, the defendant Moir had accused the plaintiff of a number of fraudulent acts. The court had to consider whether a loan made by a company to another company which was under the control of its director was illegal under the Act. Section 190 of the Companies Act 1948 (now s 330 of the Companies Act 1985) prohibited the giving of a loan to a director. Lord Denning MR considered that the company was the puppet of Dr Wallersteiner as the company was his creature and therefore that the loan should be treated as a loan made to him.

Another situation where the veil is often lifted is in group situations where the parent company and a subsidiary are treated as one entity if they carry on the same business. The principle does not seem to be consistently applied, however. In *Smith, Stone & Knight Ltd v Birmingham Corporation* (1939), the court treated a subsidiary company as the agent of its holding company (an approach that is at odds with the decision in the *Salomon* case itself).

2.2.4   Group situations

Similarly, in *Firestone Tyre & Rubber Co Ltd v Lewellin* (1957), an American company which operated through a wholly owned subsidiary in England was held liable to pay United Kingdom tax as the American company was carrying on business in the United Kingdom through the subsidiary.

In contrast, in *Harold Holdsworth & Co (Wakefield) Ltd v Caddies* (1955), the question arose as to whether the director of a holding company could be assigned duties in relation to subsidiary companies. The House of Lords held that this was indeed possible on the basis that the companies were part of the same group enterprise.

In *DHN Food Distributors Ltd v Tower Hamlets London Borough Council* (1976), the Court of Appeal had to consider a case involving the expropriation of property. A company, DHN Food Products, was formed to carry on the business of importing and distributing groceries. The premises the company traded from were in fact owned by Bronze, a wholly owned subsidiary of DHN. Bronze and DHN had the same directors. The London Borough of Tower Hamlets acquired the property to build houses on the site. Compensation was payable under the relevant legislation for loss of title. Compensation was also payable for disturbance of the business. However, compensation for disturbance of the business was only payable if the business disturbed belonged to the title holder. The operator of the business here was the holding company, the title holder was the subsidiary company.

The Court of Appeal treated the companies as one entity. Lord Denning MR said:

We all know that in many respects a group of companies are treated together for the purpose of general accounts,

> balance sheets, profit and loss account. They are treated as
> one concern ... This is especially the case when a parent
> company owns all the share of the subsidiaries, so much
> so that it can control every movement of the subsidiaries.

In *Nicholas v Soundcraft Electronics Ltd* (1993), the question
arose as to whether the withholding of money due from a
holding company to a subsidiary company and the refusal to
pay such money could amount to unfairly prejudicial conduct
in the affairs of the subsidiary company under s 459 of the
Companies Act 1985. The Court of Appeal held that, as a
matter of law, this could constitute conduct in the affairs of the
company, although on the facts it was held not to be unfairly
prejudicial. Similarly, in *Kalamazoo v Rice* (1994), the Court of
Appeal held that misrepresentations made by a holding
company to a prospective franchisee of its subsidiary could
arguably be relied upon by the franchisee to avoid a franchise
agreement subsequently entered into with the subsidiary.

The approach, however, is not consistent. In *Lonrho v Shell
Petroleum* (1982), the House of Lords considered a claim by the
plaintiff for discovery of documents in the possession of
companies that were wholly owned subsidiaries of the
defendant companies. The wholly owned subsidiaries were
incorporated and resident in South Africa and Zimbabwe (or
Southern Rhodesia as it then was). The House of Lords took
the view that even though these companies were wholly
owned subsidiaries, there was a degree of autonomy
consequent upon these companies operating overseas. It felt
that it was inappropriate to lift the veil in such a situation
distinguishing *DHN Food Distributors Ltd v Tower Hamlets
London Borough Council* (1976). Interestingly, the Court of
Appeal had taken the same view as the House of Lords and
Lord Denning MR had stated that the parent companies had
no 'power' over the subsidiaries. He considered the case to be
quite different from the *DHN* case.

Similar issues were raised in *Woolfson v Strathclyde Regional
Council* (1979). The House of Lords in this case considered the
situation where a compulsory purchase order had been made
over certain shops in Glasgow. The shops were owned by
Solomon Woolfson and by Solfred Holdings Ltd, the shares of
which were held at two thirds by Woolfson and one third by
Woolfson's wife. The shop premises were occupied by a
company called M & L Campbell (Glasgow) Ltd which
operated the business of costumiers of wedding garments. The
share capital of Campbell was 1,000 shares of which 999 of
these shares were held by Woolfson, the remaining share by
his wife. Woolfson was the sole director of Campbell and he
managed the business. His wife also worked for Campbell and

provided valuable expertise in relation to the selling of the garments. Woolfson & Solfred Holdings Ltd claimed compensation for disturbance of the business. They argued that the business carried on on the premises was truly their business, conducted by Campbell as their agent so that since they were the true occupiers of the premises, they were also entitled to compensation for disturbance. They placed reliance upon the decisions in *Smith, Stone & Knight Ltd v Birmingham Corporation* and *DHN Food Distributors Ltd v Tower Hamlets London Borough Council*.

Lord Keith in the course of his judgment in the House of Lords considered that the case was distinct from the decision in *DHN Food Distributors*. The position in that case, his Lordship said, was that compensation for disturbance was claimed by a group of three limited companies. In the case before him, the company that carried on the business, Campbell, had no control whatever over the owners of the land, Solfred & Woolfson. In fact, in commenting on *DHN Food Distributors* he said, 'I have some doubts whether in this respect the Court of Appeal properly applied the principle that it is appropriate to pierce the corporate veil only where special circumstances exist indicating that it is a mere façade concealing the true facts'.

However, the Inner House in *City of Glasgow District Council v Hamlet Textiles Ltd* (1986) allowed a hearing to proceed to determine the extent of a Scottish holding company's interest in property in Glasgow, ostensibly owned by its subsidiary company which was resident in London. The property in question had been damaged by fire and Glasgow District Council were seeking recovery of the cost of its demolition.

It may be seen that it is sometimes difficult to reconcile the decisions in this area.

There are numerous other decisions where the veil has been lifted. It is difficult to classify these cases. It is therefore appropriate to examine this *pot pourri* of cases.

2.2.5 Miscellaneous situations

A decision of all the members of a company may be binding as a company decision notwithstanding that the decision has not been taken at a company meeting. To determine if the decision is one of all the members the veil has clearly to be lifted, see for example *Re Express Engineering Works Ltd* (1920).

The veil may also be lifted to determine a company's nationality by reference to the nationality of its members. This occurred in *Re FG Films Ltd* (1953) where the court held that the film 'Monsoon' (never an international blockbuster!) was not a British film. Although the company producing it was incorporated in England, it was controlled by an American corporation.

In *Daimler Co Ltd v Continental Tyre & Rubber Co (GB) Ltd* (1916), the House of Lords decided that the company, although it was incorporated in England, was an enemy alien as all of its shareholders were German. In *Trebanog Working Mens Club & Institute Ltd v Macdonald* (1940), the device of the trust was used to circumvent the principle of separate personality. A club incorporated to provide leisure facilities for its members purchased alcohol. The alcohol was sold to the members. The club was prosecuted for selling alcohol without a licence. The court acquitted the club of the charge since it was held that there was no sale as the members in reality owned the alcohol which was purchased on their behalf by the committee of the club. It was held that the club held the alcohol as trustee for its members and that therefore the beneficial ownership in the alcohol was vested in the members collectively with the result that there was not a sale at all and therefore no criminal offence.

2.3 Companies – crimes and delicts

It has been accepted in Scotland that it is possible for companies to commit crimes and delicts. However, most crimes (particularly common law crimes) require a guilty mind (*mens rea*) and the law of delict (tort in England) usually requires the notion of *fault*.

As these are purely human actions, it is impossible for a company to form such an intention on its own. In these circumstances it appears to be necessary to attribute the *guilty mind* of an individual who is associated with the company to the company itself. Thus the individual becomes the *alter ego* of the company. This was proposed in England by Viscount Haldane in *Lennard's Carrying Co Ltd v Asiatic Petroleum Co Ltd* (1915) where he stated: '... a corporation is an abstraction. It has no mind of its own any more than it has a body of its own; its active and directing will must consequently be sought in the person of somebody who for some purposes may be called an agent, but who is really the directing mind and will of the corporation, the very *ego* and centre of the personality of the corporation ...'.

This was developed by Lord Denning when he compared a company to the human body in *HL Bolton (Engineering) Co Ltd v TJ Graham & Sons Ltd* (1957) where he distinguished between the intellectual function and the manual function. He suggested that 'directors and managers who represent the directing mind and will of the company, and control what it does' may be regarded as the company's 'brain and nerve centre' and therefore their state of mind is that of the company.

This doctrine has been applied in a number of English cases where it has been held that a company can be guilty of crimes involving dishonesty – *DPP v Kent & Sussex Contractors Ltd* (1944), *R v ICR Haulage Ltd* (1944) and *Moore v Bresler Ltd* (1944), and more recently manslaughter (the equivalent of culpable homicide in Scotland) in *R v OLL Ltd* (1995) where executive directors and managers have been held to represent the mind and will of the company (see *Student Law Review*, Summer 1995, Cavendish Publishing Ltd).

However, there is considerable inconsistency in who has been regarded as the *alter ego* of a company. For example, in *Tesco v Nattrass* (1972), a store manager employed by a chain of supermarkets was held to be another person distinct from the company, so allowing the company to succeed in a 'due diligence' defence in a prosecution brought under provisions then contained in the Trade Descriptions Act 1968. Compare this, however, to *Tesco Stores Ltd v Brent London Borough Council* (1993) where it was held that the perception of a check-out assistant could be the perception of the employing company so as to make the company guilty of an offence under the Video Recordings Act 1984.

In Scotland, in *Clydebank Co-op Society v Binnie* (1937), it was held that where a company's transport manager was aware of an employee's use of a vehicle for a purpose which was an offence under the Road Traffic Acts, the company was guilty of 'permitting' the employee to use the vehicle in the unlawful manner. It was also stated *obiter* that even if the only person aware of these circumstances had been the employee himself, his knowledge alone would have been sufficient to make the company guilty of the offence.

It is obvious that there are certain crimes such as rape, incest etc which by their nature cannot be committed by a corporate body. In the Scottish case of *Dean v John Menzies (Holdings) Ltd* (1981), a company was prosecuted for the common law crime of shameless indecency when it displayed for sale various copies of *Club International* and *Penthouse* magazine which it was alleged were 'likely to deprave and corrupt the morals of the lieges and to create in their minds inordinate and lustful desires.' The High Court of Justiciary held that a company could not feel shame. Lord Maxwell stated that the legal fiction of the controlling mind and will doctrine was not sufficiently developed in Scotland to allow for the conviction of a company for the common law crime of shameless indecency. However the question as to whether companies could be convicted of other common law crimes was left open.

In fact, more recently in the case of *Purcell Meats (Scotland) Ltd v McLeod* (1987), it was held that a company could be guilty of fraud perpetrated 'by the hands of persons unknown' provided that it could be shown that these persons were of sufficient status within the company so that their actions could be described as acts of the company.

The difficulty in deciding who might be the *alter ego* of a company has resulted in corporate prosecutions for (common law at least) crimes unlikely, and corporate conviction in cases that do go ahead difficult. The problems were focused in *R v P&O European Ferries (Dover) Ltd* (1991) where P&O Ferries along with five of its senior managers were indicted for manslaughter in respect of the *Herald of Free Enterprise* tragedy off Zeebrugge in 1987. The trial was stopped by the judge, however, because it was held that none of these managers had the necessary *mens rea* for manslaughter. Therefore those who were senior enough within the company to constitute its directing mind and will and consequently to be associated with the company as its *alter ego* did not have the appropriate guilty mind, therefore no *mens rea* could be imputed to the company.

There does, however, seem to be a growing judicial trend in cases involving corporate crime away from preoccupation with the status of the author of the human function within the company towards emphasis on the wrong which is alleged or the benefit which the company has received – see *El Ajou v Dollar Land Holdings plc* (1994), *Director General of Fair Trading v Pioneer Concrete (UK) Ltd, Ready Mixed Concrete (Thames Valley) Ltd* (1995), *R v British Steel plc* (1995) and *Meridian Global Funds Asia Ltd v Securities Commission* (1995).

For further discussion of corporate crime in Scotland see JM Ross, *Corporate Liability for Crime* (1990) SLT (News) 265.

Companies may also commit delictual acts. Not only will a company be liable for the negligence of its employees committed within the course of their employment on the basis of vicarious liability but they may also be liable in their own right. Thus a company has been held liable for defamation – *Finburgh v Moss's Empires* (1908), and for fraud – *Houldsworth v City of Glasgow Bank* (1880).

Similarly, companies may be able to sue for damages for delictual wrongs inflicted on the company, including defamation – see for example *Walker & Others v IPC Magazines* (1994), but they will only be able to recover damages for *patrimonial loss* and not *solatium* (damages for hurt feelings) – see *North of Scotland Banking Co v Duncan* (1857).

The *Salomon* Principle and the Corporate Veil

The company is a separate entity in law. It is capable of owning property, concluding contracts and committing delicts and crimes.

On occasion the so-called corporate veil is lifted and the deeds of the company are identified as those of its directors or shareholders.

Introduction

The situations where the veil is lifted may be classified as statutory or judicial.

Exceptions to the *Salomon* principle

Statutory exceptions include:

Statutory exceptions

- s 24 of the Companies Act 1985 – membership of company falls below statutory minimum;

- s 349(4) of the Companies Act 1985 – misdescription of the company;

- s 213 of the Insolvency Act 1986 and s 458 of the Companies Act 1985 – fraudulent trading;

- s 214 of the Insolvency Act 1986 – wrongful trading by a company director;

- s 216 of the Insolvency Act 1986 – prohibition on directors of insolvent companies being associated with a company with a similar name;

- s 15 of the Company Directors Disqualification Act 1986 – personal liability of a disqualified person who acts in the management of a company;

- s 117(8) of the Companies Act 1985 – liability of officers where a public company trades without a trading certificate;

- s 227 of the Companies Act 1985 – the obligation to file group accounts;

- there are many situations under the companies' legislation where obligations are placed on groups, or where rules apply to directors of companies within the same group. Wherever there is a group situation the veil is being lifted.

| Judicial exceptions | It is difficult to categorise the judicial exceptions to the *Salomon* principle. |

Certain themes can be identified, however:

- the veil is generally lifted to prevent fraud;

- sometimes the veil is lifted in a group situation, treating companies within the same group as part of the same enterprise. This is particularly true where a company is a wholly owned subsidiary of a holding company. Even here, there is no universal rule;

- sometimes the device used to lift the veil is agency, sometimes trust, sometimes in a group situation the group enterprise;

- some cases turn on their special facts eg the consent of all members is the consent of the company – *Re Express Engineering Works Ltd*, all the shareholders of a company were German therefore the company was an enemy alien – *Daimler Co Ltd v Continental Tyre & Rubber Co (GB) Ltd* decided during the First World War.

Companies and crimes and delicts

Companies may commit crimes although some crimes by their nature such as bigamy cannot be committed by companies. In relation to strict liability offences if there is a defence of due diligence in the statute the company may escape liability by demonstrating that the lack of care was that of an employee who was not part of the directing mind or will of the company. Companies may also commit delicts.

Chapter 3

Promoters

In order to set up a company, there have to be promoters. The promoters will purchase property from which the company is going to operate and undertake the preliminary steps to set the company up. They will thus be acting before the company has been formed.

3.1   **Introduction**

In Victorian Britain, there existed professional company promoters. These promoters were often dishonest and acted fraudulently. The Anglo-Bengalee Disinterested Loan and Life Assurance Company mercilessly lampooned by Dickens in *Martin Chuzzlewitt* is typical of the sort of situation that arose. A code of rules therefore developed to ensure that promoters acted with integrity in setting up the company.

There are few statutory rules in this area and indeed no statutory definition of a promoter.

In the absence of any precise definition in the statutes, resort must be had to judicial statements relating to promotion. The usual dictum referred to in defining a promoter is that of Cockburn CJ in *Twycross v Grant* (1877) where he said that a promoter is 'one who undertakes to form a company with reference to a given project and to set it going and who takes the necessary steps to accomplish that purpose'. This definition is clearly somewhat general. In *Whaley Bridge Calico Printing Co v Green* (1880), Bowen J said:

> The term promoter is a term not of law, but of business, usefully summing up in a single word a number of business operations familiar to the commercial world by which a company is generally brought into existence.

It is clear, however, that if someone is involved in the promotion of a company in a purely professional or advisory capacity, that person will not be regarded as a promoter. Thus, s 152 of the Financial Services Act 1986 (in relation to listed companies) and Regulation 13 of the Public Offers of Securities Regulations 1995 (in relation to unlisted companies) exempts from liability for untrue statements those responsible for a prospectus only in the giving of advice as to the contents of the prospectus in a professional capacity. However, a person who has accepted responsibility for any part of the prospectus or who has authorised the contents of particular parts of the prospectus will be liable. Therefore, accountants' reports given as experts may lead to liability of the expert concerned.

The old, Victorian rogue promoters responsible for finding directors to manage a company and for drafting prospectuses to raise capital from the public are largely a thing of the past. Section 57 of the Financial Services Act 1986 provides that an investment advertisement offering securities to the public can only be issued by an authorised person under the Act. Most companies are promoted as private companies by those who will subsequently be managing the business. Rules are still necessary to protect those investing in the business and to protect creditors.

3.2   Promoters' duties

Although a promoter cannot be an agent of the company, he is promoting (since it will not yet exist) he 'must put himself in the position of an agent of the company which he has promoted, and must regulate his relations towards the company according to the duty of an agent' – Lord McLaren in *Edinburgh Northern Tramways Co v Mann* (1896). Thus, a promoter owes fiduciary duties to the company which he is setting up. The duty is akin to the duty owed to the unborn child as no company is yet in existence. Most obviously where a promoter is selling property to a company, he must ensure that he discloses any profit that he is making on the deal.

The disclosure may be made to all of the shareholders, actual and potential, as was the case, for example, in *Salomon v A Salomon & Co Ltd* (1897) and in *Lagunas Nitrate Company v Lagunas Syndicate* (1899). Alternatively, the disclosure may be made to the company's directors. However, in such an instance the disclosure can only be effective if it is to an independent board of directors. In *Erlanger v New Sombrero Phosphate Co* (1878), a syndicate had purchased a lease of a Caribbean island called Sombrero. The syndicate was selling the island to a company which had been formed for the purpose. They disclosed the profit that was being made in selling the island to the company to the board of directors. There were five directors; two were abroad at the material time, two were associated with the syndicate and the fifth was the Lord Mayor of London who was too busy to give proper attention to the affairs of the company. It was held in the circumstances that this was not a full disclosure to an independent board of directors. The company was able to rescind the contract.

When a promoter discloses a profit that he is making upon a deal, he must take care to ensure that he is disclosing the entire profit that he is making from the arrangement. In certain cases, there may well be some collateral profit as well as the direct profit from the sale. It was thus in *Gluckstein v Barnes*

(1900) where a syndicate had purchased the exhibition hall, Olympia. The syndicate disclosed the profit that it was making in re-selling the hall to the company but failed to disclose a profit that it was making in relation to certain mortgages over the hall which it had purchased at a discount. This meant that when the syndicate purchased the hall there was a further reduction of £20,000 since the price of the purchase also included an amount to be set off against debts which were now owed to the syndicate. Lord MacNaghten said:

> They issued a prospectus representing that they had agreed to purchase the property for a sum largely in excess of the amount which they had, in fact, to pay. On the faith of this prospectus they collected subscriptions from a confiding and credulous public. And then comes the last act. Secretly, and therefore dishonestly, they put into their own pockets the difference between the real and the pretended price.

The case clearly represents a breach of promoters' duties and the promoter in question, Gluckstein, was held jointly and severally (with other members of the syndicate) liable to repay the secret profit.

A subscriber to the memorandum of a public company must also comply with s 104 of the Companies Act 1985 when transferring property to the company within two years of its formation. This requires the property to be independently valued by a qualified accountant and the transaction to be sanctioned by ordinary resolution of the members.

Promoters' duties continue after the company is formed. Thus, in *Mann v Edinburgh Northern Tramways Co* (1891), the Inner House held that promoters who post incorporation gave an indemnity to contractors with the company in return for a payment of £17,000 were accountable to the company for this a number of years later as they failed to formally declare the payment to the company.

A range of remedies may be available against a promoter who has breached his duty and failed to disclose the extent of the profit that he is making where he has sold property to the company. A possible remedy is for rescission of the contract of the sale between the promoter and the company. The usual bars to rescission will apply: so rescission is not available where the contract has been affirmed by personal bar, where it is impossible to restore the parties to their pre-contractual positions or where third party rights have intervened.

An alternative remedy is for the company to sue for a return of the profit. If the company wishes to keep the

3.3   Remedies for breach of promoter's duties

property in question and merely recover the profit, this is clearly the appropriate remedy to seek. This was the remedy awarded, for example, in *Gluckstein v Barnes*. The company does not have to show that it has suffered a loss in order to recover a secret profit – see *Henderson v Huntingdon Copper & Sulphur Co* (1877).

Particular problems may arise where a promoter has acquired property before the promotion began. In such a situation, where the promoter then sells the property to the company without fully disclosing the profit that is being made upon the transaction, there is a difficulty in awarding an appropriate remedy. If the company were to seek an account of profits in such a case, the question would arise as to what portion of profits properly belongs to the pre-promotion period and so would be rightfully the property of the promoter and what part of the profit could be said to belong to the post-promotion period and so belong to the company. In such cases, therefore, the view of the courts is that it is not possible to sue for an account of profits but merely for rescission of the contract, always assuming that the right to rescission has not been lost. See *Re Cape Breton* (1887) and *Ladywell Mining Co v Brookes* (1887). These decisions have been criticised notably by Xuereb in *Secret Profit – Re Cape Breton Company Revisited* (1987).

These are the two usual alternative remedies. However, in one case, the remedy of damages was awarded against a promoter. This occurred in *Re Leeds & Hanley Theatre of Varieties Ltd* (1902). In this case, the claim was for breach of duty of care in the promoter selling property to the company at an overvaluation. Damages were awarded against the promoter. This is a rare instance of damages being awarded against a promoter, but it is interesting to note that the measure of damages was the same as the profit made by the promoter.

It may be on occasion that a single shareholder can bring a claim for a wrong done to the company. Scots authority for this is found in *Hannay v Muir* (1898). The shareholder must fit within one of the exceptions to the rule in *Foss v Harbottle* (1843). This could occur where the promoters are in control of the company and are using their management and/or voting powers in general meeting to prevent an action being brought in respect of an undisclosed profit that has been made by promoters.

A further remedy may be available in the particular instance of the company's liquidation. Section 212 of the Insolvency Act 1986 permits the court to order in a liquidation that a promoter restore to the company any property or money obtained in breach of duty. This may be done on the petition of the liquidator or on the petition of a creditor or member.

A promoter cannot have a contract with the company which he is going to form. The company is not yet in existence and therefore is unable to contract. In the English case of *Re National Motor Mail Coach Company Limited, Clinton's Claim* (1908), it was accepted that there could be no contract between a promoter and his unformed company such that a promoter could claim reimbursement of expenses incurred in setting up the company. Furthermore, the court held that there could be no quasi contractual remedy in this case based on the company's having received a benefit.

Generally in such cases no problem will arise. The promoters who have been setting up the company will also be the first directors and will take care to ensure that they are reimbursed for their expenses and receive payment for the services that they have performed. In Scotland it is permissible for directors to make discretionary payments to the promoters of the company, provided that this is allowed by the company's articles and that the payments are made in good faith – see *Mason's Trustees v Poole and Robinson* (1903). Instead of making payments to promoters, directors may allot shares as a reward for what are effectively gratuitous pre-incorporation services, again provided that any allotments are made according to the articles and in good faith – *Park Business Interiors Ltd v Park* (1990). Since Scots contract law is not burdened with the English doctrine of consideration no special formalities are required to validate such contracts.

3.4 Payment for the promoter's services

Where a person enters into a contract on behalf of an unformed company, a conceptual problem arises. It is clear in such instances that the company itself cannot be bound since the company does not exist.

3.5 Pre-incorporation contracts

In *Kelner v Baxter* (1866), the plaintiff had delivered goods to the defendants. The goods had been ordered on behalf of the proposed Gravesend Royal Alexandra Hotel Co Ltd. The question arose as to whether the company was liable upon this contract. The Court of Common Pleas held that the company could not be liable since it did not exist at the time of the contract. In fact, the defendant, who had acted on behalf of the unformed company, was held liable on this contract.

Similarly, in *Tinnevelly Sugar Refining Co Ltd and Others v Mirrlees, Watson & Yaryan Co Ltd* (1894), the Tinnevelly company was being promoted by Messrs Darley and Butler.

3.5.1 Common law

Prior to incorporation they entered a contract for the supply of machinery with the defenders, purporting to act on behalf of Tinnevelly. After incorporation, Tinnevelly received the equipment, discovered that it was defective and attempted to sue the defenders for breach of contract. The Inner House held that Tinnevelly had no title to sue on a pre-incorporation contract – in the words of Lord President Robertson: 'It is in law an untenable position, for Darley and Butler could not be the agents of a non-existent company.'

This was the position at common law before statute intervened. The position was not uniform, however, and in some cases it was held that there was no contract. In *Newborne v Sensolid (Great Britain) Ltd* (1954), Leopold Newborne (London) Ltd purported to sell a quantity of ham to the defendant. The defendant refused to take delivery of the ham. The company sued for breach of contract. It transpired that the company had not been registered until the day after the contract was concluded.

The plaintiff continued the action in his own name. The plaintiff was a promoter and director of the company. It was held in the Court of Appeal that there was no contract in this case. The fact that the agreement had been signed 'Yours faithfully, Leopold Newborne (London) Ltd' and the signature of the director added beneath indicated that there was no intention that person liability should attach to the director. It was therefore held that there was no contract. Similarly in the Australian case of *Black v Smallwood* (1966) (High Court of Australia), it was held that where a contract was concluded where the purchaser was described as Western Suburbs Holdings Pty Ltd with the signatures of Robert Smallwood and J Cooper added subsequently as directors, there could be no contract between the plaintiff Black and the defendant Smallwood. In this case, all the parties believed that the company did exist whereas in fact at the time of the contract it did not. The court held that in the circumstances there could be no contract. Although a contract may take effect between the person purporting to act for the unformed company and the other contracting party, it is clear from the cases that there can be no adoption or ratification of that agreement by the company once it comes into existence. This is clear from the opinion of the Privy Council in *Natal Land & Colonisation Co Ltd v Pauline Colliery & Development Syndicate Ltd* (1904) (an appeal from the Supreme Court of Natal). The appropriate course of action in such a situation where a person acting for the company is bound is that once the company comes into existence, it should enter into a new contract on the same terms. Express *novation* of this nature was approved by the Outer House in *James Young & Sons Ltd and Liquidator v Edwards* (1902).

It has been suggested that a Scottish company might plead a *jus quaesitum tertio* (third party right) on a pre-incorporation contract. This was confirmed in *Cumming v Quartzag Ltd* (1981), in which the Inner House recognised the plea as relevant although it failed on the facts. In order to succeed with such a plea it would appear that the promoter would have had to sign the pre-incorporation contract as principal rather than as a purported agent of the company, and the contract would have to expressly provide in favour of the yet-to-be-formed company – see *Morton's Trustees v Aged Christian Friend Society* (1899). This requirement may now, however, be arguably redundant by virtue of s 36C(1) of the Companies Act 1985 (see para 3.5.2 and Hector L MacQueen, Promoter's Contracts, Agency and the *Jus Quaesitum Tertio*, 1982 SLT (News) 257).

When the United Kingdom joined the European Communities by the European Communities Act 1972, s 9(2) of the European Communities Act implemented part of the first EC Company Law Directive. Section 9(2) which has now been re-enacted with some minor amendments as s 36C(1) of the Companies Act 1985 provides:

3.5.2   Statutory provision

> A contract which purports to be made by or on behalf of a company at a time when the company has not been formed has effect, subject to any agreement to the contrary, as one made with the person purporting to act for the company or as agent for it, and he is personally liable on the contract accordingly.

This statutory provision will mean that, in both *Kelner v Baxter* and *Newborne v Sensolid* situations, the person purporting to act for the company will be liable upon the contract. However, it is not clear whether the section was intended to provide that the person purporting to act for the company will be able to hold the other party to the contractual agreement. Thus, the decision in *Tinnevelly Sugar Refining Co Ltd v Mirrlees Watson & Yaryan Co Ltd* (1894) may be unaffected.

In *Phonogram Ltd v Lane* (1982), the court had to consider the effect of what is now s 36C(1) where a company called Fragile Management Ltd was in the process of being incorporated. The company was to manage a pop group called Cheap, Mean and Nasty. The defendant was the manager of the pop group. He agreed with the plaintiffs that the plaintiffs would supply finance. He signed an agreement undertaking to re-pay the monies that had been advanced on behalf of Fragile Management Ltd if the contract were not completed before a certain time. Subsequently the plaintiffs sued the defendant for the money that had been advanced. The defendant argued he was not personally liable. It was suggested on his behalf that the contract was not 'purported' to be made by the company as it was known that the company was not in existence. Indeed it was known by both parties that the company had not yet been formed. However Lord Denning MR took the view (a view shared by Shaw and Oliver LJJ) that a contract can purport to be made on behalf of a company even though the company is known by both parties not to have been formed. He took the view that although s 36C(1) can be excluded by contrary agreement, this contrary agreement should be express. This view was shared by the other members of the Court of Appeal.

It is possible in certain situations that a promoter may act on behalf of a company to be bought 'off the shelf'. In such a situation the company does exist where the promoter is acting so that it is open to the company subsequently to ratify what the promoter has done provided that the promoter made it clear that he was acting on behalf of the company. It may be that the company subsequently alters it name; this will not change the legal situation, *Oshkosh B'Gosh Inc v Dan Marbel Inc Ltd* (1989). See, also, *Vic Spence Associates v Balchin* (1990) (para 1.1).

Promoters

There is no statutory definition of promoters. One must therefore turn to the cases. A promoter is a person 'who undertakes to form a company with reference to a given project and to set it going and who takes the necessary steps to accomplish that purpose', *per* Cockburn CJ in *Twycross v Grant* (1877).

Promoters

Promoters owe fiduciary duties to the companies they are forming. They must disclose any profit they are making from the promotion – either to the members of the company or to an independent board.

The company may sue for disgorgement of the profit or for rescission (if this is not barred) where there is a breach of this duty.

A conceptual problem arises where a person concludes a contract for the as yet unformed company. At common law, the position was confused. Sometimes, the person acting for the unformed company was held to be contractually bound but much depended on the form of words used. Since the European Communities Act 1972, the position has been standardised. Section 36C(1) of the Companies Act 1985 now provides that where a person acts for an unformed company, that person is contractually bound unless there is an agreement to the contrary.

Pre-incorporation contracts

A company cannot enforce a pre-incorporation contract unless there has been *novation* or the company can demonstrate a *jus quaesitum tertio*.

Chapter 4

Issue of Shares to the Public

Since the Financial Services Act 1986, The Stock Exchange has become a statutory-recognised regulatory body. The Stock Exchange is the competent authority in relation to listing of shares under the EC Listing Directives.

The Stock Exchange, or to give it its full official title The International Stock Exchange of the United Kingdom and the Republic of Ireland Ltd, underwent fundamental changes at the time of 'Big Bang' on 27 October 1986. Single-capacity dealing ended as did fixed-rate commissions.

The Stock Exchange currently runs two markets in company securities. These are the Listed Market and the Alternative Investment Market (AIM). The Listed Market (for those securities with an official listing) is in general utilised by large public companies. Companies with shares listed on the Listed Market must take care to ensure that they comply with The Stock Exchange Yellow Book or the rules on Admission of Securities to Listing, as it is sometimes termed. The Alternative Investment Market offers the chance for a listing for medium sized companies. Companies desiring a quotation must comply with the rules of The Stock Exchange Alternative Investment Market (Stock Exchange Green Book). The conditions for admission to the AIM are not stringent. There is no minimum trading period nor a minimum capitalisation.

The law regulating the admission of securities to the Official List of The Stock Exchange is now governed by Part IV of the Financial Services Act 1986. This Act was introduced in response to the Gower Report published in two parts, in January 1984 and March 1985. Professor LCB Gower had undertaken a review of the law on statutory protection for private and business investors in securities and other property. Part IV of the Financial Services Act 1986 replaces The Stock Exchange (Listings) Regulations 1984 which had incorporated into UK law the requirements of three EEC directives relating to the official listing of securities. These directives were the Admissions Directive (79/279), the Listing Particulars Directive (80/390) and the Interim Reports Directive (82/121). Some minor changes were made to Part IV by the Public Offers of Securities Regulations 1995.

Consistent with the entire framework of the Act which is to provide a framework of authority for Self-Regulating

4.1   Background

4.2   Public offers of listed securities

Organisations, the Act delegates responsibility for the administration of the regime in relation to listing particulars to the Council of The Stock Exchange by s 142(6) of the Act.

The Stock Exchange has delegated the functions in relation to listing particulars to its Committee on Quotations under s 142(8).

The Secretary of State has reserve power under s 192 to direct The Stock Exchange to comply with any international obligations in relation to listing particulars.

The rules in relation to listing are contained in The Stock Exchange's Admission of Securities to Listing rules, generally known as The Stock Exchange Yellow Book from the colour of its cover.

Section 143 of the Act requires where an application is made for listing of shares that this should be made to the competent authority, that is, The Stock Exchange, and that The Stock Exchange should not admit the securities to the Official List unless it is satisfied that the relevant rules are complied with. In addition to complying with the rules set out in The Stock Exchange Yellow Book, there is an overriding requirement that the listing particulars should contain such information as investors and their professional advisers would reasonably require, and reasonably expect to find, in order to make an informed assessment of:

- the assets and liabilities of the company, its financial position, profits and losses and its prospects;

- the rights that attach to those securities (s 146(1)).

There is an additional obligation to submit supplementary particulars to The Stock Exchange and, with the approval of The Stock Exchange, to publish these matters if between publication of the listing particulars and dealings opening in the company's securities significant changes occur or significant new matters arise. There is only an obligation to disclose such changes if the issuer is aware of them (s 147).

There are certain exemptions from the requirement of disclosure. These are set out in the Yellow Book and in s 148 of the Act. The Yellow Book, s 3, provides that if the information is of minor importance only and would not influence an investor then it may be omitted. Section 148 provides exemptions from disclosure on the grounds that it would be contrary to the public interest or on the grounds that it would be detrimental to the company and that non-disclosure would not be likely to mislead an investor. Section 148 also provides exemption from disclosure if the securities are debt securities such as debentures on the ground that disclosure is unnecessary given the persons likely to deal in these securities ie more experienced investors.

Section 149 requires that listing particulars and supplementary listing particulars should be registered with the registrar of companies on or before the date of their publication.

Public offers of unlisted securities are now subject to the Public Offers of Securities Regulations 1995. Part V of the Financial Services Act 1986 was intended to deal with public issues of unlisted securities but is was never brought into force. The relevant provisions of the Financial Services Act 1986 have been repealed by the Public Offers of Securities Regulations 1995 which mirror the requirements of the Prospectus Directives (89/298). These regulations were made under s 2 of the European Communities Act 1972. The regulations provide that when securities are offered to the public for the first time the offerer shall publish a prospectus available to the public free of charge.

The prospectus has to be delivered to the registrar of companies before publication.

When a prospectus is published it must contain the information required by Sched 1 to the regulations. This information includes details of the issuer, its capital and financial position.

In a similar way to the Financial Services Act 1986, in relation to listed securities, there is an overriding requirement that a prospectus must contain all information that investors would reasonably require and expect to find there for the purpose of making an informed assessment of the assets and liabilities, financial position, profits and losses and prospect of the issuer and of the rights attaching to the securities.

If an authorised person fails to comply with the requirement to publish a prospectus then the failure amounts to a breach of the Conduct of Business Rules (see s 48 of the Financial Services Act 1986), while failure by an unauthorised person is an offence. A breach of the rules is also actionable in civil law by the investor. Apart from the statutory position the other areas of potential liability for misleading prospectuses are identical to those for misleading listing particulars (see para 4.4 and Regulations 13–15 of the Public Offers of Securities Regulations 1995).

4.3   Public offers of unlisted securities

4.4 **Common law remedies for misleading listing particulars or prospectus**

If a pursuer has been induced to purchase securities on the strength of a misrepresentation in the listing particulars or prospectus, he may have a remedy for the misrepresentation.

The pursuer may seek rescission of the contract against the company. He must demonstrate a material misrepresentation of fact which has induced him to enter into the contract. Non-disclosure of a relevant fact may amount to a misrepresentation if it can be demonstrated that the omission renders the listing particulars misleading. Thus, in *Coles v White City (Manchester) Greyhound Association Ltd* (1928), a prospectus described land as eminently suitable for greyhound racing. The prospectus failed to state that the local authority would have to give planning permission for the erection of stands for viewing and for greyhound kennels. A shareholder sought rescission on the basis of the omission. It was held that the description was misleading in that the omission distorted what was actually stated.

Rescission is not dependent upon whether the person making the statement or omission is fraudulent or not and is available for fraudulent, negligent and innocent representations.

The right to rescission is lost in certain circumstances. Thus a pursuer may not rescind a contract if it is not possible to restore the parties to their pre-contractual position. This is sometimes stated as *restitutio in integrum impossibile est*. This bar to rescission will apply if the company is in liquidation, see *Oakes v Turquand* (1867). Another bar to rescission is if the pursuer affirms the contract after discovering the misrepresentation. This may occur, for example, if the pursuer votes at a meeting of members after discovering the misrepresentation, see *Sharpley v Louth and East Coast Railway Company* (1876). In a similar way, if the pursuer fails to set the contract aside promptly after discovering the misrepresentation, he will not be able to rescind – see *Caledonian Debenture Co Ltd v Bernard* (1898).

Where it can be proved that the misrepresentation was fraudulent or negligent, damages may also be awarded. It is sufficient for only one director to be guilty of the wrongful insertion – the company itself will still be responsible – *Mair v Rio Grande Estates Co* (1913).

It was formerly the case that damages could not be awarded against a company in favour of a member unless the member first repudiated the contract of membership. This was known as the rule in *Houldsworth v City of Glasgow Bank* (1880). This rule has been abolished by s 111A of the Companies Act 1985 (inserted by Companies Act 1989).

4.4.1 Damages for fraudulent misrepresentation

Damages may be claimed against a person who has accepted responsibility for a part of the listing particulars or authorised the contents of part or all of the listing particulars for a statement of fact which that person made knowing it to be false or reckless as to its truth – *Addie v Western Bank* (1867). However, fraud is notoriously difficult to prove. In *Derry v Peek* (1889), a prospectus was issued by a tramway company. The company was empowered to use horse-drawn trams in Plymouth. The prospectus stated that the company was empowered to use steam-driven vehicles. In fact, this was not the case though application had been made to the Board of Trade for permission to do so. Permission was not granted and an investor who had relied on the prospectus brought an action for damages for fraud against the directors. It was held that since the directors honestly believed the statement to be true, they were not liable in fraud.

Generally, only a subscriber who purchased shares directly from the company may seek rescission on the basis of fraudulent misrepresentation. However, if a later purchaser can show that the listing particulars were directed to encouraging purchases on the open market, he may be able to sustain an action for damages in delict where clearly no action in contract would be possible – see *Andrews v Mockford* (1896).

An action will lie in damages against a person who makes a negligent statement which causes economic loss provided there is a relationship of sufficient proximity. The range of potential defenders certainly includes the company and its directors and experts who have consented to the contents of part or all of the listing particulars.

4.4.2   Damages for negligent misstatement

The case establishing potential liability in this area is *Hedley Byrne & Co Ltd v Heller & Partners Ltd* (1964). As in the case of fraudulent misrepresentation, it is possible that the range of potential pursuers seeking damages for negligent misrepresentation will include not just those who have subscribed for shares or debentures direct from the company but also those who have purchased securities on the open market. Where the pursuer has purchased shares directly from the company he may choose to sue either in contract or in negligence – *Henderson v Merrett Syndicates* (1994). However, if the pursuer has purchased shares or debentures in the market, it seems that the scope of liability in negligence is limited. The House of Lords in *Caparo Industries plc v Dickman & Others* (1990) held that no duty of care was owed to potential investors in relation to the auditing of the company's accounts. Lord Bridge of Harwich said:

> To hold the maker of the statement to be under a duty of care in respect of the accuracy of the statement to all and sundry for any purpose for which they may choose to rely on it is not only to subject him, in the classic words of Cardozo CJ to 'liability in an indeterminate amount for an

indeterminate time to an indeterminate class' [*Ultramares Corporation v Touche* (1931)] it is also to confer on the world at large a quite unwarranted entitlement to appropriate for their own purposes the benefit of the expert knowledge or professional expertise attributed to the maker of the statement.

This principle was applied in *Al-Nakib Investments (Jersey) Ltd v Longcroft* (1990) where there was a claim against the directors of a company in relation to a share purchase on the stock market following an allegedly misleading prospectus. The court considered that the prospectus was intended to encourage subscriptions for shares so that there was no remedy for purchasers on the open market.

However, if a defender negligently divulges wrong or misleading information to the pursuer where the defender is aware of the use to which the information is to be put by the pursuer the defender may be liable – see *Diamond Manufacturing Co Ltd v Hamilton* (1969) and *Morgan Crucible Co v Hill Samuel & Co Ltd* (1991).

4.5 Statutory remedies for misleading listing particulars

The statutory remedy does not affect other common law remedies. Sections 150–52 deal with the statutory remedy in relation to listing particulars.

Section 150(1) provides liability for untrue or misleading listing particulars or supplementary listing particulars and provides that any person responsible for these is liable to compensate an investor in the securities who has suffered loss in respect of them as a result of the untrue or misleading statement or from an omission of a matter that is required to be disclosed. The section is not limited to subscribers from the company and it may well be that a person who purchases shares or debentures on the open market can recover under this section. It may even be that an investor is unaware of the content of the listing particulars or even their existence. What is crucial is that he has suffered as a result of the particulars. This would be the case if the market had reacted favourably to the misleading particulars so that the price of the shares had gone up and he had bought at that higher, inflated price.

4.5.1 Section 151(1)

Section 151 sets out six defences in relation to s 150. Section 151(1) provides that a defender will not be liable to pay compensation if he can demonstrate to the court that he had reasonable grounds for believing that the statement made was true and not misleading or that the omission was appropriate and he continued in that belief until after dealings in securities had opened. He must additionally demonstrate either:

- that he continued to hold the belief until the securities in question were acquired; or

- that they were acquired before it was reasonably practicable for him to publish a correction to potential investors; or

- they were acquired after he had taken all reasonable steps to publish a correction to potential investors; or

- the securities were acquired after such a period of time that in all the circumstances he ought reasonably to be excused.

The second defence is set out in s 151(2). This provides a defence if the defender can show that the statement was made by an expert whom he believed on reasonable grounds to be competent to make the statement and whom he reasonably believed had consented to the inclusion of the statement in the form and context in which it appeared. The defender must hold such belief until dealings in the securities in question have opened. Additionally the defender must demonstrate one of the following:

4.5.2   Section 151(2)

- that he continued to hold this belief until after the securities in question were acquired; or

- that the securities were acquired before it was reasonably practicable for the defender to issue a statement concerning the expert's lack of competence or lack of consent; or

- before the securities were acquired, he had taken all reasonable steps to issue a statement relating to the lack of competence or lack of consent; or

- that the securities were acquired after such a period of time that the defender ought reasonably to be excused.

The third defence is set out in s 151(3). The defence provides that a defender will not be liable to pay compensation if he can demonstrate that he took all reasonable steps to bring a correction, notification of a lack of competence or a lack of consent on the part of an expert, to the attention of potential investors in the securities before the securities were acquired.

4.5.3   Section 151(3)

The fourth defence provides that if a defender can demonstrate that the statement was an accurate copy of an official document, he will not be liable to pay compensation (s 151(4)).

4.5.4   Section 151(4)

If the defender can demonstrate that the pursuer had knowledge that the defender's statement was false or misleading or knew of an omission, then he will not be liable to pay compensation (s 151(5)).

4.5.5   Section 151(5)

4.5.6   Section 151(6)

A sixth defence is that if the defender can demonstrate that he reasonably believed that a change or new matter was unimportant and that supplementary listing particulars were not required, then he will not be liable to pay compensation (s 151(6)).

The persons responsible for listing particulars and supplementary listing particulars are set out in s 152. This provides that the persons responsible are as follows:

- the issuer of the securities, that is, the company;

- every person who is a director of the issuing company at the time that the listing particulars are submitted to the Stock Exchange for registration;

- persons who are named and who have authorised themselves to be named as agreeing to become directors either immediately or at some time in the future;

- every person who accepts responsibility for any part of the listing particulars (such persons will be potentially liable in relation to those parts);

- any other person who has authorised the contents of part or all of the listing particulars (such person will be liable in relation to the relevant part).

4.6   Criminal liability

It is worth noting at the outset that under s 202(1) of the Financial Services Act 1986 where an offence is committed by a company and is proved to have been committed with the consent or connivance of, or to be attributable to, any neglect on the part of: any director, manager, secretary or other similar officer of the company, or any person who is purporting to act in any such capacity; or a controller of the company, he, as well as the body corporate, shall be guilty of that offence and liable to be proceeded against and punished accordingly.

Persons involved in carrying on investment business who issue false listing particulars or a false prospectus will be guilty of an offence in certain situations (s 47). If such a person makes a statement, promise or forecast which he knows to be misleading, false or deceptive, or dishonestly conceals any material facts or recklessly makes (dishonestly or otherwise) a statement, promise or forecast which is misleading, false or deceptive if it is for the purpose of inducing another to enter into any investment agreement, he is guilty of an offence (s 47(1)). The section also makes it an offence to do any act or engage in conduct creating a false or misleading impression as to the market in or value of any investment if done to induce another to acquire, dispose of, subscribe for or underwrite those investments or to refrain from doing so or to exercise or refrain from exercising any rights conferred by those investments (s 47(2)).

It is a defence (s 47(3)) if the person concerned can prove that he reasonably believed that his act or conduct would not create an impression that was false or misleading.

The maximum penalty is seven years' imprisonment. It is an offence to publish listing particulars without a copy of them having been delivered to the registrar of companies (s 149). Under s 154 it is an offence to publish an advertisement of securities without approval of the Stock Exchange. An authorised person who contravenes the section is liable to disciplinary action whereas an unauthorised person is liable to up to two years' imprisonment.

It is an offence for a private company to issue an advertisement offering its securities to the public (s 81 of the Companies Act 1985).

The criminal law position in relation to offers of unlisted securities has been noted above (para 4.3).

Summary of Chapter 4

Issue of Shares to the Public

There are different rules applicable to the issue of shares to the public dependent upon whether the issue is to be made via the Official List of The Stock Exchange (Part IV of the Financial Services Act 1986) or via the Alternative Investment Market (AIM) or in some other way (the Public Offers of Securities Regulations 1995).

Background

The matters to be disclosed in listing particulars (Part IV of the Financial Services Act 1986) or in a prospectus are largely beyond the scope of this textbook. Part IV supplementing the Stock Exchange Yellow Book requires disclosure of such information as would enable investors 'to make an informed assessment'. The rules on disclosure in prospectuses are currently set out in the Schedule to the Public Offers of Securities Regulations.

Disclosure and remedies

The statutory remedy for misleading listing particulars (s 150 of the Financial Services Act 1986) permits recovery for misleading particulars for subscribers and those purchasing on the open market (subject to various defences). The remedy for a misleading prospectus is by way of an action for breach of statutory duty under the Public Offers of Securities Regulations 1995.

Various other remedies may be available in both cases – rescission or damages in misrepresentation, damages for fraud and damages for negligent misstatement may be available.

There are also various criminal sanctions that apply where a misleading prospectus or misleading particulars are issued.

Chapter 5

The Memorandum of Association

The memorandum (as it is generally known) is sometimes termed the external constitution of the company. This document sets out certain key features of the company's status. The memorandum is generally coupled together in the same document with the articles of association (the internal constitution of the company). Therefore, in practice, although they are referred to separately, the two parts of the constitution are submitted together to the registrar of companies.

The memorandum of association has certain compulsory clauses. These are set out in s 2 of the Companies Act 1985. It is important for both practitioners and students (whether budding lawyers or accountants) to know what these compulsory clauses are. They are as follows:

- the name of the company;

- in the case of a public company, a sub-clause stating that the company is a public limited company;

- the situate of the office of the company;

- a statement of the objects of the company;

- a statement of the limitation of liability of the company (by shares or by guarantee);

- a capital clause stating the amount of the share capital which is authorised and the division of the share capital into shares of a stated amount.

It is suggested that the compulsory clauses may be remembered by a convenient mnemonic, such as 'No Opulence On Limited Salary (= Name, Office, Objects, Limited liability, Share capital) in the case of a private company and 'No Public Opulence On Limited Salary' in the case of a public company.

In general, those setting up a company are free to choose any name they wish. They are, however, constrained by certain rules.	**5.1** **The name of the company**
A limited company must generally indicate this at the end of its name, in the case of a public company, by the words 'public limited company' and in the case of a private company by the word 'limited' (companies which register their documents in	5.1.1 Indication of the type of company

Welsh would be required to end their names with the words 'cwmni cyfyngedig cyhoeddus' or 'cyfyngedig' as appropriate) (s 25(1) of the Companies Act 1985). The words may be abbreviated respectively to 'plc' or 'ltd', s 27 of the Companies Act 1985 (the abbreviated Welsh equivalents are 'ccc' and 'cyf').

Exceptionally, a company may be permitted to omit 'limited' from the end of its name. Under the Companies Act 1948, limited companies could obtain a licence, where their work was for charity or for the public good, to omit the word 'limited'. This system ended on the 25 February 1982 but, by s 30 of the Companies Act 1985, companies with a licence on that day may continue to omit the word 'limited' from their name'. They must, however, comply with the requirements of the section. These provide that the company's objects must be the promotion of commerce, art, science, education, religion, charity or a profession together with requirements in the company's constitution that its profits, if any, or any other income be applied to the promotion of its objects and that on a winding up, the company's assets must be transferred to another body with charitable objects.

Since 25 February 1982, it has been possible for private companies limited by guarantee to register without using the word 'limited' or its Welsh equivalent at the end of its name provided they comply with the requirements of s 30.

5.1.2   Prohibited and restricted use of names

Section 26 of the Companies Act 1985 prohibits the use of certain names. A name must not in the opinion of the Secretary of State be offensive nor constitute a crime. Statutes prohibit the use of certain names and these cannot therefore be used. Restricted names in this category include use or imitation of the names of the Boy Scouts, the NSPCC and the Red Cross.

In *R v Registrar of Companies ex p Attorney General* (1991), Lindi St Claire, the famous prostitute, formed a company to carry out the service of prostitution. She initially attempted to call the company 'Prostitutes Ltd', 'Hookers Ltd' and 'Lindi St Claire (French Lessons) Ltd'. All of these titles were rejected by the registrar of companies. Subsequently the company was registered as 'Lindi St Claire (Personal Services) Ltd' and this action was then brought to challenge the registration of the company since the company's purposes were unlawful. In the upshot, the company was struck off the register.

The practice of creating 'phoenix' companies with similar names to companies which have gone into liquidation is outlawed by s 216 of the Insolvency Act 1986. Contravention of the section leads to civil and criminal consequences (see para 23.4).

The name must not be the same as one already appearing on the index of names kept by the registrar of companies (s 26 of the Companies Act 1985). The register contains names of companies registered under the Act as well as overseas companies and limited partnerships. The index is published on microfiche. In assessing whether the name is identical to a name already on the register, certain matters are ignored. These are:

- the occurrence of the definite article at the beginning of the name;

- the occurrence of the words 'company' or 'limited' or 'unlimited' or 'public limited company' or any abbreviated or Welsh form of these words;

- the typography, word division, accenting or punctuation of the name.

If a name is registered by the registrar and it is subsequently discovered that the name is too like that of an existing name, the Secretary of State can within 12 months of the registration require the company to change its name (s 28(2) of the Companies Act 1985).

Certain words and expressions require the prior permission of the Secretary of State or of some other body (s 29 of the Act). Thus permission is required from the Secretary of State for use of the words 'England', 'Scotland' or 'Wales'. Other words may require the consent of a different Minister. For example, use of the word 'university' or 'polytechnic' requires consent of the Department of Education and Science. Sometimes the body is non governmental. Thus, the General Medical Council may be asked to consent to the use of the word 'medical' in a company name. The Secretary of State's permission is also needed if the name is likely to give the impression that the company is connected with the government or with a local authority (s 26(2) of the Companies Act 1985).

The choice of name may also be limited by the possibility of a passing off action being brought against the company. If the name chosen by the company is similar or the same as the name used by an existing business, then the proprietor of that business may bring an action to injunct the company from using the name and may also seek an account of profits. Thus, in *Ewing v Buttercup Margarine Co Ltd* (1917), the plaintiff, who operated as a sole trader under the name of The Buttercup Dairy Company, sought to restrain the defendants from using the name Buttercup Margarine Co Ltd. The action was successful. To succeed in an action for passing off, the pursuer

5.1.3   Index of names

5.1.4   Specific permission required

5.1.5   Law of passing off

would have to show either evidence of confusion or an intention by the interloper to cause confusion and that he had or was likely to suffer economic loss as a result. Thus, in *Chill Foods (Scotland) Ltd v Cool Foods Ltd* (1977), the Outer House granted an interim interdict ordering a company (Cool Foods – set up by a director of Chill Foods to compete with the latter company) to desist from trading under the name Cool Foods, since it was very likely that customers would be misled into thinking that they were dealing with Chill Foods.

However, in *Salon Services (Hairdressing Supplies) Ltd v Direct Salon Services Ltd* (1988), the court recalled interdicts on the basis that confusion and therefore economic loss was unlikely to arise from a minor similarity between the names of the two companies, particularly since they traded in different areas and used different brand names for their products.

5.1.6	Trading name

Companies may trade under names other than their corporate ones. Consent is still required, however, if a connection is suggested with HM's Government or any local authority, as if the word is one of the sensitive ones set out in regulations.

The Business Names Act 1985 regulates the use of trading names. It provides that the corporate name and address must be clearly displayed on all business stationery and at company premises where customers may attend. Failure to comply with these provisions is a criminal offence and may result in the company being unable to enforce contracts against its customers – see *Thomas Montgomery & Sons v WB Anderson & Sons Ltd* (1979).

5.1.7	Failure to use the company name correctly

Sections 348–50 of the Companies Act 1985 provide for personal liability for company officers who are responsible for misnaming the company on documents used in the company's business (see para 2.2.1). It may be, however, that if a third party is responsible for the error that allows the company to deny any liability on the document the third party may be personally barred from proceeding against any company officer who merely signed the document on behalf of the company. Although this was not the decision reached in the Scottish case of *Scottish and Newcastle Breweries Ltd v Blair* (1967), it is submitted that this decision might not be followed in the light of more recent English cases such as *Durham Fancy Goods Ltd v Michael Jackson (Fancy Goods) Ltd* (1968) where an argument based on estoppel (the English equivalent of personal bar) allowed the company officer concerned to escape personal liability.

Section 28 of the Companies Act 1985 provides that a company may change its name by a special resolution. A special resolution is carried by a 75% vote in favour of those attending and voting at a meeting of which 21 days' notice has been given. A copy of the resolution should then be sent to the registrar of companies within 15 days of its passage together with a copy of the revised memorandum of association and articles of association together with a fee of £50 for re-registering the company. The registrar will then issue a new certificate of incorporation indicating the new company name. The rules on change of name are governed by the same limitations that apply to the initial choice of name.

Mention has already been made of the Secretary of State's power to require a company with a name that is similar to an existing name to change its name. In addition the Secretary of State has the power within five years of the registration of the company under a name to require the company to change its name if it has presented misleading information to him or given undertakings that are unfulfilled (s 28(3) of the Companies Act 1985).

Furthermore, under s 32 of the Companies Act 1985, the Secretary of State has the power without any time limitation to require a company to change its name if he feels that the name is misleading in relation to the type of business that is conducted by the company and that it is likely to cause harm to the public. An example of this might be if a small company is conducting business under the name of 'Consolidated Cosmopolitan Steelworks plc'.

Where the Secretary of State requires such a change of name, the company has six weeks to comply with his order but there is a right of appeal to the court.

Any change of name has no effect on the corporate personality – see *Lin Pac Containers (Scotland) v Kelly* (1982) and para 1.1.

5.2 Change of name

If the company is a public company, the second clause of its memorandum should state this to be the case. It is difficult to see what this adds to the understanding of the investing and trading public as it will be obvious from the company's name whether the company is public or not. However, it remains mandatory to have this clause in the case of public companies.

If a private company wishes to re-register as a public company, then it will be necessary to pass a special resolution to effect the change of status, altering the memorandum and articles as necessary and also to effect a change of name.

5.3 Public company status

5.3.1 Re-registration of a private company as a public company

Any application to change a private company's status to public must be delivered to the registrar of companies together with an application signed by a director of the company or the company secretary. This application should be accompanied by a copy of the altered memorandum and articles, a written statement from the auditors that at the relevant balance sheet date the company's net assets were not less than the aggregate of its called up share capital and undistributable reserves and this must not be a date more than seven months before the date of application to re-register, a copy of the relevant balance sheet together with an unqualified auditor's report, if the company has allotted shares for a consideration other than a cash consideration between the balance sheet date and the passing of the special resolution, a copy of an expert's valuation under s 103 of the Companies Act 1985, and a statutory declaration signed by the director or company secretary indicating the following:

- that a special resolution has been passed;

- that the value of the company's allotted share capital is at least £50,000;

- that every share is paid up to at least 25% plus the whole of any premium;

- that any valuation required under s 103 has been properly carried out (this provides for valuation of assets where they are exchanged for shares in a public company);

- that where shares have been allotted in exchange for services, those services have been performed;

- that where shares have been allotted in exchange for a future undertaking, that the undertaking has been performed or that there is an obligation to perform it within five years;

- that between the balance sheet date and the application to re-register, there has been no financial change in the company's circumstances whereby the company's net assets have become worth less than the aggregate of its called up share capital plus undistributable reserves.

If these documents are delivered in due order, a certificate of incorporation will then be issued confirming that the company is a public company.

5.3.2 Re-registration of a public company as a private company

A re-registration of a public company as a private company may be accomplished by special resolution under s 53 of the Companies Act 1985.

The special resolution will seek a change of status and alteration of the memorandum and articles of the company as well as the company's name.

An application should be forwarded to the registrar of companies signed by a director of the company or the company secretary together with amended copies of the memorandum and articles of association.

There is a special protection here for minorities under s 54 of the Companies Act. Holders of not less than 5% of the company's shares or not less than 50 of its members who have not voted in favour of the change of status may seek to convince the court that the alteration should not be permitted.

The requirement to state the situate of a company's office is a requirement to state the country of its registered office, not the actual address of the registered office. The situate clause must state either that the registered office is to be situated in Scotland or in England and Wales, or that it is to be situated in Wales (if it is wished to file documents in the Welsh language). This is the one matter contained in the company's constitution that can never as a matter of law be changed. That is to say, it is not possible for example to change the situate of a company's registered office from Scotland to England and Wales. Matters concerning the situate of a company's registered office do not often arise. In *Re Baby Moon (UK) Ltd* (1985), such a matter did arise. A company had been registered at Companies House in Cardiff with its situate clause stating that the registered office of the company was situated in England. However, the address of the registered office submitted to the Companies House was in Scotland. The question arose as to whether an English court had jurisdiction to hear a petition for the winding up of the company. It was held that it did have such jurisdiction as the company's constitution had stipulated for an English registered office. Harman J in the English High Court stated:

> It is quite plain that though companies registered in England ought never to have a registered office in Scotland, in this case the impossible has occurred. How that has happened, nobody on the part of the petitioner can explain, but in my judgment the jurisdiction is plainly founded and it is right that this company should answer in this court for whatever obligations it may have.

It has been suggested that it may be possible to cross-border transfer the registered office by private Act of Parliament.

5.4   Situate of the office

5.5   Objects of the company

The memorandum of the company should contain a statement of the company's objects. Historically, this statement of objects was envisaged as a short, crisp statement of what the company was set up to do. It will be seen that this turned out to be extremely wide of what occurred in practice.

The registrar of companies does not exercise any supervisory role in relation to a company's objects except to ensure that those objects are legal. Mention has already been made of *R v Registrar of Companies, ex p Attorney General* (see para 5.1.2). Registration of the company is not, however, conclusive evidence of the fact that its objects are legal, see *Bowman v Secular Society Ltd* (1917).

However, the statement of a company's objects is important for other reasons. A company may be restrained from doing something which is outside the scope of its objects clause. Thus, in *Simpson v Westminster Palace Hotel Co* (1860), a shareholder sought to restrain the hotel company from letting out rooms as office space. In the event, it was held that this was not *ultra vires* the company's objects but it was held that had it been so an injunction could have been issued. In *Stephens v Mysore Reefs (Kangundy) Mining Co Ltd* (1902), a goldmining company which was set up to mine in India was restrained from mining for gold in West Africa as this was beyond its objects clause.

A second reason why a company's statement of objects is important is that if the substratum of the company (its *raison d'être*) is destroyed, then a petitioner may apply to wind the company up on the just and equitable ground under s 122(1)(g) of the Insolvency Act 1986. Thus, in *Re German Date Coffee Company* (1882), a company was set up to work a German patent to manufacture coffee from dates. The German patent was not granted. The company did, however, obtain a Swedish patent. A petition brought by two shareholders to wind the company up on the grounds that its objects had failed was successful despite the fact that some shareholders wished to continue with the company's activities in Sweden.

An important area in relation to a company's objects clause is the question of to what extent a contract beyond the capacity of the company is enforceable, either against the company or by the company. It was formerly the case that such contracts were void at common law. Thus, in *Ashbury Railway Carriage & Iron Co Ltd v Riche* (1875), the company's objects were stated to be making, selling and hiring railway carriages. The company entered into a contract to build a railway in Belgium. The contract was approved by the shareholders at a general meeting of the company. It was held that the contract was *ultra vires* the company and that it made no difference that the shareholders had affirmed the contract as it was void *ab initio*. The company was thus able to avoid the contract and was not liable for damages to the other party to the agreement. It was also held in *General Property Investment Co v Mathieson's Trustees* (1888) that a company would never in any circumstances be barred from pleading that it did not have the capacity to do what it had purported to do. The validity of *ultra vires* contracts has been altered dramatically by statute as will be demonstrated below.

Although not as crucial as formerly when *ultra vires* contracts were void, the drafting of a company's objects clause is still important. The consequences of a company engaging in activities outside of its objects clause have just been examined. The history of objects clauses and their interpretation is largely a history of conflict between the judiciary on the one hand which wished to confine objects clauses to short crisp statements of the company's activities and entrepreneurs on the other hand who wished to provide companies with as much latitude as possible in their activities. In *Re Crown Bank* (1890), North J held that a company's *intra vires* activities were limited to its main economic activity and that other matters stated in the company's objects clause could only exist in relation to that main economic activity. The effect of this decision was at issue in *Cotman v Brougham* (1918). In this case, the House of Lords had to consider the objects clause of Essequibo Rubber & Tobacco Estates Ltd. The objects clause enabled the company to carry on virtually every type of activity. In the Court of Appeal, Lord Cozens Hardy MR had said:

> Now we are familiar with an enumeration of objects which extends the full length of the alphabet, and sometimes beyond it, so that you get sub-clauses (aa) and (bb) after you have exhausted all the other letters.

The last sub-clause of the objects clause provided that every sub-clause should be construed as a substantive object of the company and that none of the sub-clauses should be deemed to be subsidiary or auxiliary to the principal object. At issue was the matter of underwriting certain shares in an oil company. Applying the principle in *Re Crown Bank*, underwriting could only exist as an *intra vires* business in relation to rubber and tobacco. However, the statement in the company's objects clause was held to be valid with the result that the activity was held to be *intra vires*. The House of Lords thus reluctantly held the provision in the memorandum to be valid.

5.6   Drafting the objects clause

Another drafting device used to extend the scope of a company's permitted activities was at issue in *Bell Houses Ltd v City Wall Properties Ltd* (1966). The company was engaged in acquiring land and building houses. A sub-clause of the objects clause permitted the company 'to carry on any other trade or business whatsoever which can, in the opinion of the board of directors be advantageously carried on by the company in connection with or as ancillary to any of the above businesses or the general business of the company'. The plaintiff company had introduced a financier to the defendant company for an agreed fee. In this case the plaintiff company was suing for this fee. The defendants meanwhile alleged that the contract was *ultra vires* as the plaintiffs were in the business of developing property not helping others to do so. At first instance, the action of the plaintiffs for their fee was dismissed on the ground that the contract was *ultra vires*. The plaintiffs appealed to the Court of Appeal. The appeal was successful. It was held that the objects clause permitted the directors to carry on any business which they considered could be advantageously carried on with the main business. It is, however, worth stressing that this decision of itself does not permit a company to register an objects clause where the directors can simply decide that some other activity is advantageous and profitable. This is because there are limiting words in the sub-clause, namely 'in connection with or as ancillary to'. Therefore there must be some nexus between the new business and the company's principal business.

The interpretation of an objects clause was also in issue in *Re New Finance and Mortgage Company Limited (in liquidation)* (1975). The object clause of this company provided that the company could act 'as financiers, capitalists, concessionaires, bankers, commercial agents, mortgage brokers, financial agents and advisers, exporters and importers of goods and merchandise of all kinds, and merchants generally'. The company in fact ran two garages and garage shops. The company went into voluntary liquidation and Total Oil (Great Britain) Ltd sought to prove in the liquidation in relation to the sale of motor oil to the company. The liquidator rejected the proof as he contended that the purchase of the oil was *ultra vires*. The court held that the words 'and merchants generally' were broad enough to cover all types of commercial transactions and that therefore the purchase of the motor oil was *intra vires*.

The impresario, Sir David Frost has also indirectly contributed to the law in this area. In *Newstead (Inspector of Taxes) v Frost* (1983), the objects clause of a memorandum of a company authorised to carry on and execute all kinds of financial, commercial, trading or other operations was held to be valid. Some doubts were expressed on this by Viscount Dilhorne in the House of Lords but the objects clause was nevertheless upheld. At issue was the validity of a tax savings scheme entered into by David Frost with the company.

The combined effect of the jurisprudence of these various cases is to indicate that by ingenious drafting it is possible to give a company an extremely wide capacity within which to act. Such decisions inevitably led to a questioning of the law in this area. This will be examined below.

It was formerly the case (before the Companies Act 1989) that only certain changes of objects were permitted. It was necessary that the change of objects fitted within one of the permitted categories set out in s 4 of the Act. The amended section permits the members of a company by special resolution to alter the objects clause in any way. The s 4 procedure can be used to allow the company to alter any provision within its memorandum which affects the objects of the company – see *Incorporated Glasgow Dental Hospital v Lord Advocate* (1927). Section 5 of the Act permits a 15% dissentient minority to object to the court within 21 days of the resolution being passed. The court then has power to reject the alteration or to confirm it in whole or in part. The court may order the purchase of the dissentient members' interest. This purchase may be ordered by the court to be made by the company itself with the company's capital being reduced in consequence and its memorandum and articles altered accordingly.

5.7   Change of objects

It has already been noted that at common law, contracts that were outside of a company's objects clause were *ultra vires* and void. Such contracts could not be enforced by the company or against the company. See *Ashbury Iron and Railway Carriage Company v Riche*. It made no difference whether the person dealing with the company knew the company's objects or not. The whole doctrine of *ultra vires* rested on the principle of constructive notice, the rule in *Ernest v Nichols* (1857), whereby a person dealing with a company was deemed to know what was in its memorandum and articles of association. A person dealing with a company was however entitled to assume where an activity could have been executed in an *ultra vires* or an *intra vires* way that it would be executed in an *intra vires* way. Thus, in *Re David Payne & Co Ltd* (1904), where a company borrowed money that was in fact applied to its *ultra vires* business, the lender of the money was entitled to sue on the contract as he was entitled to assume that the loan was to be used for *intra vires* activities. This did not help the outsider

**5.8   *Ultra vires*
contracts and
common law**

if he actually knew the purpose of the loan, even though he might not have realised it was *ultra vires*. The combination of actual knowledge of the activity and constructive notice of its *ultra vires* nature would be fatal. Thus, in *Re Introductions Ltd* (1970), where the company went into the *ultra vires* business of pig breeding, the lender of money knowing that the purpose of the loan was for pig breeding was unable to enforce the loan (nor could the lender rely upon a substantive provision permitting the company to borrow contained in the objects clause as the court held that borrowing of itself could not stand as a substantive separate object of a company).

This distinction between substantive objects which could be perceived as ends in themselves and powers to carry out administrative acts had previously been made in the Scottish cases of *John Walker & Sons Ltd, Petitioners* (1914) and *North of Scotland & Orkney & Shetland Steam Navigation Co Ltd* (1920) where in the latter case the Inner House held that only powers which complemented objects could be included in a company's memorandum. Likewise, in *Thomson v J Barke & Co (Caterers)* (1975), Lord Dunpark held in the Outer House that a power to draw cheques expressed in the company's memorandum extended only to transactions which were *intra vires* the company's express objects, and therefore company cheques could not be used to pay a director's personal debt.

In *Re Jon Beauforte (London) Ltd* (1953), a supplier provided a company with coke. In fact the coke was used for the *ultra vires* activity of manufacturing veneered panels. The *intra vires* business was stated in the company's objects clause *inter alia* as costumiers, gown, robe, dress and mantle makers. At common law, the supplier had constructive notice of the objects clause. The order for the coke was placed on notepaper that showed that the company was in the business of manufacturing veneer panels. The court held that this combination of actual notice (by virtue of the notepaper) and constructive notice was fatal to the supplier's claim.

The whole area of *ultra vires* contracts and unauthorised acts of directors (an area that will be examined below) came up for consideration in *Rolled Steel Products (Holdings) Ltd v British Steel Corporation and others* (1986). The state of the law could scarcely be said to be satisfactory before the decision in Rolled Steel Products. The decision in this case further adds to the mosaic of rules in relation to *ultra vires* acts of a company and unauthorised acts of directors. Rolled Steel Products owed money to S Ltd. One of the directors of Rolled Steel Products (S) was also a director of S Ltd. S Ltd owed money to Colvilles Ltd which was a subsidiary of British Steel Corporation. This debt was guaranteed personally by S, the director of Rolled Steel

Products and S Ltd. Colvilles believed that S and S Ltd would have insufficient assets to pay back their debt. They therefore proposed that they would lend money to Rolled Steel Products who would use this money to pay off S Ltd who could then pay part of the debt owed to Colvilles and that Rolled Steel Products would guarantee payment of the remainder of the debt creating a debenture to secure the debt. Rolled Steel Products had a provision in its memorandum permitting it to give guarantees and security. The board resolution passed by Rolled Steel Products to grant the guarantee was only quorate by virtue of S's presence. S should have declared an interest and should not have counted in the quorum. The meeting was therefore insufficient for these purposes.

At first instance, Vinelott J held that the guarantee and the debenture were void as they were for purposes other than those authorised by the memorandum of association. This reasoning is consistent with the reasoning in *Re Introductions Ltd*.

On appeal, however, the Court of Appeal held that since the company had the power in its memorandum of association to give guarantees and to provide security, the company had contractual capacity to make the guarantee and debenture and that therefore the acts were not *ultra vires* the company. This clearly casts doubt on the decision in *Re Introductions Ltd* although it was not overruled.

The Court of Appeal went on to say, however, that the directors were acting beyond their powers in providing a guarantee and security for purposes other than those authorised by the memorandum of association and since the defendant knew of this lack of authority, they could acquire no rights under the guarantee or the debenture.

Note: although the decision in *Rolled Steel Products* was made in 1985, the relevant facts arose in 1969 and therefore were unaffected by the first statutory intervention in this area under the European Communities Act 1972.

The somewhat confused and arbitrary decisions in relation to what contracts were enforceable and what contracts were not together with the decisions on the interpretation of objects clauses prompted the government to consider statutory reform of the *ultra vires* rule and led to the commissioning of the Prentice Report which is considered below. In the meantime, however, British membership of the European Communities had necessitated reform of British company law in line with the first directive on EC company law which had been passed in 1968 (68/152).

**5.9   Section 9(1)
of the European
Communities Act
1972**

Article 9 of the first EC directive on company law provides as follows:

> (i)   Acts done by the organs of the company shall be binding upon it even if those acts are not within the objects of the company, unless such acts exceed the powers that the law confers or allows to be conferred on those organs.
>
> However, Member States may provide that the company shall not be bound where such acts are outside the objects of the company, if it proves that the third party knew the act was outside those objects or could not in view of the circumstances have been unaware of it; disclosure of the statute shall not of itself be sufficient proof thereof.
>
> (ii)   The limits on the powers of the organs of the company, arising under the statutes from a decision of the competent organ, may never be relied on as against third parties, even if they have been disclosed.
>
> Section 9(1) of the European Communities Act accordingly provided that in favour of a person dealing with a company in good faith any transaction decided on by the directors shall be deemed to be one which it is within the capacity of the company to enter into and the power of the directors to bind the company shall be deemed to be free of any limitation under the memorandum or articles of association, and a party to a transaction so decided on shall not be bound to enquire as to the capacity of the company to enter into it or as to any such limitation on the power of the directors, and shall be presumed to have acted in good faith unless the contrary is proved.

Several points should be noted in relation to s 9(1) of the ECA 1972 later re-enacted as s 35 of the Companies Act 1985. These are as follows:

• The provision only operated in favour of a person dealing with the company.

  Thus the company itself could not take advantage of the section to enforce an *ultra vires* contract.

• The section only operated where the person dealing with the company was acting in good faith.

  The section failed to contain a definition of good faith but, as is stated, there is a presumption of good faith that stands unless the contrary is proved. In *Barclays Bank Ltd v TOSG Trust Fund Ltd* (1984), Nourse J stated *obiter* that a person acts in good faith if he acts genuinely and honestly in the circumstances of the case and that it is not necessary to show that he acted reasonably to demonstrate that he acted in good faith.

- The transaction had to be decided on by the directors.

  There was no guidance given as to how this was to be determined but it seems from the decision in *International Sales & Agencies v Marcus* (1982) that provided the chain of delegation can be traced back to the board of directors, this was sufficient for satisfying the condition in the section.

In light of the obvious anomalies in the law and the ease with which companies could avoid falling into the *ultra vires* trap, the government asked Dr Dan Prentice of Oxford University to investigate the area of objects clauses and *ultra vires* with a view to the possible abolition of the *ultra vires* doctrine and recommending any necessary safeguards for investors and creditors.

Dr Prentice duly obliged the government and recommended the abolition of the doctrine with few provisos. His report was published as a consultative document – 'Reform of the *ultra vires* Rule: A Consultative Document' (1986). The Companies Act 1989 did not go quite so far as some of the radical recommendations of the Prentice Report.

Dr Prentice had recommended that companies be given freedom to alter their objects clauses in any circumstances by special resolution. This recommendation was enacted. He further recommended that companies should be able to adopt a general objects clause permitting them to operate as general commercial companies. This recommendation was enacted and accordingly s 3A permits a company's memorandum to state that its object is 'to carry on business as a general commercial company'. This means that:

(a)   the object of the company is to carry on any trade or business whatsoever, and

(b)   the company has power to do all such things as are incidental to the carrying on of any trade or business by it.

This came into effect on 4 February 1991.

The effect of the Companies Act 1985 as amended by the Companies Act 1989 is as follows.

5.10   The Prentice Report and the Companies Act 1989

The validity of an act done by a company shall not be called into question on the ground of lack of capacity by reason of anything in the company's memorandum. A transaction can thus be enforced by an outsider or by the company (s 35(1)). The section is, therefore, wider than merely encompassing the objects clause. In *Re Cleveland Trust* (1991), the memorandum restricted the payment of dividends. This restriction despite being outside of the objects clause would now be caught by s 35.

5.10.1   Company's memorandum

| 5.10.2 | Company's objects | A member may restrain the company from entering into an act which is outside the company's objects (s 35(2)). The position here has not altered and is as stated above. See *Simpson v Westminster Palace Hotel Co, Stevens v Mysore Reefs (Kangundi) Mining Co Ltd.* |

| 5.10.3 | Director's breach of duty | In so far as directors exceed limitations on their powers that flow from the memorandum, they are in breach of their duty. The company may thus be able to sue them for breach of duty (s 35(3)) – see *Maxton v Brown* (1839). However, acts that are outside the company's capacity can be ratified by special resolution and the company can ratify what they have done by a separate special resolution (s 35(3)). |

| 5.10.4 | Constructive notice | The old rule of constructive notice is abolished. Those dealing with a company are not deemed to know what the company's objects or directors' powers are. This rule is now contained in s 35B of the Companies Act 1985: |

> A party to a transaction with a company is not bound to enquire as to whether it is permitted by the company's memorandum or as to any limitation on the powers of the board of directors to bind the company or authorise others to do so.

This is added to by s 711A(1) which provides that:

> A person shall not be taken to have notice of any matter merely because of its being disclosed in any document kept by the registrar of companies (and thus available for inspection) or made available by the company for inspection.

Section 711A(2) provides 'This does not affect the question whether a person is affected by notice of any matter by reason of a failure to make such inquiries as ought reasonably to be made'.

Generally, ss 35A and 35B will protect outsiders dealing with directors who act beyond their powers, s 711A may be relevant where some other officer acts beyond his authority.

| 5.10.5 | Director's power to bind the company | Where a person deals with a company in good faith, the power of the directors to bind the company shall be deemed to be free of any limitation under the company's constitution. The outsider is not to be regarded as in bad faith by reason only of his knowing the transaction was beyond the directors' powers (s 35A). |

It should be noted that s 35A protects an outsider who deals with a company and that 'deals' is now defined as where a person is a party to any transaction or other act. This is broader than the old law and would seemingly encompass gifts, the receipt of cheques (see *International Sales and Agencies Ltd v Marcus* under the old law) and covenants.

Prentice recommended a special provision in relation to the board of directors entering into a transaction on the company's behalf with a person who is a director of the company or of the company's holding company or a person connected with such a director or a company associated with such a director. Section 322A accordingly provides that a transaction is voidable if it exceeds a limitation on the powers of the board of directors under the company's constitution if one of the parties to the transaction include (a) a director of the company or of its holding company, or (b) a person connected with such a director or a company with whom such a director is associated, at the option of the company.

5.10.6   Person connected with director

Special provision is also made for charities. By s 112 of the Companies Act 1989 in Scotland and s 98(2) and Sched 7 of the Charities Act 1993 in England and Wales, the new provisions contained in s 35 and s 35A of the 1985 Act do not apply to a company which is a charity except in favour of a person who gives full consideration in money or money's worth and does not know that the act is beyond the company's objects clause or beyond the directors' powers or who does not know at the time that the act is done that the company is a charity.

5.10.7   Charities

In most circumstances, activities that are *ultra vires* the company are enforceable both by and against the company. In the event that an outsider cannot enforce an *ultra vires* contract against the company he may have an action for breach of warranty of authority against the person purporting that the company has the appropriate capacity. The related question of directors and others acting beyond their capacity is considered below at paras 12.4 and 12.5.

Most companies are limited by shares and if it is stated that there is limited liability without any further qualification, it is assumed that this means that the company is limited by shares. If the company is limited by guarantee, the memorandum will state this and will state the amount that each of the members (guarantors) will contribute towards the payments of its debts and liabilities in the event of the company being wound up.

5.11   Limitation of liability

A private limited company may re-register as an unlimited company if all of its members agree. An application must be lodged with the registrar of companies together with the amended constitution of the company (s 49). Once a company has made a change from limited liability to unlimited liability, it cannot change back.

5.12   Change from limited liability to unlimited liability

For a public company to change from being limited to unlimited, it will first need to change to be re-registered as a private company under s 53. The members would need to pass a special resolution to alter the company's memorandum and articles. An application signed by a director or by the company secretary should then be made to the registrar together with the resolution and the amended constitution. Under s 54 there is provision for holders of 5% of the shares of a public company or 50 or more members to apply to the court to cancel the special resolution requesting re-registration as a private company provided that they have not voted in favour of the resolution. This application must be made within 28 days of the passage of the resolution. Once this change of status has been accomplished, the company may then re-register as an unlimited company under s 49.

An unlimited company may re-register as a private limited company. It must first secure the passage of a special resolution. To protect creditors, liability of past and present members remains unlimited as regards debts in existence at that time if the company should go into liquidation within three years. The resolution should be sent to the registrar together with an application signed by a director or the company secretary together with the new constitution of the company (ss 51–52 of the Companies Act 1985). An unlimited company with share capital may also apply to register as a public limited company under ss 43–48 of the Companies Act 1985, once again provided that a special resolution has been passed. Similarly an application should be made to the registrar in the prescribed manner together with the amended constitution. The company will also need to satisfy the minimum capital requirements in relation to public companies discussed above (see para 5.3.1).

5.13 Capital clause

The company's capital clause should set out the amount of authorised share capital that the company is formed with. This represents the amount up to which the company may issue shares. It is not necessary that the company should issue all of the shares. Obviously, in the case of a public company, the amount of the authorised share capital must be at least £50,000.

The clause will also divide the amount of share capital into shares of a fixed amount, for example £100,000 divided into 100,000 shares of £1 each.

5.14 Alteration of authorised share capital

Section 121 of the Companies Act 1985 provides that if it is desired to increase the authorised share capital, decrease the unissued authorised share capital, consolidate or sub-divide the shares or convert the shares into stock or vice versa, then this may be accomplished in the manner set out in Table A. Table A specifies an ordinary resolution. The power to alter the memorandum's capital provisions must be contained in the company's articles – see *Metropolitan Cemetery* (1934).

The procedure for reducing issued share capital will be examined separately (see para 9.6).

So far the compulsory clauses of the memorandum have been considered. It is possible for companies to have other clauses in their memorandum if they so desire. The effect of placing a matter into the memorandum rather than in the articles of association is to make it more difficult to alter that matter. It is still the case that it is alterable by special resolution just as it would be if it were in the articles but s 17 of the Companies Act 1985 provides that such clauses are alterable by special resolution unless:

5.15   Additional clauses in the memorandum

• the memorandum specifies otherwise; or

• the matter relates to the variation or abrogation of class rights (which is subject to a special regime which will be considered separately) (see para 6.2); or

• the alteration purports to increase a member's liability without his written consent.

In any case where an alteration is made under s 17 by special resolution, there is a right in a dissentient 15% minority to object to the alteration to the court and to seek to convince the court that the alteration should not be permitted. This application to the court must be made within 21 days of the passage of the special resolution.

The Memorandum of Association

The memorandum is sometimes called the external constitution of the company. It must contain certain compulsory clauses detailing:

- the company's name;

- that it is a public company – if this is the case;

- the situate of the registered office;

- the objects;

- a statement of limited liability; and

- the authorised share capital of the company.

It may contain additional clauses which are thus more difficult to alter than if they had been placed in the articles – a 15% dissentient minority may object to the court if the matter proposed for alteration is contained in the memorandum but could have been inserted in the articles of association (s 17 of the Companies Act 1985).

The procedures and rules relating to changing the mandatory provisions of the memorandum are diffuse.

Objects clauses and *ultra vires*

Historically, perhaps the most important clause in the memorandum has been the objects clause. This used to determine what the company could lawfully do.

Because of judicial interpretation and statutory intervention, this clause is no longer as crucial as formerly. It is possible since the Companies Act 1989 for trading companies to act as 'general commercial companies' thus affording almost total latitude.

Even for those companies with limited room for manoeuvre, activities beyond the scope of the objects clause will usually be valid. A member may however restrain a company from entering into an *ultra vires* transaction, ie before the event. Where a company does act outside of its objects clause there is usually the possibility of the company's directors being in breach of their duty. The *ultra vires* act can be ratified by special resolution and the directors may have their breach of duty ratified by separate special resolution.

Chapter 6

The Articles of Association

In addition to the memorandum of association, before a company can be registered, the company's promoters must also submit to the registrar the company's articles of association. These articles of association, as has been noted, are sometimes known as the internal constitution of the company. They cover such matters as the holding of meetings, the appointment of directors, declaration of dividends, and the appointment of the company secretary.

There exist certain model articles of association. These are set out in the Companies (Tables A–F) Regulations 1985 (SI 1985/805). Section 128 of the Companies Act 1989 makes provision for a Table G in relation to articles of association for a partnership company. A partnership company is one limited by shares whose shares are intended to be held to a substantial extent by or on behalf of its employees. Companies may elect to adopt the relevant table of articles and thus obviate the need for framing their own sets of articles. The most common form of articles is Table A. These articles are applicable to private and public companies limited by shares. In so far as a company fails to register articles or to make provision for any matter, Table A articles for the time being in force will apply (s 8(2) of the Companies Act 1985).

There are some restrictions on the articles a company may choose to adopt. Articles which are contrary to public policy are illegal and void. Thus it was held that an article purporting to exclude the jurisdiction of the court was void – *St Johnstone FC v SFA* (1965). Any conflict between the provisions of the articles and those in the memorandum will be resolved in favour of the memorandum – see *Scottish National Trust Co Ltd* (1928).

At common law a company must also act according to its articles. In *Dunn v Banknock Coal Co Ltd* (1901), the Outer House held that a company's actions which were unauthorised by its articles were *ultra vires* and therefore void, even where the actions benefited the company and were approved by the company's members. This decision is of course now subject to the new ss 35 and 35A of the Companies Act 1985 (see paras 5.10.1–5.10.7).

6.1   Alteration of the articles of association

As has been noted, a company may alter its articles of association by special resolution (s 9 of the Companies Act 1985). Indeed, any article that seems to restrict a company's freedom to alter its articles is invalid, see *Allen v Gold Reefs of West Africa* (1900), although a separate shareholders' agreement may validly restrict the alterability of the company's articles on the part of shareholders, see *Russell v Northern Bank Development Corporation Ltd* (1992). This power is subject to certain restrictions:

- a company cannot alter its articles to contravene the provisions of the Companies Act. Thus, any provision in the articles which would seek to exempt a director from liability for negligence is void by virtue of s 310. By the same token, a provision which seeks to increase the liability of a member beyond that of his original contract is void by virtue of s 16 of the Act;

- any alteration of the articles which clashes with a provision in the company's memorandum is void. See *Guinness v Land Corporation of Ireland* (1882);

- any alteration of the articles which conflicts with an order of the court is, of course, void. Thus, an order of the court under s 5 relating to changes of objects or under s 461 relating to the remedy for unfairly prejudicial conduct cannot be overridden by a change of articles;

- if the alteration of articles involves an alteration or abrogation of class rights, then in addition to the special resolution required under s 9, the company must follow the regime appropriate to variation of class rights set out in ss 125–27 (this will be considered below – see para 6.2);

- an alteration cannot affect accrued and unrealised rights of members – see *McArthur v Gulf Line* (1909);

- in addition to the statutory restrictions, the power to alter a company's articles is subject to the principle that any alteration must be *bona fide* for the benefit of the company as a whole. In *Allen v The Gold Reefs of West Africa Ltd* (1900), the company's articles of association gave the company a lien upon all partly paid shares held by a member for any debt owed to the company. A member who held some partly paid shares was also the only holder of fully paid shares in the company. Upon his death, he owed money in relation to the partly paid shares. The company altered its articles by special resolution to provide for a lien over fully paid shares. This alteration was questioned. The Court of Appeal held that the company could alter its articles provided that the alteration was in good faith. Lord Lindley MR said:

> ... the power conferred by it [s 9] must, like all other powers, be exercised subject to those general principles of law and equity which are applicable to all powers conferred on majorities and enabling them to bind minorities. It must be exercised, not only in the manner required by law, but also *bona fide* for the benefit of the company as a whole, and it must not be exceeded.

Much of the case law has centred upon a discussion of how it is to be determined whether an alteration is for the benefit of the company as a whole. In *Greenhalgh v Arderne Cinemas Ltd* (1951), it was proposed to delete a provision in the company's articles which gave members a right of pre-emption over shares that a member wanted to sell. It seemed that the majority shareholder, Mr Mallard was prompted not by what was in the company's best interest but out of malice towards a minority shareholder. The question arose as to whether the alteration was for the benefit of the company as a whole. Lord Evershed MR said that:

> ... the phrase 'the company as a whole' does not (at any time in such a case as the present) mean the company as a commercial entity, distinct from the corporators; it means the corporators as a general body. That is to say, the case may be taken of an individual hypothetical member and it may be asked is what is proposed, in the honest opinion of those who voted in its favour, for that person's benefit.

In this case, the Court of Appeal held that the alteration was valid.

This analysis does raise difficulties in determining the benefit of the individual hypothetical member. It is clear that hardship to a minority will not of itself invalidate an alteration of articles. In *Sidebottom v Kershaw Leese & Co Ltd* (1920), a minority shareholder in the company carried on a business that was competing with the company. It was proposed to alter the company's articles to insert a clause whereby a shareholder who competed with the company would be required to transfer his shares at a fair value to the directors. It was held that the alteration was valid even though it was carried out specifically against one particular member. The clause in question, of course, could apply in relation to any member.

By contrast, in *Brown v British Abrasive Wheel Co Ltd* (1919), where 98% majority shareholders wished to insert a provision in the articles requiring the minority who were not prepared to invest further capital to sell their shares as a condition of the majority's providing further capital, the alteration was held invalid. It was noted that such a provision could be used to require a minority to sell its shares at the will of the majority. The court did point out, however, that there was nothing to stop such a clause being included in the original articles submitted at the time the company was incorporated.

The cases do appear to be inconsistent. If the question is not what is for the benefit of the company as a separate corporate entity, it is difficult to conjure up a hypothetical shareholder in whose interest the alteration must be. If malevolence did not prevent Mr Mallard succeeding in *Greenhalgh v Arderne Cinemas*, why should the majority's view be overridden in *Brown v British Abrasive Wheel Co Ltd*? A possible interpretation is offered by Lord Evershed MR in the *Greenhalgh* case where he argues that if the effect of the alteration is to discriminate between the majority shareholders and the minority shareholders to give the majority an advantage, then the alteration should not be permitted.

It is now the case that ss 459–61 will provide a possible remedy to a shareholder who has been unfairly prejudiced in the conduct of a company's affairs by the use of majority voting power. In addition, courts have sometimes been willing to act to protect minority shareholders from the oppressive use of majority voting power. See *Clemens v Clemens Brothers Ltd and Another* (1976), *Estmanco (Kilner House) Ltd v Greater London Council* (1982).

A final point should be noted in relation to alteration of the articles. Notwithstanding that an alteration of the articles may result in a breach of contract by the company, an interdict (injunction in England) will not be issued to stop the alteration taking place, see *Southern Foundries (1926) Ltd v Shirlaw* (1940). The innocent party will, of course, be able to pursue a remedy in relation to the breach of contract unless the article was impliedly incorporated into the contract, thus making it unilaterally alterable by the company – see *Shuttleworth v Cox Bros (Maidenhead) Ltd* (1927) and para 6.3.1.

6.2   Variation of class rights

Variation of class rights is one of the more difficult areas in company law. It is a complex web of legal technicalities and judicial nuances. The basic principle is that an alteration of rights attached to a particular class of shares involves a special regime, which generally means that separate class consent has to be given. The principle is to protect the holders of those special rights.

The statutory rules are set out in ss 125–27 of the Companies Act 1985.

Often a company may have just one class of shares with uniform rights. In such a situation questions of class rights obviously do not arise. Often, however, there will be additional classes of shares, such as preference shares or management shares.

Defining a class of shares is difficult. Vaisey J offered a workable definition in *Greenhalgh v Arderne Cinemas Ltd* (1945) where he said 'although the word "class" is not a word of technical art, you cannot put people, whether they be shareholders or policy holders, into the same class if their claims or rights diverge'. Rights may well be attached to certain shares such as a right to a preferential dividend or a right to be paid off first in a liquidation.

6.2.1   Defining 'class' and 'rights'

The traditional view is that the rights must attach to the shares and not to the shareholders. Thus, in *Eley v The Positive Government Security Life Assurance Co* (1876), where the articles conferred the right to be a company solicitor on a shareholder, the right could not be construed as a class right – it was a personal right attaching to the shareholder. Such a case is a clear example but the rule has hardly been applied uniformly. In the Australian case *Fischer v Easthaven Ltd* (1964), which concerned a home unit company in which the unit holders were shareholders, the court considered that the relationship between a home unit owner and the company imposed a contractual duty on the company not to alter its articles so as to abrogate their rights, effectively treating them as class rights.

In *Cumbrian Newspapers Group Ltd v Cumberland & Westmorland Herald Newspaper & Printing Co Ltd* (1986), the whole question of class rights was analysed.

The case centred on the plaintiff's desire to maintain the Cumbrian newspapers independence from large national chains. The plaintiff published the *Penrith Observer* whose circulation largely confined to that market town was about 5,500 per week. Their chairman, John Burgess (later Sir John), negotiated with the defendants, who published the Cumberland and Westmorland Herald with a circulation throughout Cumbria. The negotiations involved the provision of discounted advertising arrangements for the defendants which would enhance the defendants' ability to attract advertising and the closure of the *Penrith Observer*. Sir John was anxious to protect the independence of the Cumbrian Press and so it was agreed that his shareholding of 10.67% in the defendant company entitled him to the rights of pre-emption over other ordinary shares, rights over unissued shares and the right to appoint a director. Later, the defendants wanted to cancel these special rights. The plaintiffs contended that they were class rights and therefore subject to the special statutory provisions of the Companies Act 1985.

Scott J held:

> In my judgment, a company which by its articles, confers special rights on one or more of its members in the capacity of member or shareholder, thereby constitutes the share for the time being held by that member or members, a class of shares. The rights are class rights.

The *Eley* case can therefore be distinguished on the basis that the right did not attach to Eley as shareholder.

6.2.2   Defining 'variation'

The next matter to be considered is whether the company's proposal amounts to a variation of the existing rights. Once again, fine judicial nuances abound in this area.

It should be said at the outset that not every act of a company which adversely affects the interests of a particular class of share amounts to a variation of the class rights of that share. Thus, in *White v The Bristol Aeroplane Co Ltd* (1953), the company proposed to capitalise its profits and distribute them in the form of a bonus issue of ordinary and preference shares.

The court held that the bonus issue would not affect the existing preference shareholders' rights or privileges. These rights might be affected as a matter of business practice because of the new preference stock, but this would relate to the enjoyment of the rights and not the rights themselves. Such fine legalistic reasoning is also apparent in a case decided at about the same time, namely *Re John Smith's Tadcaster Brewery Co Ltd* (1953).

Another famous case which analysed the concept of variation concerned the ubiquitous case of *Greenhalgh v Arderne Cinemas Ltd & Mallard* (1946). Mr Greenhalgh lent money to the company in exchange for 10 pence shares. These shares ranked *pari passu* with the ordinary 50 pence shares. The company later resolved to sub-divide the 50 pence shares into 10 pence shares which effectively quintupled the voting strength of the 50 pence shares.

The Court of Appeal held that the voting rights had not been varied by the resolution. The only voting right was one vote per share and this had remained the same throughout.

Such decisions demonstrate how restrictively the concept of variation of class rights has been interpreted in the cases. The area is riddled with the subtlest of distinctions. Lord Greene MR in *Greenhalgh* even said that:

> If it had been attempted to reduce that voting right (of the 10 pence share), for example, by providing or attempting

to provide their should be one vote for every five of such shares, that would have been an interference with the voting rights attached to that class of shares. But nothing of the kind had been done: the right to have one vote per share is left undisturbed.

Nothing could better illustrate the fine legalistic distinctions that are made in the cases. It is clear from Lord Greene's *dictum* that it is the means rather than the end that is all important.

Sometimes the company's constitution will set out clearly when a particular class of shareholders' consent is required. In *Re Northern Engineering Industries plc* (1994), a company's articles of association stipulated that a reduction of capital required the consent of the company's preference shareholders. The Court of Appeal held that this included the situation where it was proposed to cancel the preference shares.

If the proposal is clearly to alter the substance of the rights of a class of shareholders, the procedure that is set out in the Act must be followed. This procedure applies to variations of class rights. It is worth noting that a provision to alter or insert a new procedure relating to class rights is itself a variation of class rights, as is abrogation of rights. Both will involve the statutory procedures, see s 125(7), (8) of the Companies Act 1985.

6.2.3   Statutory procedures

In *House of Fraser plc v ACGE Investments Ltd* (1987), the issue of abrogation of class rights was discussed. In this case the company applied for a court order to confirm a reduction of capital. The petition to reduce the capital was opposed by two preference shareholders. Capital was to be returned to the preference shareholders. The court confirmed the reduction as it was merely an application of their class rights, the court taking the view that the class rights of the preference shareholders, involving as they did priority in a winding-up, had been fulfilled and not varied. The provision in the act to the effect that an abrogation amounts to a variation does not cover such a case. It was stated in the Inner House that:

> Abolition or abrogation are not appropriate expressions to describe the situation where a right and its corresponding obligation have been extinguished by performance.

The House of Lords upheld the Inner House. This case falls to be compared with the earlier decision of the Inner House in *Frazer Bros Petitioners* (1963) where it reached the opposite conclusion.

Once it is established that class rights do exist and that they have been varied, then the procedure for their alteration must then be considered. The rules under the statute are somewhat complicated and technical. If it has been established that there is a variation of class rights, then the rules for the variation are dependent upon where the rights are set out and what the rights concern:

- Variation procedure not specified in memorandum

  If the class rights are set out in the company's memorandum and the memorandum does not specify a variation procedure, or if the procedure for variation is set out in the articles of association (otherwise than on the company's incorporation), then modification of the rights can only be achieved by a scheme of arrangement under s 425 of the Act (see para 22.5) or by all the members of the company agreeing to the variation (s 125(4), (5), (7) of the CA 1985).

- Variation procedure specified in memorandum

  If the class rights and the variation procedure are both set out in the memorandum, then that procedure must be followed (s 17(2) CA 1985).

- Variation prohibited in memorandum

  If the class rights are set out in the memorandum and it contains an express prohibition on variation, then no variation can be effected except by a scheme of arrangement under s 425 of the Companies Act 1985 (s 17 of the CA 85).

- Class rights in memorandum and variation procedure specified in articles

  If the class rights are set out in the memorandum and the variation procedure is set out in the articles on incorporation, then that procedure must be followed (s 125(4)(a) of the CA 1985).

- Class rights not in memorandum and variation procedure specified in articles

  If the class rights are set out otherwise than in the memorandum (eg in the articles) and the variation procedure is set out in the articles, then this procedure must be followed (s 125(4)(b) of the CA 1985).

- Class rights not in memorandum and variation procedure not specified in articles

  If the class rights are attached to a class of shares otherwise than by the company's memorandum and the company's articles do not contain provision with respect of their alteration, they may be altered by the statutory variation procedure set out in s 125(2) of the 1985 Act whereby either:

(a) the holders of three quarters in nominal value of the issued shares of the class in question consent; or

(b) an extraordinary resolution which sanctions the variation is passed at a separate general meeting of the holders of that class,

and in either case any additional requirement is complied with.

There are special rules that apply if the class rights are set out in the memorandum or otherwise and the variation procedure is contained in the memorandum or articles and is connected with the giving, variation, revocation or renewal of an authority for the purposes of s 80 of the Companies Act 1985 (allotment of securities by directors), or with the reduction of share capital under s 135 of the Companies Act 1985. In this situation, whatever procedure is set down, the statutory procedure of s 125(2) must be complied with.

If the class rights are varied under a procedure set out in the memorandum or articles of a company, or if the class rights are set out otherwise than in the memorandum and the articles are silent on variation, dissentient minorities have special rights to object to the alteration.

They must satisfy certain conditions. The dissenters must hold no less than 15% of the issued shares of that class and must not have voted in favour of the resolution. If they satisfy this requirement and provided that they apply to the court within 21 days of consent being given or the resolution being passed, then unless the court confirms the variation, it is of no effect (s 127 of the Companies Act 1985).

It must be said that usually the court will confirm the order, but it will cancel it if it considers that the alteration has been passed by a vote which neglects the interests of the class. This is what occurred in *Re Holders Investment Trust Ltd* (1971).

In this case, Holders Investment Trust Ltd proposed to reduce its capital by cancelling its 5% cumulative preference shares in exchange for an equivalent amount of unsecured loan stock to the shareholders of that class. Almost 90% of the preference shares were vested in trustees and trusts set up by one, William Hill. They voted in favour of the resolution. They also held 52% of the ordinary stock and shares. Their vote was clearly influenced by the benefit they would receive as ordinary shareholders from the proposed variation. Megarry J held that the scheme was unfair and refused to sanction the reduction, saying 'it fell substantially below the threshold of anything that justly be called fair'.

Such cases are exceptional. It is more usual to find that what is acceptable to the majority will have to do for the minority as well.

6.2.4   Criticisms

The courts construe the concept of the variation of class rights extremely narrowly; indeed, it is arguable that their attitude is so legalistic and technical that it frustrates the very sound policy of the protection and preservation of class rights.

The statutory rules that govern the variation of class rights should be simple. Instead of this, they are technical, complex and riddled with anomalies. It is difficult to see why variations connected with the issue of shares or the reduction of share capital should be treated differently.

It would be a simple matter to provide by statute that a variation of class rights wherever the class rights are set out could be made with the consent of three quarters in value of the shareholders of the class or by an extraordinary resolution of the class concerned. Needless to say, there is not the slightest chance of this happening. The law will remain unnecessarily complex and technical.

6.3   Membership contract

Section 14 of the Companies Act 1985 provides that the effect of the articles and memorandum when registered is to constitute them into a contract which binds the company and the members as if they had been signed and sealed by each member and contain covenants on the part of each member to observe their provisions.

This provision is more important in relation to the articles than it is in relation to the memorandum. The memorandum by its nature does not generally involve contractual provisions affecting members. The effect of s 14 has been the subject of some controversy.

In *Hickman v Kent or Romney Marsh Sheep-Breeders' Association* (1915), the Association which was a registered company provided in its articles that disputes between the Association and a member of the Association should be referred to arbitration rather than being the subject of litigation in the courts. Mr Hickman, who was in dispute with the Association about his expulsion, started proceedings in the High Court. An injunction was issued to prevent the proceedings in the High Court. Astbury J held that the effect of s 14 was to create a contract between the Association and its members whereby the members agreed not to take a dispute to court.

Another illustration of the same principle is to be found in *Pender v Lushington* (1877). In this case, the articles gave shareholders the right to vote. The articles also fixed a maximum amount of votes which each member could cast, namely 100. To evade this rule, Pender transferred some of his shares into the names of nominees who were bound to vote as directed by him. The shares were registered in their name. At a meeting the chairman refused to count their votes. Pender sued for an injunction to restrain the chairman from declaring the nominees' votes invalid. He succeeded on the basis of the contract in the articles which bound the company to the shareholder. Shareholders had the right to vote as set out in the articles of association.

Section 14 only applies to the company and its members. Thus in *National Bank of Scotland Glasgow Nominees Ltd v Adamson* (1932) a creditor of a former member of a company tried to argue that a transfer of the debtor's shares was invalid, because the transfer had not been effected in accordance with provisions in the company's articles. However, it was held that the creditor had no title to sue, since any irregularity in the transfer was a domestic matter and could not be challenged by an outsider.

Thus far the principle seems straightforward. A member can sue in relation to matters set out in the articles and also can be sued by the company in the same way. However, it seems the matter is not so simple. In *Eley v Positive Government Security Life Assurance Co* (1876), Eley had been named as company solicitor in the articles of association. He had been appointed as such but was subsequently removed. Eley was a member of the company and he sought to enforce the rights set out in the articles. He was unsuccessful. The court held that he was an outsider and could not enforce the contract in his capacity as a solicitor. The articles only gave him rights in his capacity as a member. It is not clear from the decision whether the position would have been different had he sued as a member. In the later case of *Beattie v E & F Beattie Ltd* (1938), the articles of the company provided for any dispute between a member and the company to be referred to arbitration. A director of the company who also held shares in the company sought to restrain legal proceedings against him on the basis of this article. The Court of Appeal held that he must fail as he was seeking to enforce the terms of the articles as an outsider, that is, as a director rather than as a member. It is thus said that the articles of association cannot be enforced by a member or against a member in relation to outsider rights and obligations. In *Salmon v Quin & Axtens Ltd* (1909), the company's articles gave the power of management to the board of directors but provided that joint managing directors each had a power of veto over certain key decisions. Salmon, one of the managing directors, sought to enforce this right of veto in relation to a board resolution. He sued the company on behalf of himself and other shareholders to restrain the company from acting on the resolution in breach of the article. The court held that he would succeed. He was thus able to enforce his right as a director by suing upon the membership contract. The case is clearly at odds with the later decision in *Beattie v E & F Beattie Ltd*.

It has been suggested that, in Scotland, a third party may be able to rely on provisions contained in a company's constitution on the basis that it creates a *jus quaesitum tertio* if its provisions clearly demonstrate an intention to benefit the third party and are irrevocable (which of course is only possible by inclusion of the provision in the memorandum rather than in the articles) – see *Stair Memorial Encyclopedia*.

6.3.1   The effect of s 14

There has been much discussion about these cases and the effect of s 14. Professor Gower takes a traditional view that the membership contract is only enforceable in relation to membership rights and obligations in the narrow sense. Lord Wedderburn (Shareholders' Rights and the Rule in *Foss v Harbottle* (1957)) in contrast takes the view that a member always has the right to have the articles and memorandum enforced. He takes the view that there is one basic membership right to have the articles and memorandum enforced. Other academics have joined the fray. GD Goldberg ((1972) 33 MLR 362) and Dr GN Prentice ((1980) 1 Co Law 179) have put forward a qualified version of Wedderburn's thesis that a member can sue in respect of a right set out in the articles. Goldberg argues that a member has a contractual right to have the affairs of the company conducted by the appropriate organ while Dr Prentice contends that it is necessary to ask whether the particular provision affects the power of the company to function. These contentions may help to rationalise the decision in *Salmon v Quin & Axtens Ltd*. However, there is no evidence that the judges were thinking in this way.

A different view is put forward by Roger Gregory ((1981) 44 MLR 526) who argues cogently that there are two lines of cases supporting different views and that the cases are irreconcilable. This view is probably closest to the truth.

An interesting case that is perhaps consistent with either theory and which illustrates the breakdown that there has been between membership and management rights in small private companies is *Rayfield v Hands* (1960). In this case, a provision in the articles stated that every member who wished to transfer his shares should notify the directors of this and that the directors would be obliged to purchase the shares at a fair value. In this company all of the shareholders were directors.

The plaintiff informed the directors of his wish to sell his shares and then when they refused to take them as stipulated under the articles he sought to enforce the article against them. The court held that the article imposed a contractual obligation against the directors in their capacity as members.

On occasion, the company's memorandum and articles may form the basis of a quite separate contract. This was the case, for example, in *Muirhead v Forth and North Sea Steamboat Mutual Insurance Association* (1893) where a company was able to rely on its altered articles as terms incorporated into a contract of insurance, and in *Re New British Iron Company ex p Beckwith* (1898) where directors were able to imply a contract on the same terms as the articles when suing for their remuneration.

However, if this is the case then the contract incorporating the terms of the company's articles may well be on alterable terms since the articles are freely alterable by the company. Thus in *Swabey v Port Darwin Gold Mining Company* (1889) the court took the view that the company could alter its articles and so affect the terms of the contract for the future.

In some cases, it may be that there is an implied term that the contract is concluded on the basis of the articles as they are at a particular date. Therefore, later variation of the articles will not affect the terms of the contract. Thus, in *Southern Foundries (1926) Ltd v Shirlaw* (1940), both the Court of Appeal and the House of Lords held that it was a breach of contract to alter the articles of the company so as to affect the contract of employment between the appellant and the respondent.

Quite apart from the controversy concerning the types of rights and obligations that can be enforced via the membership contract, the s 14 contract has other special features. In some respects it is quite unlike an orthodox contract.

6.3.2   Special features

The court has no jurisdiction to rectify the articles even though they do not represent the intention of those signing them, as was held in *Scott v Frank F Scott (London) Ltd* (1940) and *Bratton Seymour Service Co Ltd v Oxborough* (1992). In this respect, the contract is quite different from a normal contract. However, if the understanding of the members differs materially from the constitutional arrangements of the company, this may be a basis for winding the company up on the just and equitable ground under s 122(1)(g) of the Insolvency Act 1986. In the New Zealand case of *Re North End Motels (Huntly) Ltd* (1976), a retired farmer subscribed for half of the share capital of the company on the basis that he would have an equal say in its management. He found, however, that he was in a minority on the board of directors and he successfully petitioned to wind the company up on the just and equitable ground.

It used to be the case that a member could not sue for damages for breach of his membership contract while remaining a member. This was a rather unusual feature of the membership contract of a company. A member was limited to the remedies of interdict or declarator. This was the rule in *Houldsworth v City of Glasgow Bank* (1880). However s 131 of the Companies Act 1989, altering the Companies Act 1985, now provides that 'a person is not debarred from obtaining damages or other compensation from a company by reason only of his holding or having held shares in the company or any right to apply or subscribe for shares or to be included in the company's register in respect of shares' (s 111A).

The s 14 contract is, of course, subject to the provisions of the Companies Acts and so the articles cannot defeat the provisions of the legislation. Furthermore, the company's articles and memorandum are alterable by special resolution and so this means that the terms of the s 14 contract can also be altered.

The Articles of Association

The articles of association together with the memorandum forms the company's constitution. The articles are sometimes termed the company's internal constitution. They govern the internal workings of the company.

Although the articles are said to be freely alterable – in fact by special resolution under s 9 of the Companies Act 1985 – there are various restrictions that apply:

Alteration of the articles

- the alteration must not contravene the companies' legislation;

- the alteration must not conflict with the company's memorandum;

- the alteration must not be 'at odds with' a court order;

- a special regime applies if the alteration varies class rights;

- at common law an alteration of the articles must be put forward *bona fide* for the benefit of the company as a whole.

Where rights are attached to a particular class of share, a special procedure applies for varying those rights.

Variation of class rights

First, it must be determined that there is a separate class of shares involved. The courts adopt a broad approach to this question as in *Cumbrian Newspapers Group Ltd v Cumberland & Westmorland Herald Newspaper & Printing Co Ltd* (1986).

Secondly, the question arises as to whether there is a proposed variation of rights attaching to those shares. Here the court adopts a restrictive approach so that if what is to be varied is the enjoyment of rights rather than the rights themselves then the variation of class rights regime does not apply. For example, a proposed reduction of a preference dividend would be a variation of class rights whereas a proposal to increase the voting strength of management shares as against ordinary shares would not be a variation of the rights of the ordinary shareholders.

Thirdly, if there is a proposed variation of class rights, then in addition to passing a special resolution of all of the shareholders there needs to be a separate class consent. This will generally be expressed by an extraordinary resolution of the class concerned or by three quarters consent of the class concerned. There are some variations on this theme, however.

Fourthly, even if there is a separate class consent given, it is still generally open to a dissentient 15% of the class to apply to the court to seek to stop the variation. They may be able to do so, for example, by demonstrating that the holders of the shares of the class concerned have voted in a particular way as they are also shareholders of another class (see *Re Holders Investment Trust Ltd* (1971)).

Membership contract

The provisions of the articles and also of the memorandum constitute a contract between the company's members and the company and between the members *inter se* (s 14 of the Companies Act 1985).

There is controversy as to whether the contract is enforceable in relation to all rights and obligations set out in the constitution or merely so-called membership rights and obligations.

There are other special features about the membership contract.

There can be no rectification even if there is a fundamental misunderstanding of the provisions of the company's constitution, although the circumstances may justify a winding up order.

It is no longer the case that a member cannot sue his company for damages whilst remaining a member.

Chapter 7

Shares and Payment of Capital

Where a company is limited by shares, the capital of the company is divided into shares. These are units of a given amount defining a shareholder's proportionate interest in the company. The nature of a share was discussed in *Borland's Trustee v Steel Bros & Co Ltd* (1901) where Farwell J said:

> The share is the interest of the shareholder in the company measured by a sum of money, for the purpose of liability in the first place, and of interest in the second, but also consisting of a series of mutual covenants entered into by all the shareholders *inter se* in accordance with (what is now s 14 of the Companies Act 1985).

A share falls into the category of incorporeal (intangible) moveable (not land or anything permanently attached to land) property in Scotland. In England, it is referred to as personal property. Under s 186 of the Companies Act 1985, in Scotland, a share certificate issued under the company's seal is sufficient evidence of title (ownership) to the shares referred to unless the contrary is shown.

The main features of a share are as follows:

- a right to dividends declared on the shares;

- generally (unless it is a non-voting share) a right to vote at general meetings;

- on the liquidation of the company or on a reduction of capital the right to receive assets distributed to shareholders of that class;

- an obligation to subscribe capital of a given amount which will sometimes be the nominal value of the share if the share is issued at par and sometimes will be in excess of this if the share is issued at a premium (the issue of shares at par and at a premium will be discussed below at para 7.11);

- rights of membership attached to the shares as defined in the company's memorandum and articles (discussed above in relation to the s 14 membership contract at para 6.3);

- a right to transfer the share in accordance with the articles of association at para 7.6.

An individual becomes a shareholder either by subscribing to shares (directly or indirectly receiving an allotment from the

7.1   The nature of a share

7.1.2   Main features

company) or by receiving a transfer of shares from an existing shareholder.

7.2   Different classes of shares

Often a company will only have one class of share. These will be ordinary shares or the equity of the company. On occasion, the company may have more than one class of share. The classes will be differentiated by reference to rights to dividend, rights to repayment of capital, rights to vote, etc. Where this is the case, matters of the variation of class rights may arise where it is proposed to alter the company's articles and that alteration varies the rights attaching to a particular class of share (these matters are considered under Variation of Class Rights at para 6.2).

7.2.1   Preference shares

It is perhaps appropriate here to say something about the nature of a preference share which is probably the most common type of share other than ordinary shares.

The most common feature of a preference share is that it confers a right to a preferential dividend up to a specified amount, for example 8% of its paid up value. This dividend is paid before any dividend is paid on the ordinary or equity share capital of the company. Preference shares may also have other preferential rights such as preferential voting rights or a right to repayment of capital in priority to other shares on a winding up.

The rights of the preference shares will depend upon what is set out in the terms of issue or in the articles of association (or conceivably the memorandum) of the company.

In relation to dividends, the preference share holder is only entitled to a preferential dividend when this dividend is actually declared – see *Monkland Iron & Coal Co Ltd v Henderson* (1883). Even if there are available profits there is no obligation upon the directors to declare a dividend (the question of dividends is considered separately (see Chapter 8). If, however, a dividend is not declared in any given year in relation to preference shares, the right to that dividend is carried forward. This presumption of the preference dividend being cumulative can be rebutted by a provision in the articles or in the terms of issue but in the absence of any express statement, it is assumed that the right to a preference dividend is cumulative. Thus, in *Ferguson & Forester Ltd v Buchanan* (1920), where there were two classes of preference shares, one of which was expressly cumulative (A class) and the other not (B class), it was held by the Inner House that B class shares were implied cumulative since there was no express provision to overcome the general presumption that preferential shares are cumulative. Therefore, if a preference dividend of 8% is not paid in Year one, the right to that dividend carries forward into Year two and so on.

However, unless specifically provided for in the articles, no interest will be payable on the arrears – *Partick Gas Co v Taylor* (1888). Preference shareholders will have no right to payment of arrears if the company enters liquidation before the arrears are declared.

If the preference dividend is paid in full, there is no further right to any additional dividend unless the terms of issue or articles say so. If there is such a right to an additional dividend, the preference shares are termed participating preference shares.

In relation to capital, there is no automatic priority for preference shares in a winding up or in a reduction of capital. The right only exists if the terms of issue or the articles set out such a right. If preference shares are given a priority in a winding up, then once their capital has been returned, this is exhaustive of their rights unless the terms of issue or the provisions of the articles provide otherwise ie preference shares do not participate in any surplus assets on a winding up.

The possible types of class of shares are virtually infinite. It is not uncommon for a company to have *redeemable preference shares*. These shares are shares that mirror preference shares except they are redeemable at a set date or at the option of the company.	**7.3 Other classes of shares**

A company may issue *deferred* or *founders' shares*. These shares rank after ordinary shares in respect of dividends and sometimes in relation to a return of capital. They will usually, however, have additional voting rights. Typically they would be taken up by a company's promoters.

Many large public companies have separate management shares, eg the Savoy Hotel Group. These shares carry additional voting rights and they are thus able to outvote the ordinary shares of the company. In other respects, their rights will often be the same as the ordinary shares, for example in relation to dividends and return of capital.

The methods which may be adopted in order to issue shares depend upon the type of company concerned. Private companies are prohibited by s 170 of the Financial Services Act 1986 for advertising their securities (shares or debentures) for sale unless the Secretary of State has made an exemption order. Section 89 of the Companies Act 1985 also prevents companies from issuing shares in contravention of pre-emption rights unless these are disapplied (see para 7.5).	**7.4 Issue of shares**

Private companies are therefore restricted as to how they issue shares.

Public companies may advertise their securities, although any advertisements are subject to rules imposed by the Companies Act 1985, the Financial Services Act 1986 and the Public Offers of Securities Regulations 1995 (see Chapter 4). They are still subject to s 89 of the Companies Act 1985 regarding pre-emption rights, but if these are disapplied the company may make its shares available for subscription by the public at large.

Section 84(1) of the Companies Act 1985 requires that any proposed issue of share capital by a public limited company be subscribed for in full before any allotment takes place. Public companies making a direct offer (inviting the public to subscribe to shares directly from the company) will therefore have any issue underwritten. This ensures that there is someone available to take up any surplus should the issue be undersubscribed. Section 97 of the Companies Act 1985 as amended by the Financial Services Act 1986 allows the issuing company to pay an underwriting commission (subject to a statutory limit) in these circumstances, provided that it is authorised by the articles.

Public companies whose pre-emption rights have been disapplied may also make an offer for sale where the shares are allotted to an issuing house who in turn issue the shares to subscribers from the public at large. Section 84(1) of the Companies Act 1985 is obviously satisfied by such a mode of issue.

Where there are negotiations between an issuing company and a subscriber the usual contractual rules of offer and acceptance apply – *Premier Briquette Co v Gray* (1922). An advertisement of securities will normally amount to an invitation to treat and a statement of intention to subscribe will not amount to an offer – *Millen & Sommerville v Millen* (1910). An application to subscribe to shares will normally be an offer and may be withdrawn before acceptance (which will occur when the allotment takes place) unless this is precluded by the terms on which applications to subscribe are invited – *Chapman v Sulphite Paper Co* (1892).

Before a contract is concluded, Scots law requires proof that an acceptance has been received by an offeror – *Mason v Benhar Coal Co* (1882). Allotment will generally be carried out by the directors. Before the directors may allot shares they must be given the power to do so. The Companies Act 1985 s 80 provides that such powers may be granted by the articles or by an ordinary resolution for a minimum period of five years, stating the (maximum) number of securities that may be allotted. In private companies, however, s 80A of the Companies Act 1985 allows directors' powers of allotment to be extended indefinitely by elective resolution (see para 15.5.9).

The process of allotment will be completed when the subscriber receives his share certificate and has his name entered on the Register of Members. If, however, a person's name wrongfully appears on the Register of Members he must challenge the entry without delay, otherwise he may be personally barred from denying his membership – *Re Scottish Petroleum Co* (1883).

There is now a general requirement to offer shares on a subsequent issue of shares after the first subscription to shareholders on a pre-emptive basis. The provision applies to equity securities (s 89 of the Companies Act 1985). The section only applies in relation to equity shares that are fully paid up in cash. The section also applies to options to purchase equity shares and also to the issue of securities that are convertible into equity shares. The pre-emption requirements may be excluded by the memorandum or articles of association of private companies (s 91).

7.5   Pre-emption rights

It is possible in relation to both private and public companies for the pre-emption requirements set out in s 89 to be disapplied by special resolution under s 95(2) of the Companies Act 1985. If the directors have authority to allot shares under s 80, then a special resolution may be passed either that s 89 should not apply to a specified allotment of equity securities or that the subsection shall apply to the allotment with a certain modification. In a similar way, it is possible that the company's articles of association or a special resolution may disapply the pre-emption provisions generally under s 95(1) of the Act where the directors have authority to allot shares under s 80.

Shares are freely transferable unless the company's articles impose restrictions on transfers. It was formerly the case before the Companies Act 1980 that private companies had to restrict the transferability of their shares in some way as a condition of their private status. This requirement was swept away by the Companies Act 1980.

7.6   Transfer of shares

If the articles contain no restriction at all, then the motive of the transferor in disposing of his shares is immaterial. In *Re European Bank, Masters Case* (1872), 12 days before a banking company stopped business, a shareholder transferred shares to his son-in-law. The shares were partly paid shares. The court held that the transfer could not be set aside. The court would not inquire into the *bona fides* of the transferor. In *Re Smith, Knight & Co* (1868), the court held that the directors of the company have no discretionary powers except those that are given to them by the company's constitution to refuse to register a transfer which has been made *bona fide*.

| 7.6.1 | Restrictions on transferability |

What happens where there is some restriction on transferability? The restriction may take one of many forms. Articles of association may give the directors an absolute discretion to refuse to register a transfer of shares. This was the position in the Scottish case of *Stewart v Keiller* (1902) which was mirrored in England in *Re Smith & Fawcett Ltd* (1942) (see para 11.7). In this case, the court held that the directors had a total discretion as to registering transfers. The only limitation on their discretion was that it should be exercised *bona fide* in the interest of the company. The Court of Appeal refused to draw an inference that it was being exercised *mala fide*. It is clear that where the directors have an absolute discretion to refuse to register a transfer, the courts are reluctant to interfere. It should be noted, however, that a refusal to register a transfer of shares may justify a petition under ss 459–461 (considered under Minority Protection, Chapter 14).

However, in *Dodds v Cosmopolitan Insurance Co* (1915), the Inner House opined that directors had satisfied a duty incumbent upon them by refusing to register a transfer attempted on the day notice of a resolution proposing a creditors' voluntary winding up (see Chapter 23) was to be sent to members. This case may be compared to *McLintock v Campbell* (1916) where the Inner House upheld a transfer on the eve of liquidation of the company concerned. Here, a director who was aware of his company's hopeless position fraudulently induced his housekeeper to purchase his shares on which a liability of £20,000 in uncalled capital was owed. A share transfer was duly executed and the company went shortly into insolvent liquidation. It was held that there were no grounds upon which the liquidator could challenge the transfer since the transaction between the director and his housekeeper was external to the company.

Sometimes, the refusal to register may only be exercised on certain grounds. A familiar power is one that the directors can exercise if, in their opinion, it is contrary to the interests of the company that the proposed transferee should become a member.

In *Re Bede Shipping Co Ltd* (1917), which concerned a Newcastle based steamship company, the court held that such a power only justifies a refusal to register on grounds that are personal to the proposed transferee. It does not, for example, justify a refusal to register transfer of single shares or shares in small numbers because the directors do not think it is desirable to increase the number of shareholders. The refusal to register was exercised on the ground that the directors did not want the shares to be held by many people. Lord Cozens-Hardy MR cited Chitty J in *Re Bell Bros* (1895) with approval:

> If the reasons assigned are legitimate, the court will not overrule the directors' decision merely because the court itself could not have come to the same conclusion, but if they are not legitimate, as, for instance, if the directors state that they rejected the transfer because the transferor's object was to increase the voting power in respect of his shares by splitting them among his nominees, the court would hold the power had not been duly exercised.

If a transfer is concluded between the parties but refused by the directors the transferor holds the shares in trust for the benefit of the transferee. He, therefore, must accept and pass on dividends accruing on these shares – *Stevenson v Wilson* (1907).

Occasionally, the restriction on transfer may be one of pre-emption giving other shareholders the right to purchase the shares of the transferor at a fair value before they are offered elsewhere. This situation arose in *Curtis v JJ Curtis & Co Ltd* (1986) in the New Zealand Court of Appeal. Here, the company's articles of association provided that a shareholder who wished to transfer his shares to an outsider had first of all to offer them to existing shareholders. This was not done. Cooke J held that a perpetual injunction would be granted against the transferor preventing him from transferring them other than in accordance with the articles.

7.6.2 The issue of pre-emption

A pre-emption clause was the restriction which was utilised in *Rayfield v Hands* (1960) to preserve control in a few people in a small company. Similarly, in *Greenhalgh v Mallard* (1943), an article provided that if a member wished to transfer his shares to a non-member, they must first be offered to existing members. Another article provided that if a member wished to sell his shares, he must notify the fact to the directors. A member transferred his shares to other members. Greenhalgh, another member, sought to have the transfers declared invalid on the ground that the restriction on transfer of shares applied to sales to existing members as well as to non-members and in this case the shares had not been first offered to members as a whole.

This argument was rejected by the Court of Appeal because the articles were not sufficiently clear to restrict a transfer to existing members. The restriction was held to apply only to the case of sales of shares to non-members.

Lord Greene MR stated:

> Questions of constructions of this kind are always difficult, but in the case of the restriction of transfer of shares I think it is right for the court to remember that a share, being personal property, is *prima facie* transferable, although the conditions of the transfer are to be found in the terms laid down in the articles. If the right of transfer, which is inherent in property of this kind is to be taken away or cut down, it seems to me that it should be done by language of sufficient clarity to make it apparent that this was the intention.

The issue of pre-emption also came up in *Tett v Phoenix Property Investment Co Ltd & Others* (1984) where the articles of association of the company restricted the right of the shareholder to transfer his shares. On the facts of the case, it was held that the directors had offered the shares to existing shareholders and the offer had not been taken up so that sale elsewhere was effective. Registration of the transfer was appropriate.

The courts will lean against an interpretation of any power in the directors which hampers the right to transfer shares.

On the other hand, the courts will not carry out a literal construction so far that it defeats the obvious purpose of the provision. Thus, in *Lyle & Scott Ltd v Scotts Trustees* (1959), where the articles provided for a right of pre-emption in the other shareholders where a shareholder was desirous of transferring his ordinary shares, and some shareholders sold their shares to a takeover bidder and received the purchase price and gave him irrevocable proxies to vote on their behalf, the House of Lords held that in the context 'transferring' meant assigning the beneficial interest and not the process of having a transfer registered. The shareholders had indicated their intention to sell their shares and could not continue with the sale without giving the other shareholders their right to exercise their pre-emption rights.

The Outer House held in *Williams v MacPherson* (1990) that if a transfer in breach of the articles was entered in the Register of Members the company was personally barred from subsequently objecting to the transfer. The court also held that if a transferee is informed of the company's execution of a transfer, and the transferee chooses to ignore it, he is likewise personally barred from challenging the transfer.

It is most important, if the company wishes to protect some shareholders from the effect of shares being held by others, to ensure that the power of refusal to register a transfer of share also applies on transmission (cases where shares pass on death or bankruptcy).

In *Safeguard Industrial Developments Ltd v National Westminster Bank Ltd* (1982), a shareholder held the balance of control between two rival brothers. He died leaving the shares to one of the brothers' children. The question arose as to whether pre-emption applied on transmission or simply where a shareholder wished to transfer his shares during his lifetime.

The court held that the provision could only apply in respect of transfer not transmission. Careful wording is therefore needed to protect companies and their shareholders in such a situation.

If, on the true construction of the company's articles, the directors are only entitled to reject on certain prescribed grounds, and if it is proved that they have rejected on others, the court will interfere as in *Re Bede Steam Shipping Co Ltd*. Interrogatories may be administered to determine on which of certain prescribed grounds the directors have acted but not as to their reasons for rejecting on those particular grounds, see *Sutherland (Jute) v British Dominions Land Settlement Corporation Ltd* (1926).

7.6.3   Directors' rights to reject on prescribed grounds

However, if the directors do state their reasons, the court will investigate them to determine whether they have acted on those grounds. They will overrule their decision if they have acted on considerations which should not have influenced them.

Even where the right to refuse is a qualified one, in certain situations the directors may not be obliged to give their reasons. In a case concerning Tottenham Hotspur Football Club, it was established that even if the directors can only refuse to register a transfer on certain grounds, they cannot be obliged to give the reason if the articles provide they need not do so (*Berry & Stewart v Tottenham Hotspur Football & Athletic Co Ltd* (1935)).

In relation to transfer generally, it should be noted that a refusal to register a transfer must be a positive act of the board. In *Re Hackney Pavilion Ltd* (1924), the two directors of the company were divided on the question of whether the proposed transfer should proceed. The company secretary was asked to write to the executrix's solicitors and return the transfer documents indicating that the transfer could not go

7.6.4   Positive act of board

ahead. The High Court ordered that the transfer must go ahead. Astbury J said:

> Now the right to decline must be actively exercised by the vote of the board *ad hoc*. At the actual board meeting there was a proper quorum but as the board was equally divided, it did not and could not exercise its rights to decline.

In such situations, the transfer must therefore go ahead.

7.6.5   Refusal must be exercised within a reasonable time

Another restriction on refusal of registration of a transfer is that the refusal must be exercised within a reasonable time. This rule has been given statutory force in s 183(3) of the Companies Act 1985 which provides that the refusal must be exercised within two months after the date the transfer is lodged with the company. During this two month period, however, the transferee cannot claim to be registered as a member even though there are no directors so that the company cannot exercise the right to refuse to register – see *Re Zinotty Properties Ltd* (1984).

The Jenkins Committee recommended in 1962 that directors should also be obliged to give a reason for refusing to register a transfer and also that the refusal must be notified within five weeks. These recommendations have never been implemented.

However, s 459 of the Companies Act 1985 probably enables members to apply for a remedy in cases where directors fail to register a transfer of shares and this failure constitutes unfair prejudice to the members concerned. This may now enable a member to obtain a remedy in cases such as *Re Smith & Fawcett Ltd* (see para 11.7). Other transfer situations may involve this section. Section 459 was involved in *Re a Company (No 007623 of 1984)* (1986) where a rights issue was made which the petitioning shareholder was unwilling to accept.

Hoffmann J held that the remedy was to offer to sell his shares to the other members under pre-emption provisions. The pre-emption provisions of this company contained a mechanism for determining a fair value of the shares by means of a valuation conducted by auditors. This procedure should have been employed without recourse to the courts. The inference of the decision is that a remedy would have been available under s 459 had there been no pre-emption provisions.

The area of law relating to share transfer, and particularly restrictions on transferability, is increasingly important as more and more people buy shares and as more and more set up their own businesses where they may wish to keep control and ownership within a tightly-knit group.

Share warrants are freely transferable. Share warrants are negotiable instruments and can be transferred simply by delivery. Share warrants are not common although they may become more so given the United Kingdom's membership of the European Community. The holder of the share warrant can simply surrender the share warrant for cancellation by the company. Where this happens, the company must then register the holder's name in the register of members (s 355(2)).

The Companies Act 1989 creates various offences relating to forged share warrants in Scotland.

7.7   Share warrants

The Second EC Directive on Company Law (1977/91) necessitated a change in British company law in relation to payment for shares and the classification of companies. These changes were incorporated into British law by the Companies Act 1980, the provisions of which are now consolidated into the Companies Act 1985.

The rules on payment for shares bear more strictly upon public companies than on private companies.

Section 99(1) of the Act requires that shares should be paid up in money or money's worth. Section 99(2) of the Act provides that a public company may not accept an undertaking from a person to do work or perform services in relation to payment for shares.

Section 100 of the Act restates a rule that is of long standing. Shares may not be issued at a discount. This rule is already clearly stated in common law. In *Klenck v East India Mining Co* (1888), the Inner House held that shares could not be issued at a discount. This was confirmed by the House of Lords' decision in the English case of *Ooregum Gold Mining Co of India Ltd v Roper* (1892). That is to say, that the company must always obtain at least the nominal value (or par value) of the share in payment. Section 100(1) simply provides a company's shares shall not be issued at a discount. If shares are issued in contravention of the section, the allottee is liable to pay the company the amount of the discount with interest at the appropriate rate (currently 5% per annum), see s 100(2) and s 107 of the Act.

There are some exceptions to the rule that shares cannot be issued at a discount. It is possible to issue shares to underwriters under s 97 of the Act at a discount of up to 10% on the par value of the shares (see para 7.4). Another exception is that a company may issue debentures at a discount (debentures are considered in Chapter 18). The debentures may be convertible into shares. Provided that the right to convert is not immediate, there will be no contravention of s 100, see *Koffyfontein Mines Ltd v Mosely* (1911).

7.8   Payment for shares

In a public company, when shares are allotted, they must be paid up to at least one quarter of their nominal value plus the whole of any premium. Where shares are issued partly paid, ie some of the nominal value or a premium or both remains unpaid, the amount that is unpaid may be called up by the company. However, it may be that a limited company by special resolution determines that a portion of the share capital that has not been called up shall only be called up if the company is wound up and if this is the case that amount can only be called up in the event of the company being wound up (s 120 of the Act).

A public company cannot allot shares in exchange for non-cash consideration which may be transferred more than five years after the date of the allotment (s 102(1)). Furthermore, if a public company issues shares in exchange for non-cash assets, then the consideration for the allotment must be independently valued. This statutory provision (s 103(1)) only applies to public companies. Private companies may accept any consideration for allotment, including specific assets, goodwill, know-how, or services – see *Cameron v Glenmorangie Distillery Co Ltd* (1896). However, there is a common law rule that all companies must only issue shares for non-cash assets if the value of those assets is at least equal to the value of the shares. In general, however, in a private company the courts will not interfere with the valuation placed upon those assets.

It may do so, however, if there is fraud, see *Re Wragg* (1897), or if the consideration is clearly inadequate, for example, the consideration is open-ended as in *Hong Kong & China Gas Co Ltd v Glen* (1914).

If a share certificate is issued in respect of partly paid shares which *prima facie* suggests that the shares it represents are fully paid, the company (or its liquidator) will be personally barred from claiming that the shares are not fully paid against a shareholder (either a transferee or a subscriber) who has received the certificate in good faith and who does not have notice of the defect – see *Scottish Heritages Co* (1898) and *Penang Co v Gardiner* (1913).

7.9   Securities over shares

Shares may be issued by the holder as security against a debt. In order to achieve this, the shareholder must create an assignation in security over the shares. The way to achieve this is to transfer an executed (completed by both parties) share transfer form to the creditor whose name will then be entered on the register of members – see *Guild v Young* (1884). As far as the company is concerned, the creditor replaces the debtor as member in respect of the assigned shares. The debtor will, however, be entitled to have the shares transferred back to him upon satisfaction of the debt.

If the company officer who initially issued the share certificates to the debtor was not authorised by the company to do so, this will not affect the assignee in security's (creditor's) title to the shares – see *Clavering v Goodwin, Jardine & Co* (1891).

A company in Scotland (unlike an English company) has a common law right of retention or lien over its shares whether fully or partly paid – see *Bell's Trustee v Coatbridge Tinplate Co* (1886). This may be extended or restricted by the articles. For example, articles will usually provide for a lien only to be exercisable over partly paid shares. Unless the articles provide otherwise, shares subject to a lien cannot be sold by the company to satisfy a debt owed to the company: in such cases the company can do no more than refuse to register a transfer. Under s 150 of the Companies Act 1985 a public company in general cannot create or exercise a lien over its shares unless the shares are fully paid.	**7.10 Retention or lien over shares**
Shares may sometimes be issued at a premium. Shares are issued at a premium if they are issued at more than par or nominal value. The amount of any premium must be fully paid on allotment if an issue is in a public company. The amount of the premium is paid into a share premium account. For most purposes, the share premium account is treated just as if it were ordinary share capital. There are certain exceptions to this principle. They are that the money in a share premium account may be used to pay up fully paid bonus shares or to pay off the company's preliminary expenses or to pay up any commitment or discount allowable on the issue of shares or debentures of the company or in providing for the premium payable on redemption of debentures of the company.

There is no statutory rule requiring a company to obtain the best possible premium on an issue of shares in the way that there is a similar rule to obtain at least the par value and therefore not to issue shares at a discount. Yet, if shares are issued at well below the price that they could attain in the market, this may constitute a breach of directors' duties. | **7.11   Issue of shares at a premium** |
| Section 88 of the Companies Act 1985 provides that where a company limited by shares or limited by guarantee with share capital has issued shares, then a return of allotments must be made stating the number and nominal amount of the shares and the names and addresses of the allottees and the amount, if any, that is still payable on the shares or in the case of shares | **7.12   Return of allotments** |

allotted as fully or partly paid up otherwise than in cash, a contract in writing and a return stating the number and nominal amount of shares so allotted and the extent to which the shares are to be treated as paid up together with the consideration for which they have been allotted. This information should be passed to the registrar of companies within one month after the allotment for registration. There is a penalty in default.

Shares and Payment of Capital

A share is the interest of the shareholder in a particular company. There are various different types of shares such as ordinary, preference, deferred and management shares.

Introduction

Private companies are restricted in the methods they may use in order to issue shares. Public companies may advertise their shares but may not be able to allot shares unless an issue is fully subscribed or underwritten.

Issue of Shares

The normal contractual rules of offer and acceptance apply.

When shares are issued, the directors must take care to ensure that the statutory pre-emption provisions are honoured. These pre-emption provisions may be excluded or modified in various ways. Shares are said to be freely transferable but, in the case of private companies, it is often the case that there are various restrictions on transferability.

Transfer of shares

Sometimes, the restriction on transferability will give the company's directors the power to refuse to register a transfer. The power may be a general power of refusal or it may be exercisable on specified grounds. It is a power to refuse – so, if the directors are evenly split, the transfer must go ahead. If the directors have a general power to refuse, they cannot be obliged to give reasons for their refusal to agree to the transfer.

Sometimes, the restriction provides that shares must first be offered for sale to existing members. If this is so, the provision will be construed strictly (as it will in all cases of restriction on transfer) so that if it is desired to restrict shares being transmitted in cases of death and bankruptcy this would have to be set out clearly.

When shares are issued, the directors must also take care to ensure that the company receives full payment for the shares. Here again, there are statutory provisions to ensure that the company receives payment in full. In particular, shares must not be issued at a discount ie at less than par value.

Payment for shares

Once shares have been issued, a return of allotments has to be made to the registrar of companies setting out the shares that have been issued and the consideration that has been received.

Chapter 8

The Payment of Dividends

The payment of dividends used to be a matter to be decided by commercial prudence and the company's constitution. The memorandum of association generally made no express provision, although almost invariably the articles of association did.

Under Table A, articles of association, and most other forms of articles, it is provided that the basic power to pay dividends lies with the company in general meeting. It is granted the power to pay a dividend up to the amount recommended by the directors. Article 102 of Table A provides:

> Subject to the provisions of the Act, the company may by ordinary resolution declare dividends in accordance with the respective rights of the members, but no dividend shall exceed the amount recommended by the directors.

Generally, directors will be granted the power to declare interim dividends. Article 103 of Table A provides:

> Subject to the provisions of the Act, the directors may pay interim dividends if it appears to them that they are justified by the profits of the company available for distribution.

If the dividends are to be paid otherwise than in cash, express authority is required. Article 105 of Table A is an example of such a provision. It provides:

> A general meeting declaring a dividend may, upon the recommendation of the directors, direct that it shall be satisfied wholly or partly by the distribution of assets and, where any difficulty arises in regard to the distribution, the directors may settle the same and in particular may issue fractional certificates and fix the value for distribution of any assets and may determine that cash will be paid to any member upon the putting of the value so fixed in order to adjust the rights of members and may vest any assets in trustees.

This point was at issue in *Wood v Odessa Waterworks Co* (1889) where the company's articles empowered dividends 'to be paid' by directors. This was interpreted as meaning 'paid in money'. A member was then able to rely on this article in challenging a distribution that was made in a non-cash form by the issue of bonus debentures.

8.1 Distributable reserves

8.1.1 The company's constitution

Dividends are payable, in the absence of any provision to the contrary, to those members who are on the register at the time the dividend is declared.

Another question that needs to be considered in relation to provisions in the memorandum or articles is from which profits are dividends payable. Some articles, for example, specify 'the profits of the business', which is taken to mean that dividends can only be paid out of trading profits and not out of capital profits.

The proportional distribution of any declared dividend among the shareholders will also depend upon the articles. In *Hoggan Tharsis Copper & Sulphate Co* (1882), it was held that where there was no express provision in the articles the dividend would be allocated according to the extent to which each share was paid up, or, if the company did not have a share capital, equally among the members.

8.1.2   The Stock Exchange

In addition to the requirements set out in the company's constitution, The Stock Exchange provides rules for companies that are listed or are dealt with on the Alternative Investment Market. The Stock Exchange requires that the date of any board meeting at which the declaration or recommendation of payment of a dividend is expected to be decided must be notified to The Stock Exchange in advance; it will then publish the information. The Stock Exchange issues a schedule of suitable dates to assist in settlement of transactions and to permit securities to be traded 'ex-dividends' from a convenient date.

8.1.3   Statutory provisions

If the regime relating to the payment of dividends used to be somewhat lenient, that changed with the Companies Act 1980. Amendments were made by the Companies Act 1981 and the provisions are now consolidated in the Companies Act 1985.

A company may not make a distribution which includes paying a cash dividend except out of the profits available for distribution (s 263(1) of the Companies Act 1985).

The statutory provisions of the Companies Act 1985 apply to distributions. These are defined in s 263(2) to include any distribution of the company's assets to its members. The definition is an extremely wide one and covers any benefits in cash or in kind. However, the following are expressly excluded:

- an issue of fully or partly paid bonus shares;

- the redemption or purchase of any of the company's shares otherwise than out of distributable profits;

- reductions of capital;

- distributions of assets to members of the company on its winding up.

The profits available for distribution in both private and public companies are accumulated, realised profits not previously distributed or capitalised, less accumulated, realised losses not previously written off in a reduction or reorganisation of capital (s 263(3)). Two key points about this provision should be noted:

- The use of the word 'accumulated' in relation to profits and losses applies to a continuous account

  In particular, directors should ensure that previous years' losses are made good before a distribution is made. This reverses the position in *Ammonia Soda Co Ltd v Chamberlain* (1918). In this case, a distribution of revenue profits was made in a trading year even though there was an accumulated deficit from earlier years which had not been made good.

  The plaintiff company, which had been incorporated for the purpose of acquiring, developing and working as brineland an estate in Cheshire, sued to recover dividends which the company alleged had been wrongly paid. The Court of Appeal held that there was no law that prohibited a company from distributing the clear net profit of its trading in any year without making good trading losses of previous years.

- Profits must be realised

  Directors should ensure that any income whether from trading or from capital must have actually been received by the company. This gives statutory recognition to the decision in *Westburn Sugar Refineries Ltd v IRC* (1960). However, this was not previously the case in England – see *Dimbula Valley (Ceylon) Tea Co Ltd v Laurie* (1961).

A further restriction in s 264 of the Companies Act 1985 only applies to public companies. Distributions may only be made so long as the value of the company's net assets does not fall below the aggregate of its called up share capital plus its undistributable reserves.

Undistributable reserves are defined in s 264(3) as:

- the share premium account;

- the capital redemption reserve;

8.2   Undistributable reserves

- the amount by which the accumulated unrealised profits not previously used by paying up bonus shares or by transfers of profits before 22 December 1980 to the capital redemption reserve fund exceed accumulated unrealised losses (so far as not previously written off in a reduction or reorganisation of capital duly made); and

- any other reserve which the company is prohibited from distributing by any enactment or by its memorandum or articles.

This means, in effect, that a public company must maintain its capital and take account of any changes in the value of its fixed assets.

Previously, a dividend could be paid out of realised profits without the need to make good any capital loss realised or unrealised, for example, as in *Lee v Neuchatel Asphalte Co* (1889). This is now no longer the case in relation to public companies.

In relation to fixed assets, even for private companies there is an obligation to make provision for depreciation. The accounting rules introduced by the Companies Act 1981 require provision for depreciation of fixed assets. Dividends for all companies will need to make allowance for depreciation, therefore (Sched 4, para 19 of the Companies Act 1985).

Certain types of company are dealt with separately.

| 8.3 | **Investment companies** | 'Investment companies', in a new category created by the Companies Act 1980, are subject to a special regime and may ask for a different basis of distribution of profits. The rules (ss 265–67 of the Companies Act 1985) are only applicable if the company has a listing, and it must have notified the registrar of companies of its status and declare this on its letterheads. |

An investment company must comply with the following conditions:

- its business consists of investing its funds principally in securities with the aim of spreading investment risk and giving its members the benefit of the results of the management of its funds (s 266(2)(a));

- none of its holdings in companies (other than in other investment companies) represents more than 15% by value of its total investment (s 266(2)(b));

- the distribution of capital profit is prohibited by its memorandum or articles (s 266(2)(c));

- the company has not retained during any accounting reference period more than 15% of its investment income from securities unless required to do so by the Act (s 266(2)(d)).

The aim of the different rules is to relieve investment companies of the problem they might encounter in connection with the net value test applicable to a public company. Securities, the assets of investment companies, are subject to fluctuation in value which might take the value of assets below the net value level. Yet, since such companies receive considerable income from dividends, due allowance must be made for this fact.

An investment company may make a distribution out of its accumulated realised revenue profits not previously used by distribution or capitalisation, less its accumulated realised losses, whether realised or not, not previously written off in a reduction or reorganisation of capital if at that time the value of its assets is at least equivalent to one and a half times its total liabilities and to the extent that the distribution does not reduce the value of its assets below that amount (s 265(1) of the Companies Act 1985). The advantage of this basis for distribution is that realised and unrealised capital losses do not have to be taken into account in determining the amount available for distribution. However, the company can only distribute realised capital profits on a winding up.

Insurance companies (as defined in the Insurance Companies Act 1982) which carry on a long term business are also subject to special rules. Any amount which is properly transferred to a company's profit and loss account from a surplus or a deficit on its long term business funds is to be treated as a realised profit or a realised loss as appropriate (s 268(1) of the Companies Act 1985).	**8.4 Insurance companies**
It is for the directors of any company, who will be the ones making a recommendation (if any) to pay a dividend, to ensure that these rules are complied with. A dividend will be based on a company's profits, losses, assets and liabilities as well as provisions (for example, for depreciation) and share capital and reserves. Basically the directors must determine if there is an accumulated realised profit from which a dividend can be declared. In assessing whether there is such a profit, they should refer to the company's relevant accounts (s 270 of the Companies Act 1985). Generally the most recent audited annual accounts will be the relevant ones, and the	**8.5 Accumulated realised profit by reference to accounts**

last annual accounts must have been laid before the company in general meeting. The accounts must have been properly prepared   or prepared subject only to matters which are not material, and the auditors must have made a report on the accounts to the members.

If the auditors' report is qualified, then they must state in writing whether, in their opinion, the substance of the qualification is material for determining the legality of the proposed dividend. However, if the distribution infringes s 263 or s 264, the directors will need to refer to such 'interim accounts' as are necessary to decide whether a dividend can be paid. In all cases, these accounts must enable a reasonable judgment to be made and in the case of a public company the accounts must have been 'properly prepared' and a copy of them must have been delivered to the registrar of companies (they need not, however, be audited).

If a distribution is to be made during a company's first accounting reference period, or before any accounts have been laid before a general meeting or delivered to the registrar, 'initial accounts' may be prepared to assess whether there is a profit available for dividend. The 'initial accounts' need not be audited but if the company is a public one, auditors must report on whether the accounts have been properly prepared. A copy of these initial accounts and auditors' report must be delivered to the registrar.

8.6	**Wrongful payment of dividend**

There are various consequences of a wrongful payment of dividend. There are no criminal sanctions for a breach of the rules, but if a shareholder knows or has reasonable grounds for believing at the time of the distribution made to him that the distribution is in contravention of the Companies Act, then he is liable to repay it (or the offending part of it) to the distributing company (s 277 of the Companies Act 1985).

In *Precision Dippings Ltd v Precision Dippings Marketing Ltd* (1985), the plaintiff company, which was a wholly owned subsidiary of the defendant company, paid a cash dividend of £60,000 to the defendant. The relevant accounts, the company's last annual accounts, were qualified. The last annual accounts showed sufficient distributable profits to finance the dividend but no statement on the materiality of the qualification had been made by the auditors as the Act required.

Subsequently, the company went into creditors' voluntary liquidation and the auditors then issued a written statement to the effect that the qualification in their report was not material. The plaintiff company, through its liquidator, sued to recover the dividend on the ground that it was paid in contravention of the statute and was *ultra vires*. The Court of Appeal held that the company had paid a dividend in contravention of the statute. The auditors' written statement had to be available before a distribution was made, and the absence of such a statement was not a mere procedural irregularity that could be waived or dispensed with. The dividend payment was *ultra vires* and, as the defendant company received the money with notice of the facts as a volunteer, it held the money as constructive trustee for the plaintiff company.

Section 277 of the 1985 Act does not deal with the position of directors responsible for the payment of dividends. A director who is responsible for an unlawful distribution could be liable to the company for a breach of duty. In *Liquidators of the City of Glasgow Bank v MacKinnon* (1882), the Inner House acknowledged that a director authorising the payment of a dividend out of capital may be guilty of negligence. However, the case failed on its facts as there was insufficient evidence to prove that dividends had been paid out of capital. In *Flitcroft's Case* (1882), the question of directors' liability for the wrongful payment of the company's dividends arose. For several years the directors had presented to the shareholders in general meeting reports and balance sheets in which various debts the directors knew were bad were entered as assets, so that an apparent profit was shown in the company's accounts, although in reality there were no profits. The general meeting relied on the accounts to pass resolutions to declare dividends. The company was wound up and the liquidator sought to have the directors make good the wrongful payment of dividends. The Court of Appeal held that the directors were liable for these wrongful payments and must reimburse the company the full amount of the dividend.

8.6.1   Directors' liability

However, this principle only applies where the director knows about the circumstances of the payment. An innocent director is not liable to repay a dividend that has been wrongfully paid.

In *Re Denham & Co* (1884), Crook, a director whose name appeared on the company's reports, never attended board meetings nor took any active part in the preparation or issue of the company's reports or balance sheets, although at one meeting he did formally propose the resolution to declare a dividend. It was found that the company had been paying dividends out of capital. The court held, however, that Crook was not personally responsible for the company's reports and balance sheets and the dividends paid under them. He had no reason to suspect any misconduct and was not guilty of negligence. As Chitty J said:

> As regards Crook, who acted as a director throughout the period of the four years when the dividends were paid, it is not charged against him that he was guilty of actual fraud, or that he was in fact party or privy to the fraud committed, and I am satisfied, on the evidence, that he had not any suspicion of it ... The auditors are not before me on the present occasion, still I am bound to say that from the evidence, such as it is, it does appear that the auditors themselves were to some extent cognisant of and parties to the fraud. Mr Crook was, however, entitled to trust them, there was nothing at all to arouse his suspicions that they were not doing their duty.

Similarly, in *Dovey v Cory* (1901), a director who agreed to the payment of dividends out of capital, and who relied on the advice of a fellow director and general manager of the company by whose statements he was misled and whose integrity, skill and competence he had no reason for suspecting, was held not to be liable in negligence. In the course of his judgment, the Earl of Halsbury LC made it clear that directors are also entitled to trust their auditors:

> I cannot think that it can be expected of a director that he should be watching the inferior officers of the bank or verifying the calculations of the auditors themselves. The business of life could not go on if people could not trust those who are put into a position of trust for the express purpose of attending to details of management.

8.6.2   Auditors' liabilities

In addition to directors, the company's auditors may also be liable for the wrongful payment of dividends. The auditors will only be liable to the company if they have facilitated the improper payment of a dividend.

As Lindley LJ said of the auditor in *Re London & General Bank Ltd (No 2)*: 'It is nothing to him whether the dividends are properly or improperly declared provided he discharges his own duty to the shareholders.' In that case, dividends had been paid out wrongfully, and the company's assets were overstated in the balance sheet. The court found that the auditors had been negligent in respect of a particular year's report – certain loans which were not realisable were entered in the accounts at face value. The auditor was held liable to repay the dividends in question.

An auditor's liability is generally limited to situations where the auditors are in breach of their contractual duty in relation to the company's annual audit and where this negligence facilitates the payment of a dividend out of capital.

An auditor may be clearly liable to the company for breaches of his contract with the company which has resulted in the wrongful payment of dividends. Lopes LJ spoke of the auditors' contractual duties in those terms in *Re Kingston Cotton Mill Co (No 2)* (1896):

> It is the duty of an auditor to bring to bear on the work he has to perform that skill, care and caution which a reasonably competent, careful and cautious auditor would use. What is reasonable skill, care and caution must depend on the circumstances of each case. An auditor is not bound to be a detective or ... to approach his work with suspicion or with foregone conclusion that there is something wrong. He is a watchdog, but not a bloodhound. He is justified in believing hired servants of the company in whom confidence is placed by the company.

The rules have been made much stricter since 1980. No criminal liability attaches to directors or others simply for the wrongful payment of dividends. Any member knowingly receiving a dividend wrongfully paid is liable to repay it. Directors may, however, find themselves liable for breach of their duties to the company and auditors may also be in breach of their contractual duty to the company, their client.

The Payment of Dividends

The payment of dividends used to be a matter to be decided largely by reference to the company's constitution. The Companies Act 1980 introduced statutory controls for the first time. Since that date, dividends can only be paid out of accumulated realised profits less accumulated realised losses. This applies to private and public companies. Public companies also have to maintain the value of their capital assets before paying any dividend but private companies are also obliged to make provision for depreciation under the accounting rules.

Where dividends are paid wrongfully, recipients will be obliged to pay back the sum where they know of the circumstances. Directors who have recommended payment of an unlawful dividend may be responsible as may auditors who have facilitated payment of an unlawful dividend.

There are special rules for investment companies and for insurance companies.

Chapter 9

The Maintenance of Capital

Certain aspects of maintenance of capital have already been considered. The rules relating to the issue of shares and payment for those shares have been considered. It is now proposed to consider certain other rules relating to the maintenance of capital, namely the provision of financial assistance to acquire a company's shares and the company purchasing its own shares.

Section 151 of the Companies Act 1985 provides that where a person is acquiring or proposing to acquire shares in a company, it is not lawful for the company or any of its subsidiaries to give financial assistance directly or indirectly for the purpose of that acquisition before or at the same time as the acquisition takes place (s 151(1)). Section 151(2) further provides that where a person has acquired shares in a company and a liability has been incurred for the purpose of that acquisition, it is not lawful for the company or any of its subsidiaries to give financial assistance directly or indirectly for the purpose of reducing or discharging that liability.

9.1 Financial assistance towards the purchase of a company's own shares

The penalty for breach of this provision is as follows:

- *conviction on indictment*: a fine in relation to the company and in relation to an officer of the company two years' imprisonment and/or a fine;

- *on summary conviction*: a fine up to the statutory maximum in relation to the company; in relation to an officer of the company six months' imprisonment and/or a fine up to the statutory maximum.

Section 152 sets out the different forms of financial assistance. These may include:

9.1.1 Forms of financial assistance

- a gift;

- a guarantee, security or indemnity other than an indemnity in relation to the indemnifier's own neglect or default;

- a release or waiver;

- a loan;

- a novation of or an assignment of rights;

- any other financial assistance whereby the net assets of the company are reduced to a material extent or given by a company which has no net assets.

This last provision would, for example, cover a situation where the company purchased an asset from the purchaser of the shares at a much higher value than the true value of the asset to put the purchaser in funds to purchase shares in the company, see *Belmont Finance v Williams (No 2)* (1980).

| 9.1.2 | Consequences of a breach of s 151 |

As has been noted, there are criminal sanctions applying where there is a breach of the section. In addition, the transaction itself is unlawful and void. There are various other consequences:

- any guarantee issued in connection with the transaction is itself void, see *Heald v O'Connor* (1971);

- the company may sue its directors for breach of duty as they are liable in a similar way to trustees in relation to misapplication of trust funds, see *Selangor United Rubber Estates Ltd v Cradock (No 3)* (1968) and *Belmont Finance v Williams Furniture* (see above);

- furthermore, other persons receiving corporate property with knowledge that it is being applied for a wrongful purpose are liable to the company on the basis of constructive trust, see *Selangor United Rubber Estates Ltd Co v Cradock* and *Belmont Finance v Williams Furniture*;

- there is also the possibility that the company can sue for conspiracy if two or more persons have got together to accomplish the unlawful act, see *Belmont Finance v Williams Furniture* (see above).

| 9.1.3 | Exceptions |

There are certain exceptions to the basic prohibition contained in s 151:

1 If the provision of the financial assistance is not principally to give assistance for the acquisition of the shares but an incidental part of some larger purpose and the assistance is given in good faith in the interests of the company, then it does not fall foul of s 151. Under this exception, assistance in management buy-outs would generally be legitimate but asset stripping of the company to enable the purchaser of the shares to cancel or reduce an obligation would not.

It should be noted that the exception applies not simply to giving assistance which is an incidental part of some larger purpose but cancelling or reducing a liability where this is an incidental part of some larger purpose.

In *Brady v Brady* (1989), the House of Lords adopted a restrictive approach to this exception.

2 Dividends lawfully paid.

3   The allotment of bonus shares.

4   A reduction of capital in the company confirmed by court order under s 137.

5   A redemption or purchase of shares under the Act.

6   Anything done in pursuance of a court order under s 425 (compromises and arrangements with creditors and members).

7   Anything done under an arrangement made in pursuance of s 110 of the Insolvency Act 1986 (acceptance of shares by a liquidator in a winding up as consideration for sale of the property).

8   Anything done under an arrangement between a company and its creditors which is binding on the creditors under Part 1 of the Insolvency Act (Voluntary Arrangements).

9   If the lending of the money is part of the ordinary business of the company then the lending of such money is not illegal.

10 The provision by a company in good faith in the interest of the company of financial assistance for the purposes of an employees' share scheme is not illegal.

11 This has been extended to enable companies to facilitate transactions in shares by *bona fide* employees or former employees of the company or of another company in the same group or to facilitate transactions in shares by the wives, husbands, widows, widowers, children or stepchildren (up to 18 years of age) of such employees or former employees.

12 The making by the company of loans to persons (other than directors) employed in good faith by the company with a view to enabling those persons to acquire fully paid shares in the company or of the company's holding company.

Exceptions 9, 10, 11 and 12 are qualified in the case of public companies by s 154 which provides that the giving of financial assistance is only permitted if the company's net assets are not reduced or to the extent that they are reduced the assistance is provided out of distributable profits.

There is a special overriding exception in the case of private companies. Section 155 of the Act provides that private companies may give assistance towards the acquisition of shares subject to certain conditions (see *Brady v Brady*). The financial assistance must come from distributable profits. A subsidiary

9.1.4   Overriding exception in the case of private companies

company cannot provide financial assistance towards the purchase of shares in the holding company if it is also a subsidiary of a public company which is itself a subsidiary of that holding company. This provision is clearly designed to prevent evasion of the requirements that apply more strictly to public companies.

Approval of the manoeuvre is needed by special resolution in general meeting unless the company is a wholly owned subsidiary. Where the financial assistance is to be given by a company towards the acquisition of shares in its holding company, then the holding company and any other company which is both the company's holding company and a subsidiary of that holding company must also approve the manoeuvre by special resolution in general meeting except in a case where the company is a wholly owned subsidiary. Where the company is a wholly owned subsidiary there are no shareholders needing protection.

The directors of the company which is proposing to give the financial assistance must provide a statutory declaration and where the shares to be acquired are shares in the company's holding company, the directors of that company as well, together with the directors of any other company which is both the company's holding company and a subsidiary of that other holding company should make the statutory declaration as set out in s 156. The statutory declaration should state that the directors have formed the opinion that immediately following the assistance there will be no ground on which the company will be found unable to pay its debts and if it is intended to wind the company up then the debts will be paid within 12 months of the commencement of the winding up or in any other case that the company will be able to pay its debts as they fall due during the year immediately following that date (ie the date of the assistance). An auditors' report should be annexed to the effect that the directors' statutory declaration is not unreasonable in all the circumstances after enquiring into the state of affairs of the company. The statutory declaration and auditors' report should be delivered to the registrar of companies together with a copy of any special resolution that is required and if no resolution is required to be passed, it should be delivered within 15 days of the making of the declaration. This special resolution should be passed within the week following the statutory declaration (s 157 of the Companies Act 1985). If a director makes a statutory declaration without having reasonable grounds, he is liable on conviction on indictment to two years' imprisonment and/or a fine, and on summary conviction to six months' imprisonment and/or a fine not exceeding the statutory maximum. However, provided that all of the required particulars have been delivered to the registrar of companies it is not fatal to the validity of the exercise that the prescribed forms have not been used (see *Re NL Electrical Ltd* (1994)).

An application may be made to the court for the cancellation of a resolution by the holders of 10% in nominal value of the company's issued shares or any class of those shares or 10% of the company's members if the company is not limited by shares. The applicants must not have voted in favour of the resolution. The court may confirm the resolution or cancel the resolution. It may as a condition of confirming the resolution require that the dissentients be bought out (s 157(2) of the Companies Act 1985).

Although a company is prohibited subject to the provisions of the Act from purchasing its own shares, the company may in certain circumstances acquire its own shares. Thus a company may acquire its shares as a gift. Furthermore, the company's articles may provide for the forfeiture of shares or the acceptance of shares in lieu of forfeiture where sums are owed to the company.

9.2   A company's purchase of its own shares and the issue of redeemable shares

In addition to the rules that allow a company to purchase or redeem its shares in certain circumstances, a company may acquire its shares in a reduction of capital made under the Companies Act or in pursuance of a court order under s 5 in relation to an alteration of objects or s 54 in relation to a public company altering its status to become private or under ss 459–461 in relation to the remedy for unfairly prejudicial conduct.

It was once a basic article of faith of British company law that a company could not purchase its own shares. This was the rule in *Trevor & Another v Whitworth & Another* (1887), reflected in Scotland in *General Property Investment Co Ltd v Matheson's Trustees* (1888). This was a rule which was restated as recently as the Companies Act 1980 (see, now, s 143 of the Companies Act 1985). However, in the Companies Act 1981, new provisions were introduced permitting a purchase of a company's own shares and altering the rules on issue of redeemable shares, subject to certain conditions. These rules are now contained in Chapter VII of the Companies Act 1985.

9.3   Redeemable shares

Section 159 of the Act allows a company to issue redeemable shares of any class. The company must be limited by shares or limited by guarantee with a share capital and there must be authority in the company's articles. No redeemable shares may be issued if there are no issued shares of the company which are not redeemable (s 159(2)). The shares must be fully paid. Section 160 of the Act provides that redeemable shares can only be redeemed out of distributable profits of the company or out of the proceeds of a fresh issue of shares made specifically for the purpose of the redemption and the premium payable on redemption must be paid out of distributable profits of the company. If the redeemable shares were issued at a premium, any premium payable on their redemption may be paid out of the proceeds of a fresh issue up to the amount equal to the aggregate of the premium received by the company, or the current amount of the company share premium account, whichever is the less.

Where shares are redeemed, they are treated as cancelled on redemption. The amount of the company's issued share capital is diminished accordingly.

Section 171 of the Companies Act 1985 allows private companies to redeem shares out of capital. A private company must be authorised to do so by its articles. It may make a permissible capital payment for redemption. The directors must make a statutory declaration specifying the amount of the permissible capital payment and stating that having made full enquiry into the affairs and prospects of the company they have formed the opinion that immediately following the payment there will be no grounds on which the company could be found unable to pay its debts and having regard to the prospects for the year immediately following that date it is their view that there are financial resources available to the company to enable the company to carry on business as a going concern and that accordingly it will be able to pay its debts as they fall due throughout that year (s 173(3)).

A special resolution must also be passed (s 173(2)). This special resolution must be passed on the date of the statutory declaration or within one week immediately following it (s 174(1)). The statutory declaration must be supported by and have annexed to it an auditors' report (s 173(5)). The auditors' report should state that the auditors have enquired into the company's state of affairs and the amount specified in the declaration as the permissible capital payment and that they are not aware of anything to indicate that the opinion expressed by the directors in the declaration is unreasonable in all the circumstances.

Under s 175, within the week following the date of the resolution, there should be publicity given to this by notice in the *Gazette* stating that the company has approved a payment out of capital specifying the amount of the permissible capital payment, stating that the statutory declaration of the directors and the auditors' report required are available for inspection at the company's registered office and stating that any creditor of the company may within five weeks following the resolution apply to the court under s 176 for an order prohibiting the payment.

Under s 176, any member of the company other than one who voted in favour of it and any creditor may object to the court and apply for a cancellation of the resolution. The court may make such order as it sees fit.

Section 173(6) of the Companies Act 1985 provides that a director who makes a declaration without having reasonable grounds for doing so is liable to imprisonment for up to two years and/or a fine on indictment and imprisonment of up to six months and/or a fine up to the statutory maximum on summary conviction.

Section 162 provides that a company limited by shares or limited by guarantee with share capital may if authorised to do so by its articles purchase its own shares (this includes redeemable shares). In the same way as applies to redemption of shares, the shares must be fully paid and any purchase must be financed out of distributable profits or the proceeds of a fresh issue. Purchased shares are treated as cancelled in the same way as redeemed shares. A company may not purchase any of its shares if as a result of the purchase it is left without members other than members holding redeemable shares.

9.4 The purchase by a company of its own shares

The rules on the financing of the purchase of shares are the same as in relation to the redemption of shares. The procedure differs according to whether the purchase is an off market purchase or a market purchase. A purchase is off market if the shares are purchased other than on a recognised investment exchange or are purchased on a recognised investment exchange but not subject to a marketing arrangement on that investment exchange (s 163(1) the Companies Act 1985). A market purchase is a purchase made on a recognised investment exchange other than a purchase which is an off market purchase (s 163(3) of the Companies Act 1985).

The procedure for an off market purchase is that the company must obtain authority by special resolution to make the contract to purchase the shares. If the company is a public company, the authority must specify a date on which the authority is to expire and this must not be later than 18 months from the date on which the resolution is passed. The contract should be available for inspection at the company's registered office for not less than 15 days ending with the date of the meeting at which the resolution is passed and also at the meeting itself. The details made available should include the names of members holding shares to which the contract relates. When the resolution is voted upon, a member who holds shares to which the resolution relates should refrain from voting.

Section 165 provides that a company may enter into a contract to purchase its own shares on the happening of a certain contingency, for example, the retirement of an employee, but such a purchase must be authorised by special resolution.

If the purchase is a market purchase, then the required resolution is an ordinary resolution (s 166). The resolution should set out the maximum number of shares authorised to be acquired and the maximum and minimum prices for the acquisition of the shares and a date on which the authority is to expire (this must not be later than 18 months from the date of the resolution).

In both cases, within 28 days from the date on which the shares are purchased, the company must deliver to the registrar of companies a return in the prescribed form setting out the number of shares of each class that have been purchased, the nominal value of those shares and the date on which they were delivered to the company. In the case of a public company, the return should also state the aggregate amount paid by the company for the shares and the maximum and minimum prices paid in respect of shares of each class purchased.

Private companies may purchase their own shares out of capital in just the same way as they may redeem shares out of capital. The rules have been examined above.

9.5   Other protections related to a company's purchase of its own shares

Section 23 of the Companies Act 1985 provides that in general a company cannot be a member of its holding company.

Companies are prohibited from dealing in the rights to purchase their own shares. The company cannot thus traffic in the rights to purchase a member's shares and so create a market in relation to such contracts.

Section 76 of the Insolvency Act 1986 provides that in the event of the company's going into liquidation where there has been a payment out of capital towards a redemption of shares or a purchase of a company's own shares, then if the winding up commenced within a year of the date when the relevant payment was made, then the person from whom the shares were redeemed or purchased and the directors who signed the statutory declaration made in accordance with the redemption or purchase are liable to contribute to the company's assets to enable the insufficiency to be met. The person from whom the shares were redeemed or purchased is liable to contribute an amount not exceeding the amount of the payment in relation to the shares and the directors are jointly and severally liable with that person to contribute that amount. This, of course, only applies where the company has insufficient assets to pay its debts and liabilities and the expenses of the winding up.

If a company wishes to reduce its issued share capital, it must have authority in its articles. A special resolution is needed.

9.6   Reduction of capital

Although the s 135 procedure may be used for any reduction of capital – see *Westburn Sugar Refineries* (1951) and *Lawrie v Symington* (1969) (where a substitution for loan stock was held to be a deferred reduction of capital), there are three expressly recognised types of reduction:

(a) to extinguish or reduce liability on any of the company's shares which are not paid up; or

(b) to cancel any paid up share capital which is lost or unrepresented by available assets; or

(c) to pay off any paid up share capital which is in excess of the company's needs (s 135(2)).

In cases (a) and (c), the company is actually giving something back to the shareholders, either an actual return   of capital or cancelling an existing liability. In case (b), nothing is being returned to the shareholders, there is merely a recognition of the fact that the company's paid up share capital is unrepresented by the company's assets.

The procedure is that the special resolution is passed and the company then applies to the court for confirmation of the resolution. In Scotland the court will, as a general rule, remit the proposed reduction to a 'reporter' (usually a solicitor of appropriate standing) who will point out to the court any points which give cause for concern. The court will consider the position of creditors under (a) and (c) above and has a general discretion to consider the position of creditors. The court shall settle a list of creditors and shall ascertain as far as possible the names of creditors and the nature and amount of their debts and may publish notices fixing a day when the creditors who are not entered on the list of creditors may claim to be so entered. If a creditor who is on the list and whose debt is not discharged does not consent to the reduction, the court may dispense with the consent of that creditor on the company's securing payment of his debt or claim either by admitting the full amount of the debt or making provision for

9.6.1   Procedure

it or by providing an amount fixed by the court. The court has discretion where it considers that the company is sufficiently financially buoyant to dispense with giving creditors the opportunity to object – see *Anderson, Brown & Co* (1965).

Once the court is satisfied that every creditor has been provided for, it may make an order confirming the reduction on such terms and conditions as it thinks fit (s 137(1)).

The court may as a condition of granting the order require that the company add the words 'and reduced' after the end of its name. The court may also make an order requiring the company to publish as the court directs the reasons for the reduction of capital or such other information as the court thinks expedient to give proper information to the public. Section 138 of the Act requires that the registrar of companies on production to him of the court order confirming the reduction and delivery to him of a copy of the order and of a minute showing the amount of the share capital, the number of shares into which it is to be divided and the amount of each share, and the amount at the date of the registration deemed to be paid up on each share, shall register the order and the minute. The reduction takes effect from the time of registration.

Note that if a company has more than one class of share, it is important also to consider class rights (see para 6.2) although the courts have seemed to be unwilling to interfere with a reduction which affects shareholder's rights. In *Balmenach Glenlivett Distillery v Croall* (1906), the Inner House allowed a reduction which altered the shareholders' relative rights because they were satisfied that minority interests were protected. See, also, *Wilsons & Clyde Coal Co v Scottish Insurance Corporation* (1949) where the House of Lords reached a similar decision to that in *House of Fraser plc v ACGE Investments Ltd* (1987) even although there was substantial opposition to the repayment of the preference shares and the reduction was not necessary to further the interests of the company.

However, if a company's articles specify that a reduction of capital amounts to a variation of class rights, the relevant procedure must be followed – see *Northern Engineering Industries* (1993).

Where a company wishes to return capital to members it should consider whether it is better to purchase its own shares or formally to reduce the capital. In the former case, it is not possible to purchase part of a share, only complete shares, whilst in a reduction of capital it is possible to return capital in respect of part of a share. On the other hand a formal reduction of capital involves application to the court.

The Maintenance of Capital

In general, it is not permissible for a company to provide financial assistance for the purpose of acquiring shares in the company or of its holding company. There are various exceptions to this general rule. In particular private companies are permitted within limits to provide financial assistance for the purchase of the company's own shares.

Financial assistance towards the purchase of a company's own shares

All companies may, subject to satisfying certain conditions, issue redeemable shares and may also purchase their own shares. In the case of public companies, this can only be financed out of distributable profits or out of the proceeds of a fresh issue. In the case of private companies the purchase may be financed out of capital.

Purchase of a company's own shares and the issue of redeemable shares

Companies may reduce their issued capital by special resolution followed by application to the court. The court will consider the position of creditors in deciding whether to approve the reduction.

Reduction of capital

Chapter 10

Directors

The company is not a natural person. Therefore, somebody needs to act on behalf of the company. The division of powers between the shareholders in general meeting and the directors will be considered later. Suffice it to state at this juncture that the power of management is largely left with the directors where Table A applies (see Table A, Article 70). The purpose of this section of the textbook is to consider the role of directors, the appointment of directors, the removal of directors and directors' duties.

10.1 Management of the company

The first directors will generally be appointed in writing by the subscribers to the company's memorandum. They may otherwise be appointed by a meeting of those subscribers. In any event, the incorporation of the company cannot be accomplished until a statement of the first directors and company secretary has been submitted to the registrar of companies (s 10 of the Companies Act 1985).

10.2 The appointment of directors

Public companies must have at least two directors and a private company must have at least one director. The single director in the case of a private company cannot also be the company secretary.

Subsequent directors may be appointed in accordance with the articles. Table A provides for appointment of additional directors by ordinary resolution in general meeting. The board of directors may appoint people to casual vacancies between annual general meetings but where this is done, the people appointed to such vacancies must stand down at the next annual general meeting and be subject to re-election by ordinary resolution.

Changes in directors and registered details of directors (for example a change of address) must be notified to the companies registry within 14 days of the change.

Directors will not become employees of the company purely by virtue of their directorships. However, executive and managing directors will be presumed to be employees unless the opposite is proved – see *Anderson v James Sutherland (Peterhead) Ltd* (1941).

Unlike company secretaries, directors do not need to have a particular qualification to serve even in a public company.

10.3 Qualification of directors

However, there are some negative conditions that must be considered.

Table A provides that a person may be disqualified from office if he becomes insane or bankrupt and also the board may remove a director who has been voluntarily absent from board meetings for a period of six months or more.

Sometimes, directors are required to hold qualification shares. A director has two months within which to get the relevant number of shares. If he does not do so, his office is automatically vacated at the expiry of this period (s 291 of the Companies Act 1985).

A failure by the company to hold a general meeting may result in the directors automatically losing office. This was held by the Lord Ordinary in *Alexander Ward & Co v Samyang Navigation Co* (1973). The case was later appealed to the House of Lords who reversed the decision of the Lord Ordinary without challenging this particular point.

In addition, there are statutory disqualifications from office. By virtue of the Company Directors Disqualification Act of 1986, both undischarged bankrupts and those disqualified by the court are ineligible to serve. Disqualification of directors will be considered below at para 10.6. In addition persons aged over 70 can only be elected or re-elected as directors of public companies or private companies that are subsidiaries of public companies if special notice is given (special notice will be considered below at para 10.5).

10.4	**Removal from office**

Section 303 of the Companies Act 1985 provides that a director may always be removed from the board of directors by ordinary resolution in a general meeting notwithstanding anything that is stated in the company's articles or in any contract with the director. This provision was first introduced in the Companies Act 1948 in response to the recommendations of the Cohen Committee of 1945.

At first sight, it seems to be a very powerful weapon in the hands of shareholders but its apparent power is subject to certain very real restrictions.

10.4.1	Weighted voting provisions

Although the section prohibits the exclusion of removal by ordinary resolution, it does nothing to counteract normal principles of company law that may make that power very difficult to exercise. Thus in British company law it has always been possible to weight votes attaching to shares. This may therefore be used to give a minority shareholder who is a director the power to block his removal. In *Bushell v Faith* (1970), the House of Lords held that a weighted voting provision was valid in this context. Shares were held in a property company which owned a block of flats in Southgate, North London by two sisters and a brother. The shares were held equally. The sisters wished to remove the brother from the board of directors. In normal circumstances, they would have had no problem as they had more than half of the shares. However, there was a provision in the articles of association that stated on a resolution to remove a director, his shares would carry three votes each. The House of Lords held by a majority of four to one that this provision was valid. The effect of this was therefore to block the brother's removal as a director. It is perhaps worth noting that the senior Law Lord, Lord Morris of Borth-y-Gest, dissented in this case. He said the effect of finding that weighted voting was permissible in such circumstances was to drive a coach and horses through the intention of the legislature. It is possible that a shareholder could in appropriate circumstances use such a weighted voting provision as the basis of a petition under ss 459–61 of the Companies Act 1985.

By the same token, it would seem that other devices may be used. For example, a quorum provision that stated that the meeting was *inquorate* in the absence of the director threatened with removal would not be contrary to the Companies Act 1985. However, it may well be that a shareholder wishing to remove a director may be able to use such a provision as the basis of a petition under ss 459–461 of the Companies Act 1985 as being unfairly prejudicial. In *Re BML Group Ltd* (1994) there was a shareholders' agreement which contained a provision that the meeting was only quorate if B or his proxy was present. B was removed as a director in his absence and he issued proceedings under s 459 contesting his removal. The Court of Appeal held that those wishing to remove the director could not use a s 371 application to the court (see para 15.4.5) to override the shareholders' agreement as the section could not be used to override class rights. The shareholders' agreement attached rights to shares and this has the same effect as if the class rights were contained in the company's articles.

10.4.2   Quorum provisions

The section is stated by s 303(5) to be without prejudice to the removed director's rights to compensation for breach of contract. It was formerly the case that directors would have lengthy service contracts at high remuneration and that therefore at least in private companies it would be extremely expensive to dispense with their services. Section 319 of the Companies Act 1985 now provides that a long term service contract, that is one that is expressed to last for five years or more, must be approved by the members in general meeting.

10.4.3   Compensation provisions

Removal may still prove expensive for the company, see *Shindler v Northern Raincoat Co Ltd* (1960), *Southern Foundries Ltd v Shirlaw* (1940). It may be that the company has concluded a service agreement with the director in which there is a liquidated damages provision specifying how much is payable to the director in the event of breach of the service agreement. In such an instance the director may sue for the sum as a debt provided it is not a penalty, see *Taupo Totara Timber Co Ltd v Rowe* (1978), a Privy Council decision on appeal from New Zealand.

10.4.4   Voting agreements

A director may have entered into voting agreements with other shareholders whereby they agree to vote as directed by him in specific instances. If this is the case, the director may ensure that they vote as promised: see *Stewart v Schwab* (1956) (South Africa) and see, on voting agreements in a different context, *Russell v Northern Bank Development Corporation Ltd* (1992).

10.4.5   Petition to complain of a removal

If the company is a quasi partnership company, it may be that the director if he is also a member can petition under ss 459–61 of the Companies Act 1985 on the grounds that his removal from office is unfairly prejudicial to his interests as a shareholder. This was one successful ground for the petition in *Re a Company* (1986) for example. In *Re Bovey Hotel Ventures Ltd* (1981), an excluded director succeeded in a petition to purchase the shares of the excluding director. In *Re Bird Precision Bellows Ltd* (1986), it was accepted by the parties concerned that the company was a quasi partnership. The petitioning shareholders had been excluded from office as directors. The court held that in the circumstances of the case the conduct amounted to unfair prejudice and it was ordered that the petitioner's shares be purchased by the respondents at a fair value.

If, however, the court does not find that the company is a quasi partnership (that is, where the petitioning member has no legitimate expectation by virtue of his membership to participate in the management) the petition will fail – see *Gammack v Mitchells (Fraserburgh) Ltd* (1983).

In order to pre-empt a removal under s 303, the director concerned would need to threaten that if removed he would seek a remedy under ss 459–61.

10.4.6   Petition for a winding up order

In a similar way under s 122(1)(g) of the Insolvency Act 1986, a director-member who is removed from a quasi partnership company may seek to wind the company up on the just and equitable ground. Such a petition was successful in *Ebrahimi v Westbourne Galleries Ltd* (1973). In this case, Ebrahimi and Nazar had run a successful partnership business selling carpets and tapestries. They decided to incorporate. The business flourished.

Later Nazar sought the entry of his son, George, into the business and it was so agreed. Some shares were transferred from Ebrahimi and some from Nazar. Discord soon followed and Nazar and George excluded Ebrahimi from the business and removed him as a director. Furthermore the considerable profits of the business were paid out as directors' salaries rather than in the form of dividends. Exclusion as a director therefore kept Ebrahimi away from the profits. He sought a winding up order under the Act. The House of Lords held unanimously that his petition would be granted.

In most circumstances, director members in such a situation will now petition under ss 459–61. The just and equitable winding up remedy is after all a 'sledge hammer' remedy. Furthermore, s 125(2) of the Insolvency Act 1986 requires the court if it is of the opinion that the petitioner is entitled to relief to decide whether it is just and equitable that the company should be wound up, bearing in mind the possibility of other forms of relief. The court if it comes to the conclusion that it would be just and equitable that the company should be wound up in the absence of any other remedy must make a winding up order unless it is of the opinion that the petitioner is acting unreasonably in not pursuing that other remedy. In most circumstances, it will surely be unreasonable for a petitioner not to seek a remedy in such a situation under ss 459–61 of the Companies Act 1985. However, in both the Scottish case of *Hyndman v RC Hyndman Ltd* (1989) and its English equivalent of *Virdi v Abbey Leisure Ltd* (1990), the court considered that a refusal by the shareholder to accept an offer to buy his shares where he feared that the valuation would be wrong was not unreasonable.

10.5 Special notice

Special notice is required in three situations in company law. The removal of a director is one of these circumstances. The other two are the removal of the company's auditors and the election or re-election of a director aged 70 or above in a public company or in a private company which is a subsidiary of a public company.

Special notice is defined under s 379 of the Companies Act 1985. It provides that special notice (that is, 28 days notice of the resolution) has to be given to the company by the person who proposes the relevant resolution. The notice is given by depositing a copy of the proposed resolution at the company's registered office.

If the resolution concerns the removal of a director, the resolution must be forwarded forthwith to the director in question. He may make representations in writing which are then to be circulated to every member of the company to whom notice of the meeting is to be sent. If for some reason it is not possible to circulate his representations, they must be read out at the meeting. An exception to this situation is where the representations contain defamatory matter in which case application may be made to the court which would then decide if it thought appropriate that circulation was inappropriate.

Notice of the resolution to remove the director would then be included in the notice of the meeting that is to be called. The director who is threatened with removal would be allowed to speak in his defence at the meeting.

In all three situations where special notice is appropriate, the resolution that is needed is an ordinary resolution.

In general, if the requirements of special notice are not complied with, the meeting and the removal of the director at such a meeting will be void. However, this gives way to the principle that the court will not interfere with the decision that is reached at such a meeting if it is clear that had the correct procedures been followed, the decision would have been the same, see *Bentley-Stevens v Jones* (1974).

The mere serving of special notice by a member who wishes to propose a resolution to remove a director will not of itself entitle that member to have the resolution circulated. Were it otherwise, any vexatious member (perhaps planted by a rival company) could embarrass the company by requiring meetings to be held to discuss his proposed resolution. In *Pedley v The Inland Waterways Association Ltd* (1977), Pedley who was a solicitor (and so should arguably have known better) proposed the removal of the entire board of the company. He served special notice. Not surprisingly the board did not wish to call the meeting. They did not do so. Pedley argued that this was a contravention of the provisions of the Act. He was unsuccessful. In order to ensure that a meeting is held, a person serving special notice will need to fit within one of the categories of those able to call meetings. These circumstances will be considered subsequently at Chapter 15.

The Companies Act 1989 has introduced a new regime whereby private companies need not call meetings if all their members agree on a particular course of conduct. These situations will be considered subsequently at para 15.5.4. At this stage, suffice it to say that there are certain exceptions where even in private companies meetings will need to be held if members are unanimous and these exceptions include the proposed removal of a director. The director has, after all, the right to speak in his own defence, a right that can only properly be secured if a meeting is held.

The Company Directors Disqualification Act 1986 governs the position on disqualification. Section 1 of the Act sets out the basic thesis whereby a person may be disqualified from being

- a director; or

- a liquidator or administrator; or

- a receiver or manager; or

- in any way directly or indirectly concerned or taking part in the promotion, formation or management of a company.

There are various periods of disqualification which may be meted out depending upon the ground of disqualification. The period of disqualification runs from the date of the disqualification order.

Sections 2–5 of the Act deal with disqualification for general misconduct in connection with companies.

10.6.1   Disqualification for general misconduct

Section 2 provides for disqualification upon the conviction of an indictable offence which is in connection with the promotion, formation, management or liquidation of a company or with the receivership or management of a company's property.

The disqualification order may be passed by a court winding up the company or by a court before or upon a person being convicted of an offence. The maximum period of disqualification is five years in the case of a court of summary jurisdiction and 15 years in any other case.

Section 3 of the Act permits disqualification for persistent breaches of companies' legislation. A person is to be taken to be persistent in default if it is conclusively proved that in the five years ending with the date of the application he has been adjudged guilty of three or more defaults in relation to Companies Act provisions. The default may either involve conviction of a particular provision or a default order being made against the person in question under one of the following:

- s 242(4) – failure to deliver company accounts;

- s 713 – failure to make returns;

- s 69 of the Insolvency Act 1986 – failure of a receiver to make returns (s 69 only applies in Scotland – its English equivalent is found in s 41 of the Insolvency Act 1986);

- s 170 of the Insolvency Act 1986 – failure of a liquidator to make returns.

The maximum period of the disqualification under s 3 is five years.

Section 4 allows the court to disqualify for fraudulent trading (see para 23.2) or for fraud in relation to the company by an officer, liquidator, receiver or manager or breach of duty by such officer, liquidator, receiver or manager.

The maximum period of the disqualification under s 4 is 15 years.

10.6.2   Disqualification for unfitness

Sections 6–9 of the Act provide for disqualification for unfitness.

It is provided that the court must make a disqualification order against a person when application has been made if it is satisfied that a person has been a director of a company which has become insolvent and that his conduct as a director of that company (either taken on its own or together with his conduct as a director of any other company or companies) makes him unfit to be concerned in the management of a company. Application under s 6 is made by the Secretary of State for Trade and Industry or if the Secretary of State so directs by the official receiver.

A company is taken to be insolvent if:

- the company goes into liquidation at a time when its assets are insufficient to pay its debts and liabilities and the expenses of the winding up; or

- an administration order is made in relation to the company; or

- a receiver of the company is appointed (note that in England this presumption only applies where an administrative receiver is appointed – Scots law makes no distinction between receivers and administrative receivers).

There is a duty upon the liquidator, the administrator or a receiver as is appropriate (and in England the official receiver) to inform the Secretary of State for Trade and Industry if it is considered that a director is within the section. Schedule 1 of the Act provides for the matters that are relevant for determining the unfitness of directors. These are:

1   Any misfeasance or breach of any fiduciary or other duty by the director.

2   Misapplication or retention of property by the director or any conduct by the director giving rise to an obligation to account for money or other property.

3   The extent of the director's responsibility for the company entering into any transaction that is liable to be set aside under Part XVI of the Insolvency Act which deals with provisions relating to debt avoidance (Part XVI of the Insolvency Act 1986 only applies in England).

4   The extent of the director's responsibility for failure by the company to comply with one of the various provisions that are set out relating to the keeping of records and the making of an annual return.

5   Failure to approve and sign the company accounts.

6   The extent of the director's responsibility for the company entering into a transaction which may be set aside as a gratuitous alienation or unfair preference under ss 242–43 of the Insolvency Act 1986 or any other rule of law in Scotland (the English equivalents are found in ss 127 and 238–40 of the Insolvency Act 1986).

7   Failure to comply with one or more of the obligations under the Insolvency Act relating to the provision of a statement of affairs, co-operation with the liquidator, etc.

Note: the matters set out in 6 and 7 above relate specifically to where the company has become insolvent. The other matters are applicable in all cases and may thus arise where the director's conduct in another (possibly solvent) company is being examined.

The maximum period of disqualification under the section is 15 years and the minimum period is two years.

Section 8 provides for disqualification of a director after an investigation of a company (see Chapter 21). If it appears to the Secretary of State from a report made by inspectors that it is expedient in the public interest that a disqualification order should be made against a person who is or has been a director or shadow director, he may apply to the court for such an order to be made against that person. The court may make such an order if it is felt that the director is unfit.

The disqualification period here is subject to a maximum of 15 years' disqualification.

Section 9 of the Act provides that where a court is to determine whether a person's conduct as a director or shadow director makes him unfit to be concerned in the management of a company, the court shall again have regard in particular to the matters mentioned in Part I of the First Schedule to the Act, and if the company is insolvent, the factors set out in Part II of the Schedule which deals with matters applicable where the company has become insolvent are appropriate.

In *Re Sevenoaks Stationers (Retail) Ltd* (1991) the Court of Appeal set out certain principles on disqualification for unfitness. Dillon LJ said at p 328:

> I would for my part endorse the division of the potential 15 year disqualification period into three brackets, which was put forward by Mr Keenan for the official receiver to Harman J in the present case and has been put forward by Mr Charles for the official receivers in other cases, *viz:*
>
> (i)   the top bracket of disqualification for periods over 10 years should be reserved for particularly serious cases. These may include cases where a director who has already had one period of disqualification imposed on him falls to be disqualified yet again;
>
> (ii)   the minimum bracket of two to five years' disqualification should be applied where, though disqualification is mandatory, the case is relatively not very serious;
>
> (iii)   the middle bracket of disqualification for from six to 10 years should apply for serious cases which do not merit the top bracket.

In *Secretary for State for Trade and Industry v Gray and another* (1995), the Court of Appeal allowed an appeal where the first instance judges had considered that the future protection of the public did not merit a period of disqualification. The Court of Appeal stated that if the respondents' conduct fell below the standard appropriate for persons considered fit to be directors then it was the judge's duty to make a disqualification order.

An example of a disqualification for unfitness is provided by *Re Firedart Ltd* (1994), where F, the director, had continued trading through the medium of the company when it was insolvent, had received excessive remuneration and had failed to keep proper accounting records. The appropriate period of disqualification was held to be six years.

10.6.3   **Disqualification in other cases**

Sections 10–12 deal with other cases of disqualification. Section 10 provides that where there has been participation in wrongful trading or fraudulent trading such that a person is held liable to make a contribution to a company's assets, then whether or not an application for an order is made, the court may if it thinks fit make a disqualification order against the person to whom the declaration of liability relates. The maximum period of the disqualification is 15 years.

Section 11 of the Act provides that it is an offence for a person who is an undischarged bankrupt to act as a director. This provision has been interpreted so as to extend to any person directly concerned with the management of the company's affairs (*Drew v HMA* (1995)). Section 12 provides that where a person fails to make a payment as provided for in an administration order of the county court, the court may make a disqualification order against the person concerned in revoking the administration order. The period may not exceed two years.

Section 13 provides that a person who acts in contravention of a disqualification order is guilty of an offence which on conviction on indictment is punishable by up to two years' imprisonment and/or a fine and is punishable on summary conviction by imprisonment of not more than six months and/or a fine up to the statutory maximum.

Section 14 of the Act provides that where a company is guilty of an offence of acting in contravention of a disqualification order and it is shown that the offence occurred with the consent or connivance or is attributable to any neglect on the part of any director, manager, secretary or other officer of the body corporate or any person purporting to act as such, he shall be guilty of an offence as well as the body corporate.

Section 15 provides that a person who is disqualified and continues to act is personally responsible for all the relevant debts of the company.

There is a register of disqualification orders which is kept by the Secretary of State in pursuance of s 18 of the Act.

A disqualification order is not made principally to punish a director but 'to protect the public against the future conduct of companies by persons whose past records as directors of insolvent companies have shown them to be a danger to creditors and others' – *per* Browne Wilkinson V-C in *Re Lo-Line Electric Motors Ltd* (1988).

10.6.4   The purpose of disqualification

Thus courts have rarely disqualified directors for periods even approaching the maximum possible under the Act and have frequently allowed disqualified directors to continue on the board of a company which relies on their personality. A recent example occurred in *Secretary of State for Trade and Industry v Henderson* (1995). In this case, a medium length disqualification order of seven years was held appropriate where a director had over a period of years failed to file accounts or pay National Insurance contributions. Meanwhile, the company was encountering increasing financial distress, yet the particular director took as part of his remuneration package a Jaguar XJ6 and a BMW 730, and entertained his family on a regular basis in a bar/restaurant owned by the company at the company's expense. The court concluded that the director was living off the company's creditors. And in

Secretary of State for Trade and Industry v Palfreman (1995) a director of an insolvent company which had failed to pay taxes was the subject of a three year disqualification order but was nevertheless allowed by the Outer House to remain on the boards of two other companies, provided that his presence on these boards was monitored by an independent solicitor who was also to be appointed to the respective boards.

10.7   Directors' loss of office and compensation payments

Where a director loses office, he may nevertheless be awarded a golden handshake sum. Sections 312–16 deal with this area.

Section 312 provides that it is not lawful for a company to make a payment to a director by way of compensation for loss of office or in connection with his retirement without particulars of the proposed payment being disclosed to members of the company and their approval being given to that payment.

It may be organised in a slightly different way. Under s 313, it is not lawful in connection with the transfer of business for a payment to be made to a director by way of compensation for loss of office or as consideration for or in connection with his retirement without the consent of the members being provided as set out above.

Section 314 provides that if a payment is proposed to a director as compensation for loss of office in connection with the transfer of any or all of the shares in a company where an offer has been made to the shareholders generally or an offer made with a view to the obtaining of the right to exercise or control the exercise of at least one third of the voting power of the company, then the particulars of the proposed payment must be brought to the attention of the company's shareholders and sent out with the notice of the offer made for their shares.

The provisions on golden handshakes clearly require full disclosure to the shareholders of the company. Under s 312 and s 313, the unlawful payment is held on trust for the company. In the case of s 314 the payment is held on trust for the assenting shareholders (s 315).

It should be noted that the provisions on golden handshakes do not apply to payment of compensation for breach of a contract of service by court order (s 303(5)) or to a *bona fide* settlement of a claim under s 303 or where a director sues for a liquidated sum set out in the contract as payable in the event of breach, see *Taupo Totara Timber Co Ltd v Rowe* (1978), a Privy Council decision on appeal from New Zealand (see s 316(3)).

The law in this area is not likely to set the pulse racing. The rules are technical and complex. They are summarised here.

The rules in this area were significantly tightened by the Companies Act 1980. They are now consolidated in the 1985 Act.

There is no need to define the term 'loan'. The term 'quasi loan' is defined in s 331(3) of the Act as a transaction under which one party agrees to pay or agrees to reimburse expenditure incurred by another party, on terms that the borrower will reimburse the creditor or in circumstances giving rise to a liability on the borrower to reimburse the creditor. For example, a company pays a director's credit card bill and the director agrees to reimburse the company. A credit transaction is where the creditor supplies goods or sells land under a hire purchase agreement or a conditional sale agreement or leases or hires land or goods in return for periodical payments or otherwise disposes of land or supplies goods or services on the understanding that payment is to be deferred. An example of this would be if a company lets a house to a director.

There is a general prohibition on all companies making loans to directors or entering into any guarantee or providing any security in connection with a loan to a director of a company or a director of its holding company. There are certain exceptions which will be considered below.

The Act contains additional restrictions which apply to relevant companies. A relevant company is defined as:

- a public company;

- a subsidiary of a public company;

- a subsidiary of a company which has as another subsidiary a public company;

- a company which has a subsidiary which is a public company.

In relation to these companies, it is prohibited to make a quasi loan to a director of the company or of its holding company or to make a loan or quasi loan to a person connected with such a director or enter into a guarantee or provide any security in connection with the loan or quasi loan made by any other person for such a director or a person so connected. Furthermore, a relevant company shall not enter into a credit transaction as creditor for a director of it or its holding company or a person so connected or enter into any guarantee or provide security in connection with a credit transaction made by any other person for such a director or a person so connected.

10.8 Loans, quasi loans and credit transactions in favour of directors

10.8.1   Connected persons

Section 346 defines 'connected persons' as follows:

1 a spouse, child or step-child;

2 a body corporate with which the director is associated (this means if he holds more than one fifth of the voting share capital);

3 a person acting as trustee of any trust the beneficiaries of which include the director, his spouse or any children or step-children or a body corporate with which he is associated or of a trust whose terms confer a power on the trustees that may be exercised for the benefit of the director, his spouse or any children or step-children or any such body corporate;

4 a person acting as partner of the director or of any person set out above.

Certain reciprocal transactions are prohibited. It is not permitted to enter into an arrangement whereby the company will make available some benefit to the director of another company in return for that company making available a benefit to the directors of the company conferring the benefit.

10.8.2   Exceptions to s 330

There are certain exceptions to s 330. These are as follows:

• Inter company loans in the same group (s 333).

• Loans to directors which in aggregate for each director do not exceed £5,000 (s 334).

• Loans made to directors to provide them with funds to meet expenditure incurred or to be incurred for the purposes of the company provided that in the case of relevant companies the amount in aggregate does not exceed £20,000. The loans must have the prior approval of the company and must be repayable within six months of the conclusion of the next annual general meeting (s 337).

• Loans and quasi loans made by money lending companies (s 338). If the business of the company includes the making of loans or quasi loans or the giving of guarantees in connection with loans or quasi loans, the company is a money lending company. For the exception to apply, the loan or quasi loan or guarantee must be made in the ordinary course of the company's business and the terms must not be more favourable than the terms which it would be reasonable to expect the company to have offered to a person of the same financial standing but unconnected with the company.

• In the case of money lending companies which are not recognised banks, there is an overall limit of £100,000. This ceiling applies in aggregate with other loans etc to each director. In the case of recognised banks, there is no ceiling. In the case of all money lending companies, it is possible to make loans of up to £100,000 on favourable terms for house purchase or improvement if loans of that description are ordinarily made by the company to its employees and on no less favourable terms.

- Short term quasi loans. Section 330 does not prohibit a company from making a quasi loan to one of its directors or to a director of its holding company if it contains a term requiring the director to reimburse the creditor within two months of the charge being incurred and the aggregate of the amount of that quasi loan and any other quasi loan which is outstanding does not exceed £5,000. It should be recalled that this exception only applies to relevant companies since there is no prohibition on non-relevant companies from making quasi loans (s 332).

- It is also provided that minor business transactions are exempted (s 335). Section 330 does not prohibit a company from entering into a credit transaction for a person if the aggregate of the relevant amounts does not exceed £10,000. This exception is provided that the transaction is entered into in the ordinary course of business and the value of the transaction is not greater and the terms on which it is entered into are no more favourable than that or those which it is reasonable to expect the company to have offered to a person of the same financial standing but who is unconnected with the company.

10.9 Consequences of breach of the loan, etc, provisions

Section 341 provides that if a company enters into a transaction or arrangement in contravention of s 330, the transaction or arrangement is voidable at the instance of the company unless restitution of the money or asset is no longer possible or unless there are rights acquired *bona fide* for value and without notice of the contravention of the statute on the part of the creditor.

Criminal liability is provided for by s 342 which provides for both imprisonment and a fine.

Finally, in this area of the law, it is worth noting that loans, quasi loans and credit transactions of any type must be disclosed in the company's annual accounts (s 232 of the CA 85).

Directors

The appointment of directors is a matter which is generally settled by the articles of association.

    Public companies must have at least two directors and private companies must have at least one director.

Appointment of directors

Section 303 of the Companies Act 1985 provides for the removal of directors from the board of directors by ordinary resolution in general meeting.

    There are various provisos which may affect the exercise of this power:

- the possibility of weighted voting shares;

- a carefully drawn quorum provision;

- compensation payable for breach of contract;

- voting agreements;

- a ss 459–61 petition by a shareholder/director;

- a winding up petition on the just and equitable ground (s 122(1)(g) of the Insolvency Act 1986) by a shareholder/ director;

- the procedural niceties of the special notice procedure.

Removal of directors

The Company Directors Disqualification Act 1986 provides for disqualification from office as:

- a director; or

- a liquidator or administrator; or

- a receiver or manager; or

- a person concerned in the promotion, formation or management of a company.

Disqualification may arise on various grounds. It may be from conviction of an indictable offence connected with the running of a company, persistent breach of filing provisions of the companies legislation or for fraudulent trading. In addition, directors may be disqualified on the ground of unfitness following the insolvency of their company or following a company investigation. There are various guidelines which are

Statutory disqualification

set out in a schedule to the Act which are relevant in determining unfitness.

An undischarged bankrupt cannot act as a director.

Directors' loss of office and compensation payments

Golden handshake payments for directors have to be disclosed to members and assented to (ss 312–16 CA 85).

Loans

There are strict rules restricting loans, quasi loans and credit transactions in favour of directors and connected persons. Transactions in breach of the provisions are void and criminal liability may result. There are certain exceptions.

Chapter 11

Directors' Duties

The first question that needs to be considered in relation to the duties of directors is the question of to whom those duties are owed. The traditional view in British company law is that directors owe their duties to the providers of capital, that is to say to the shareholders. This duty is owed to the shareholders as a body and not to individual shareholders. Thus, in *Percival v Wright* (1902), where certain shareholders approached the directors asking them to purchase their shares at a time when secret takeover negotiations were going on, the directors failed to mention this to the shareholders. In subsequent litigation, it was held that the directors were not in breach of duty to the shareholders. The directors owed their duty to the shareholders as a body and the court took the view that premature disclosure of the takeover negotiations would have been detrimental to the shareholders. The position is different if the approach is made by the directors to the shareholders. In such a situation the directors constitute themselves as fiduciaries *vis à vis* the shareholders, see *Briess v Woolley* (1954), *Allen v Hyatt* (1914).

Other jurisdictions have taken a more liberal view of the duty owed to individual shareholders. Thus, in *Coleman v Myers* (1972), the New Zealand Court of Appeal held that the managing director and chairman of a company owed fiduciary duties to the shareholders of the company in a takeover situation. Indeed, even in Great Britain, it seems that in certain situations, the courts are willing to hold that a duty is owed to individual shareholders. This seems to be the case in takeover situations, see *Gething v Kilner* (1972). However, in *Dawson International plc v Coats Patons plc* (1989) Lord Cullen in the Court of Session held that during the course of a takeover bid the directors are not under a positive duty to recommend acceptance of the highest offer but 'if ... directors take it upon themselves to give advice to current shareholders, ... they have a duty to advise in good faith and not fraudulently'. However, it has been held in Scotland that if the articles require directors to act as agents for shareholders wishing to sell their shares, the directors owe the shareholders a duty of disclosure, even if the articles provide that the shares must be valued by independent auditors – see *Munro v Bogie* (1994).

Note that the decision in *Percival v Wright* in relation to purchase of shares by directors is obviously now subject to legislative provisions on insider dealing (although these provisions in general apply only to quoted companies – see Chapter 13) and indeed the proposition that directors of a company may purchase the shares of other shareholders without disclosing pending negotiations for the purchase of the company has been doubted by Browne-Wilkinson V-C in *Re Chez Nico (Restaurants) Ltd* (1991).

The traditional interpretation of directors' duties that they are owed only to the providers of capital has now been qualified by statute.

Section 309 of the Companies Act 1985 provides that:

(i) The matters to which the directors of a company are to have regard in the performance of their functions include the interests of the company's employees in general as well as the interests of its members.

(ii) Accordingly the duty imposed by this section on the directors of a company is owed by them to the company (and the company alone) and is enforceable in the same way as any other fiduciary duty owed to a company by its directors.

The Bullock Committee, the Committee of Inquiry on Industrial Democracy had recommended (Cmnd 6706) that directors duties should be extended to take account of the interests of employees. This is the only recommendation of the Bullock Committee to have been implemented.

Although the provision does seem at first flush to be a radical provision, the reality is otherwise. The enforcement of the duty still rests with the members as s 309(2) makes clear. The provision does, however, mean that where directors have taken account of the interests of employees in performing their functions they cannot now be called to account on the basis that their decision and subsequent action have been *ultra vires*, see *Parke v The Daily News* (1960), a decision which is anyway specifically overruled by statute in s 719 of the Companies Act 1985.

11.2   Duties to creditors

In normal circumstances, it seems that no duty is owed at common law to creditors. In *Liquidator of West Mercia Safetywear Ltd v Dodd* (1988), however, it was held that a duty was owed by a director of an insolvent company to the company's creditors. The court acted on the principle that had been applied in various commonwealth authorities such as *Walker v Wimborne* (1976) and *Kinsela v Russell Kinsela Pty Ltd* (1986).

In *Nordic Oil Services v Berman* (1993), the Outer House held that the directors of a company did not owe a duty of care to creditors in the ordinary course of events unless there was a specific agreement to that effect or some other special relationship of proximity was established. In this case a company had leased an aircraft which had been detained under statute where the company had been unable to pay route, navigational and aircraft charges to the Civil Aviation Authority and the British Airports Authority. The owners of the aircraft had to pay those fees themselves in order to release the impounded aircraft. The court pointed out the the lessee company could have obtained contractual guarantees from the directors (which are frequently sought).

There is no clear principle in British company law in relation to duties owed to creditors and dicta in the cases are inconsistent. Section 214 of the Insolvency Act 1986 does, however, make it a statutory duty for directors and shadow directors of companies to take steps to minimise the loss to creditors where they ought to know that the company has no reasonable prospect of avoiding insolvent liquidation. If they fail to do so they may be called to account to make a contribution towards the company's assets in liquidation.

The leading case of the duty of care and skill is *Re City Equitable Fire & Insurance Co Ltd* (1925). The company had experienced a serious depletion of funds and the managing director, Mr Bevan, was convicted of fraud. The liquidator, however, sought to make other directors liable in negligence for failing to detect the frauds. Romer J in what has become the classic exposition of directors' duties of care and skill set out three propositions:

11.3   The duty of care and skill

> There are, in addition, one or two other general propositions that seem to be warranted by the reported cases:
>
> (1)   A director need not exhibit in the performance of his duties a greater degree of skill than may reasonably be expected from a person of his knowledge and experience. A director of a life insurance company, for instance, does not guarantee that he has the skill of an actuary or of a physician. In the words of Lindley MR, 'if the directors act within their powers, if they act with such care as is reasonably to be expected from them, having regard to their knowledge and experience, and if they act honestly for the benefit of the company they represent, they discharge both their equitable as well as their legal duty to the company', see *Lagunas Nitrate Co v Lagunas Syndicate* (1899). It is perhaps only another way of stating the same

proposition to say that the directors are not liable for mere errors of judgment.

(2)   A director is not bound to give continuous attention to the affairs of his company. His duties are of an intermittent nature to be performed at periodic board meetings and at meetings of any committee of the board upon which he happens to be placed. He is not, however, bound to attend all such meetings, though he ought to attend whenever in the circumstances, he is reasonably able to do so.

(3)   In respect of all duties that, having regard to the exigencies of business, and the articles of association, may properly be left to some other official, a director is, in the absence of grounds for suspicion, justified in trusting that official to perform such duties honestly ...

11.3.1   Standard of care and skill

In relation to the first principle set out by Romer J, the decision in *Re Denham & Co* (1883) is illustrative. In this case a director recommended the payment of a dividend out of capital. As has been seen (Chapter 8), this is not something that is permissible! The director was held not liable in negligence. As was stated in the case, the director was a country gentleman and not an accountant. Although such cases resound with Victorian echoes, it is probably the case that little has changed. The circumstances in the Scottish case of *Liquidators of City of Glasgow Bank v MacKinnon* (1882) were similar. However, the case failed on its facts and the possibility of a director being held liable in negligence in such circumstances was left open.

In England, s 13 of the Supply of Goods and Services Act 1982 introduced a statutorily imposed implied term that the supplier of services would provide services of a reasonable standard. Directors were exempted from this provision before it even came into force by Statutory Instrument 1982 No 1771. In *Dorchester Finance Co Ltd v Stebbings* (1989) (a decision that was reached some 10 years before it was fully reported), Foster J held that the duties owed by non-executive directors were the same as those owed by executive directors. In this case an executive director and two non-executive directors all had relevant accounting experience. The two non-executive directors signed blind blank cheques which the executive director then used to further his own ends and those of companies which he controlled. It was held that all three directors had been negligent.

There is some reason for believing that some change in the law is occurring. In s 214 of the Insolvency Act 1986, an objective standard of care is introduced in relation to directors and shadow directors where the company is insolvent.

Note – many of the provisions of the companies' legislation apply to 'shadow directors' as well as directors. Section 741 of the Companies Act 1985 provides that a shadow director means a person in accordance with whose directions or instructions the directors of the company are accustomed to act.

However, a person is not deemed a shadow director by reason only that the directors act on advice given by him in a professional capacity.

In *Norman v Theodore Goddard* (1991), Hoffmann J accepted that the standard in s 214 applied generally in relation to directors and that the relevant yardstick was what could be expected of a person in the position of the director carrying out those functions. The standard may well be different from what could be expected of that particular director. In the event, Hoffmann J held that the director of the property development company acted reasonably in accepting information from a senior partner in the city solicitors, Theodore Goddard.

In relation to Romer J's second proposition, *Re Cardiff Savings Bank, Marquis of Bute's Case* (1892) provides a stark example of this principle at play. In this case the Marquis of Bute was appointed president and director of the Cardiff Savings Bank when he was only six months old. At this age, clearly little could be expected from him in terms of corporate control. In the next 38 years the Marquis only attended one board meeting and during this time massive frauds were perpetrated by another director. The court held that the Marquis was not liable for breach of duty in failing to attend board meetings as he had not undertaken to do so.

11.3.2   Continuous attention

The third proposition set out by Romer J seems unexceptionable. It permits delegation to experts. Thus, in *Dovey & Metropolitan Bank (of England and Wales) Ltd v Cory* (1901), where a director, John Cory, had delegated the task of drawing up the accounts to others, it was held that he was entitled to rely on those accounts in recommending the payment of a dividend which subsequently turned out to be illegal.

11.3.3   Delegation

The umbrella term 'fiduciary duties' is used to cover many aspects of the director's duty to act in good faith for the benefit of the company as a whole. There are certain statutory provisions that affect this area as well as the common law and equitable principles. First, it is proposed to consider some of the statutory provisions that impact in this area.

Section 317 of the Companies Act 1985 requires a director to disclose any interest he has in a contract between the

11.4   Fiduciary duties

company and him. This is extended to cover persons connected with him. Connected persons are:

- the director's spouse or infant child;

- a company with which the director is associated (that is to say, he controls more than 20% of the voting capital);

- a trustee of a trust whose beneficiaries include the director himself or a connected person;

- a partner of the director or of a connected person (see s 346).

A shadow director is required to comply with s 317 in the same way as a director.

Failure to comply with s 317 renders the director or shadow director liable to a fine for non-compliance.

It should be noted that where disclosure to the board is required under s 317, this means disclosure to the full board and not disclosure to a sub-committee of the board. This principle derives from the House of Lords decision in *Guinness plc v Saunders and Another* (1990). In *Movitex Ltd v Bulfield & Others* (1986), the interpretation of a company's articles in relation to s 317 arose. The articles of association provided that directors could vote at board meetings where there was a question of entry into a contract in which they had an interest if they were interested in a contract with another company of which they were directors or other officers, members or creditors. Vinelott J held that this could apply to cases where the directors were both members and directors of the other company and that therefore the exception applied in the case before him.

Where the company only has one director, compliance with s 317 is by means of a declaration at a director's meeting even though there is only one director (see *Neptune (Vehicle Leasing Equipment) Ltd v Fitzgerald* (1995)).

Compliance with s 317 does not of itself entitle a director to keep any profit deriving from the contract. Most articles including Table A provide that if a director fails to disclose his interest, the contract is voidable at the option of the company. Table A also provides that provided there has been disclosure of the director's interest in the contract, the director may keep any benefit accruing from it. In fact, in *Liquidators of West Lothian Oil Co v Mair* (1892), an article providing that no contract between a director and the company could be voidable by virtue only of the director's relationship with the company was upheld. The common law position is illustrated by the case of *Aberdeen Railway Co v Blaikie Brothers* (1854). In this case, Mr Blaikie, who was chairman of the board of directors, induced the company to enter into a contract whereby it would buy railway track equipment from a partnership called Blaikie Brothers of which he was the managing partner. He did not disclose this. It was held that the company could repudiate the contract even though the contract was concluded on market terms.

In addition to complying with s 317 of the Companies Act 1985, some contracts involve compliance with s 320 of the Act as well. Such contracts require approval by the members in general meeting and are termed substantial property transactions. If the director or shadow director is to sell to or purchase from the company one or more non-cash assets that are substantial, then prior approval from the company in general meeting is needed. A transaction is substantial if the market value of the asset exceeds the lower of £100,000 or 10% of the company's net asset value as set out in the last balance sheet. Transactions worth less than £2,000 are never substantial. Section 320 as well as applying to shadow directors also applies to connected persons as defined above. If the director or connected person is also a director of the company's holding company, then the transaction must also be approved by the holding company in general meeting before its conclusion. In the same way, substantial property transactions with a director of a company's holding company also need prior approval.

If a substantial property transaction does not receive prior approval or approval within a reasonable period of the contract being concluded, then it is voidable at the option of the company and the director concerned is liable to make good any profit to the company and indemnify the company against any loss.

Directors must not place themselves in a position where their personal interest is seen to conflict with their duty to the company. The leading case in this area is the House of Lords decision in *Regal (Hastings) v Gulliver* (1942). Regal owned a cinema in Hastings. The company's solicitor considered that it would be a sound business move to acquire two other cinemas in the town. He suggested this to the directors. The company had insufficient funds. However, a scheme was hatched and a subsidiary was created for the purpose of acquiring the two other cinemas. The directors of Regal put up some money to subscribe for shares as did the company solicitor. The move proved to be a successful one and ultimately the shares of Regal and its subsidiary were sold to a purchaser. The

11.5   Use of corporate opportunities

directors made a profit on the sale as did the company solicitor. The company under its new management then proceeded to start an action against the former directors for damages in respect of the secret profit made on the sale of the shares. It was proved that the directors had acted from sound motives and there was no *mala fides*. The House of Lords held that the directors who acquired a beneficial interest in the shares were liable to disgorge their profits back to the company (ie back to the purchaser who willingly paid the asking price for the business!) as this profit had been made at the expense of the company. The company's solicitor, as he was not a director, was not subject to any fiduciary duties and was therefore not liable to disgorge. It had, of course, been his idea in the first place!

The decision is in many ways a horrendous one. It is the triumph of form over substance. If the directors had obtained the consent of the company in general meeting to what they were doing, no complaint would have been possible. Furthermore, had the directors sold the business as a going concern rather than sold the shares, the purchaser would not have been in a position to bring the action as the company. The decision is a comedy or rather tragedy of errors! However, it does establish the very clear principle that directors should not let their personal positions conflict with their duties to the company.

In the Scottish case of *Henderson v Huntingdon Copper Co* (1877), the House of Lords held that a director who received £10,000 from the vendor of mines which the company had purchased was liable to hand over this secret commission to the company since this had not been disclosed to the company and there was no evidence to demonstrate that the director had rendered services to the company which could justify the payment.

Later cases illustrate the same point. In *IDC v Cooley* (1972), Cooley was an architect with the East Midlands Gas Board. He left to become a director of IDC. He was subsequently approached by the Eastern Gas Board. They wished him to do some work for them by designing a gas holder at Ponders End! They did not wish to deal with IDC and made it quite clear that the offer was only applicable to Cooley in his personal capacity. Because Cooley was tied to IDC by contract, he went to his management and told them that he was desperately ill and sought leave to terminate his contract. This was agreed to. Whereupon Cooley convalesced by designing the gas holder! IDC then brought this action for disgorgement of profit. IDC was successful. One can in some ways sympathise with IDC.

Clearly Cooley was dishonest and the prospect of his profiting from his dishonesty is not an attractive one. The decision though must be questionable as it is unlikely that Cooley had here taken a corporate opportunity as the Eastern Gas Board was clear it did not wish to deal with IDC but only with Cooley. The judge, Roskill J, said that Cooley should have stayed with IDC and sought to convince the Eastern Gas Board to change its mind.

Another interesting decision in this same line of cases is *Horcal Ltd v Gatland* (1984). In this case, Gatland, who was a director, was nearing retirement. The board of directors other than Gatland had just decided to make a golden handshake payment to him on his retirement. Gatland subsequently, when a person rang up to arrange for some building work, diverted the contract to himself and undertook to execute it on his own account without putting it through the company books. Later, when the customer rang up to complain that the work was faulty after Gatland had retired from the company, it became obvious what he had done. Horcal Ltd then brought this action to (1) obtain disgorgement of the profit on the contract, and (2) obtain reimbursement of the golden handshake. The company was successful in obtaining disgorgement of the profit. That much is clear. However, the company was not successful in obtaining a return of the golden handshake. The judge said that at the time when the golden handshake payment was agreed to by the board, Gatland had evil thoughts but there had been no evil deeds! The decision on this point seems surprising. Surely, had the board known of these evil intentions, the golden handshake payment would not have been made.

Some cases present much simpler legal questions. In *Cranleigh Precision Engineering v Bryant* (1964), the director concerned had been working on a revolutionary above ground swimming pool. He left the company taking the plans and designs with him and developed the swimming pool on his own. The company later brought this action to seek disgorgement of profits he had made from developing the swimming pool for his own purposes. It is clear that the company should succeed, as indeed it did.

Questions of criminal law may also arise in such cases. Directors may well be guilty of theft in instances where they are appropriating company property to themselves.

If the board of directors considers a proposed activity or transaction and turns it down *bona fide* and then an individual director takes it up and exploits it, it is clear that this is not exploitation of a corporate opportunity. It has ceased to be a corporate opportunity when turned down by the company. See *Peso Silver Mines Ltd v Cropper* (1966), from the Supreme Court of Canada. In *Island Export Finance Ltd v Umunna* (1986), Hutchinson J said that the question of whether a director was liable to disgorge a profit to his former company from a corporate opportunity was to some extent a question of timing. Umunna had been managing director of the company and when he resigned the company had some hopes of doing business with the Cameroon authorities. Umunna resigned hoping to do business with the Cameroon authorities. At this time there were no specific corporate opportunities. It was held that Umunna could take it on his own account.

11.6   Competing with the company

From the position of strict logic it would seem that directors should not be directors of competing companies, nor to compete on their own account or through a partnership. They would be placed in an invidious positions where corporate opportunities arose as to which of the two companies they should favour with the opportunity. As is so often predictably the case, the only British authority on the point indicates that there is no principle of law that prevents a director from being a director of two competing businesses, see *London & Mashonaland Exploration Co Ltd v New Mashonaland Exploration Co Ltd* (1891). The decision is an old one and is open to question. Yet, the decision was approved by Lord Blanesburgh *obiter* in *Bell v Lever Brothers Ltd* (1932). Commonwealth authority is inconsistent on the point. Some cases follow the *Mashonaland* case, others indicate that directors may not be directors of competing companies, see *Abbey Glen Property Corporation v Stumborg* (1976) from Canada. In other areas of the law, it seems that it is not possible for senior employees to compete by holding two employments in similar lines of business. Thus, in *Hivac Ltd v Park Royal Scientific Instruments Ltd* (1946), senior employees engaged on sensitive work in wartime were prohibited from working for competing employers. They were normally engaged in work on midget valves for deaf aids. During the war the work had wartime applications.

In partnership law, partners may not compete with their partnerships. The logical position should be that directors should not be able to compete with their company, either as directors of other competing businesses or as partners within a firm or indeed acting on their own account. The *Mashonaland* case is reviewed and criticised by Michael Christie in *Modern Law Review* (1992).

On occasion, the question of whether directors have exercised their powers for a proper purpose may arise. The most common example of the exercise of directors' powers that is subject to the fiduciary duty of directors is the power to issue shares.

Generally, this power is given to the directors. If directors do have the power to issue shares, this power must be given to them and the power may only operate for up to five years (s 80 of the Companies Act 1985). An exception to this is in the case of private companies whose members may unanimously decide that the power to issue shares given to the directors should be unfettered in terms of time limit. The power to issue shares is given for the purpose of raising necessary capital for the company. Any other purpose is not *prima facie* a legitimate exercise of that power. However, the courts have recognised that other purposes may be validated by the company in general meeting. Thus for example it is an improper purpose to issue shares to defeat a takeover bid but the exercise of the issue of shares for this purpose may be validated by the company in general meeting. In *Hogg v Cramphorn Ltd* (1967), a takeover bid was proposed which the directors genuinely believed not to be in the best interest of the company. To block the takeover bid, the directors issued 5,000 additional shares which were to be held on trust for the employees of the company. The court held that the issue was not a proper exercise of the directors powers and therefore invalid. However, the court ordered that a meeting of the members should be held which could if it considered it appropriate validate the issue.

At this company meeting, the new shares would not be able to vote. In the event the issue was ratified. A similar conclusion was reached in *Bamford v Bamford* (1970). It is not every issue of shares for extraneous purposes that can be validated, however. If the purpose of the issue of shares is clearly to further the directors' or majority shareholders' own personal interests, the issue cannot be validated by the company in general meeting, see *Howard Smith Ltd v Ampol Petroleum Ltd* (1974) (a Privy Council case from Australia). In this case there were rival bids for the share capital of a company. The majority shareholders favoured one bid. The directors who favoured a different bid issued additional shares to the bidding company to place the majority shareholders in a minority position. The Privy Council held that the issue was an improper exercise of their powers as it was designed to thwart the wishes of the majority shareholders.

In *Clemens v Clemens Brothers Ltd* (1976), two shareholders held the entire share capital of a company and the majority

11.7   Directors' exercise of powers for a proper purpose

11.7.1   Power to issue shares

shareholder used her voting power to pass a resolution authorising the issue of new shares to an employee trust scheme. This was held to be invalid. The effect of the new issue of shares was to reduce the other shareholders' holding (that of her niece) to less than the 25% stake where she had been able to block a special resolution. Foster J considered that the exercise of the majority's voting power in this case was being used inequitably against the minority shareholder and this was held to be invalid.

In an earlier unreported decision, *Pennell, Sutton and Moraybell Securities Ltd v Veluda Investments Ltd* (1974) (noted in 1981 MLR 40 by Burridge), the majority proposed to increase the share capital of the company. The minority had sought a declaration that this constituted a fraud on the minority and asked for an interlocutory injunction. The minority succeeded. Templeman J held that there was a *prima facie* case of abuse of powers by the company's directors and the judge considered that the company was a quasi partnership company based on mutual trust and confidence.

| 11.7.2 | Power to refuse to register a transfer of shares |

There are, however, other examples of the exercise of directors' powers that are subject to the same fiduciary duty. In *Re Smith & Fawcett Ltd* (1942), the question arose as to the exercise of the directors' power to refuse to register a transfer of shares. By the articles of association, the directors had unlimited discretion to refuse to register a transfer. The appellant sought to register 4,001 shares in his name after the death of his father who had previously held the shares. The directors refused to register the transfer but offered to register a transfer of 2,001 shares provided that the applicant sold the other shares to one of the directors at a price proposed by the directors of the company. The High Court held that the directors were acting within their discretion and this was upheld by the Court of Appeal.

In a similar way, the question of the exercise of directors' powers arose in *Lee Panavision Ltd v Lee Lighting Ltd* (1992). In this case, the plaintiffs had acquired an option to purchase the defendants. The plaintiffs also had a management agreement by which they ran the defendants' business and they also nominated the company's directors. It was clear that the option to purchase the business was not to be exercised and that the management agreement would therefore be terminated. Since the plaintiffs wished to continue managing the business, they ensured that the directors of the defendants voted in favour of a second management agreement perpetuating the plaintiffs' control of the company. Subsequently, the directors of the defendants were removed from office and the defendants announced that they did not consider themselves bound by the second management agreement. The plaintiffs sought an injunction to prevent breach of the second agreement. The defendants alleged that the directors had not disclosed their interest in the agreement. Harman J held that the agreement was void at the instance of the defendants and that the agreement had not been entered into in the interests of the defendants. This was upheld by the Court of Appeal. Harman J had also held that it was voidable on the basis of the failure of the directors to declare their interests to a board meeting. The Court of Appeal took the view that there was no breach of s 317 since the interest of the directors was known to all members of the board.

The powers of directors that are subject to directors' fiduciary duties also extend to other areas:

11.7.3   Other powers

- the power to borrow money and grant securities, see *Rolled Steel Products (Holdings) Ltd v British Steel Corporation* (1986);

- the power to call general meetings;

- the power to provide information to shareholders; and

- the power to make calls on partly paid shares.

Even where there is no breach of duty in relation to the exercise of powers by directors there is the possibility of a petition alleging unfair prejudice under ss 459–61 of the Companies Act 1985.

In addition to liability to the company, directors may be directly liable to outsiders.

11.8   Personal liability of directors

Directors may be contractually liable as follows:

11.8.1   Contractual liability

- **Breach of warranty of authority**

  If directors indicate to outsiders that they have authority to conclude a particular transaction on behalf of the company and no such authority exists, then the director (or indeed other person) is liable for breach of the warranty of authority.

- **Collateral guarantee**

  Often when directors conclude a contract on behalf of their company, they will also give a collateral guarantee. This is particularly the case where a company borrows money from its bank and the bank requires security from the company's officers. In such a situation, if the primary liability fails, the outsider may sue the guarantor on the collateral guarantee.

- **Pre-incorporation contracts**

  As has already been examined (see para 3.5), where a person (perhaps a future director) concludes an agreement on behalf of an as yet unformed company that person will be liable on the agreement unless there is an express contrary intention (s 36C(1) of the Companies Act 1985).

11.8.2   Delictual liability

Directors may be delictually liable as follows:

- **Fraud**

  A director may be liable in fraud to subscribers and even purchasers on the open market in relation to statements made in a company prospectus or listing particulars under the principle in *Derry v Peek* (see para 4.2.8).

- **Negligent misstatement**

  In a similar way a director may be liable in delict for negligent misrepresentations made to subscribers and purchasers under the principle in *Hedley Byrne v Heller* for misstatements in a prospectus or listing particulars (see para 4.2.9).

- **Personal skill and care of directors**

  In rare circumstances where a director has warranted his own personal skill and care, he may be liable to the outsider notwithstanding that the contract has been concluded with the company rather than with the director. Thus, in *Fairline Shipping Corporation v Adamson* (1975), where Mr Adamson owned a refrigerated store used by a company of which he was managing director, he warranted to Fairline Shipping Corporation that the perishable goods stored in the company's refrigeration would be safe. In fact the goods were ruined. It was held that he was personally liable. The company itself could not pay damages as it had gone into liquidation.

11.8.3   Statutory liability

Personal liability to outsiders may also arise under statute:

- **Misstatements or omissions in listing particulars or prospectus**

  Under the Financial Services Act 1986, s 150 provides that compensation may be ordered to be paid by directors in relation to misstatements or omissions in listing particulars.

  Directors may be personally liable to pay compensation in relation to prospectuses under Regulation 14 of the Public Offers of Securities Regulations 1995.

- **Failure to repay subscription monies**

  Directors may be personally liable for failure to repay subscription monies for shares under s 83(5) of the Companies Act 1985 where a minimum subscription has not been received in response to a prospectus (see also s 84(3) of the Companies Act 1985). The sections provide for liability to repay with interest after 48 days from the issue of the prospectus.

- **Irregular allotment of shares**

  Directors may be personally liable for irregular allotment of shares under s 85(2) of the Companies Act 1985 following the allotment of shares where there has not been a minimum subscription or a full subscription if that is required consequent upon a prospectus issue.

- **Improper use of the company name**

  Directors may be liable for improper use of the company name. Under s 349(4) of the Companies Act 1985, any misdescription of a company name by an officer and this includes any abbreviation of the company name other than *de minimis* exceptions (see para 2.2.1) will be liable for the transaction or other arrangement involving the misdescription. Thus, there was liability in *British Airways Board v Parish* (1979) where the word 'limited' was omitted from the company name by a company officer.

There are of course other areas where there may be personal liability of directors in relation to company debts (for example, under s 26 of the Bills of Exchange Act 1882 – compare *Brebner v Henderson* (1925) with *McLean v Stuart & Others* (1970)) but these areas generally involve a contribution to the company's assets in liquidation rather than a direct payment to the outsider. Thus, directors may be liable for fraudulent trading under s 213 of the Insolvency Act 1986, for wrongful trading under s 214 of the Insolvency Act 1986 and for acting in contravention of a disqualification order under s 15 of the Company Directors Disqualification Act 1986.

11.8.4   Other liability

It has been noted above that a company's articles and any contract with the director may not limit a director's liability for negligence, see s 310 of the Companies Act 1985 (see para 6.1). Companies may, however, provide insurance for directors in such situations, see s 310(3) of the Companies Act 1985 inserted by the Companies Act 1989. This provides that a company may indemnify an officer or auditor against liability incurred by him in defending any proceedings (whether civil or criminal)

11.9   Limiting the liability of directors

in which judgment is given in his favour or he is acquitted or in proceedings under s 144(3) where the court grants relief to a director who has acquired shares as a nominee of the company and is liable to pay on those shares but has acted honestly and reasonably and is relieved in whole or in part or under s 727 (discussed below) where an officer, auditor or employee of the company is relieved in whole or in part.

Notwithstanding this, it is open to the court to grant relief to an officer if it is proved that the officer acted honestly and reasonably and ought in all the circumstances to be excused in the whole or in part, s 727 of the Companies Act 1985. This matter was discussed in *Re Duomatic Ltd* (1969). The company in this case had three directors. The articles of the company required directors' remuneration to be determined by the general meeting. One director Elvins drew salary without the approval of the company in general meeting, assuming that it would be agreed at the subsequent annual general meeting. In fact, the company went into liquidation before the annual general meeting could be held. He also made a gratuitous payment to Hanley, another director, without complying with s 312 of the Companies Act 1985 which requires disclosure of golden handshakes to the company in general meeting and approval of the payment by the company in general meeting, and in addition he drew in excess of the agreed limit on his drawings from the company.

It was held that Elvins would be relieved from liability for drawing the unauthorised salary as it was reasonable for him to follow the established practice. He was not relieved from liability in relation to the payment of the compensation payment as he should have sought legal advice in relation to this matter and he was also liable for the excessive drawings from the company. In relation to this last matter, he had neither been honest nor reasonable.

An alternative course of action for the company where a director has acted in breach of duties (provided the breach of duty is not fraudulent) is to ratify what the director has done. This has the effect of negating any breach of duty. This is what occurred in *Hogg v Cramphorn* and *Bamford v Bamford* (see para 11.7.1). In relation to matters that are *ultra vires* the company, the possibility of ratification is now open to the company. The act itself must first be ratified by special resolution and then the unauthorised act of the director must also be ratified by special resolution (see para 5.10).

Directors' Duties

Traditionally, directors are said to owe duties to the providers of capital (the shareholders). However, s 309 of the Companies Act 1985 provides that the directors must take account of the interests of employees. Some cases suggest that directors should take account of the interests of creditors.

Introduction

The law in this area resounds with Victorian echoes. Little has been expected of directors in terms of care and skill, in the past – see *Re City Equitable Fire & Insurance Co Ltd*. More recently, there have been suggestions that an objective standard of care is expected of directors – see s 214 of the Insolvency Act 1986 and *Norman v Theodore Goddard*.

Duty of care and skill

The standard expected of directors in relation to honesty, integrity and good faith is in stark contrast to the standard expected in relation to care and skill.

Fiduciary duties

Some of the rules are statutory. Directors are required to disclose to the board any interest they have in a contract to be concluded with their company (s 317). Certain substantial property transactions involving directors require prior approval (s 320).

Directors must not allow their own personal interest to conflict with their duty to the company. This rule is applied strictly.

In theory, a director should not be able to compete with his company but the cases are inconsistent.

Directors' powers should be exercised in a fiduciary way, for example the power to issue shares.

Directors may on occasion be liable to outsiders in contract, in delict or by statute.

Personal liability of directors to outsiders

It is not possible for a company by its articles or by contract to exempt directors from liability for negligence.

Limiting directors' liability

Negligence may be ratified by ordinary resolution.

Furthermore, s 727 permits the court to grant relief to directors where they have acted honestly and reasonably and where in all the circumstances the action ought to be excused in whole or in part.

Chapter 12

Powers of Directors

Generally, companies will delegate considerable powers of management to the directors of the company. Table A, Article 70 provides:

> Subject to the provisions of the Act, the memorandum and the articles and to any directions given by special resolution, the business of the company shall be managed by the directors who may exercise all the powers of the company. No alteration of the memorandum or articles and no such direction shall invalidate any prior act of the directors which would have been valid if that alteration had not been made or that direction had not been given.

The company will obviously delegate only such powers as it itself has. Thus the directors are not competent to engage in *ultra vires* transactions. As has been seen, however, *ultra vires* transactions may be ratified and the breach of directors' duties may be ratified by a separate special resolution. Furthermore, the directors can only validly act in the interests of the company and for the purposes for which the powers are conferred upon them as has been noted, see *Hogg v Cramphorn Ltd* (1967), *Bamford v Bamford* (1970) (at para 11.7).

The powers delegated to the directors are delegated to them collectively. It is open to the directors, of course, to sub-delegate powers to individual directors or, indeed, to others.

In general, the directors are vested with management by the members. Their removal from office is by an ordinary resolution passed in general meeting following special notice, see s 303 of the Companies Act 1985. Directors may exercise their powers of management while they are in office, see *Salmon v Quin & Axtens* (1909). Where companies have articles like Article 70 of Table A, however, this permits directions to be given by special resolution to the directors.

In other circumstances, it is sometimes the case that the members have to fill a void. The members in general meeting may have power to initiate legal proceedings where the company for some reason failed to do so. In *Marshalls Valve Gear v Manning Wardle & Co* (1909), the directors failed to initiate legal proceedings against one of their number. The members were permitted to override this failure and to bring the proceedings on behalf of the company. By contrast, in *John*

12.1 Introduction

12.2 Control of the directors

Shaw & Sons (Salford) Ltd v Shaw (1935), the Court of Appeal refused to allow the members to override the decision of the directors to commence legal proceedings.

The House of Lords in *Alexander Ward & Co v Samyang Navigation Co* (1975) allowed two members to raise proceedings to protect the interests of the company when the company had no directors. In *Re Argentum Reductions (UK) Ltd* (1975), Megarry J declined to decide whether the members had reserve powers where the directors were unable to act stating at p 189 'there are deep waters here'.

The cases are far from consistent. On occasion the courts have permitted the members to act where there is deadlock on the board of directors. Thus, in *Baron v Potter* (1914), the company had two directors who were not on speaking terms. It was impossible to hold constructive board meetings. Canon Baron refused to attend board meetings with Potter. Potter tried to call a general meeting. Baron intended to boycott this meeting but his train was met by Potter at Paddington who proceeded to try to hold a meeting on the platform. He proposed Charles Herbert, William George Walter Barnard and John Tolhurst Musgrave as additional directors. Baron objected and Potter purported to use his casting vote as chairman. The court held that this was an ineffective meeting. In the circumstances, it was held that in view of the deadlock on the board of directors, the powers were exercisable by the members in general meeting. In a similar way in *Foster v Foster* (1916), there was a dispute over which of two directors should be appointed as managing director of the company. There were three directors in all. The articles gave the power to appoint a managing director to the board of directors. However, directors could not vote on a matter in which they had a personal interest. It was accordingly not possible to pass the resolution. The general meeting accordingly could fill the vacuum.

It is open to the members of the company in general meeting to ratify matters that have been performed by the directors. It is possible to use this power of ratification in relation to *ultra vires* acts by special resolution. It is possible to use the power of ratification in relation to acts that are beyond the directors' authority by ordinary resolution provided that the directors are not acting fraudulently, see *Hogg v Cramphorn Ltd, Bamford v Bamford* and *Grant v United Kingdom Switchback Railways Co* (1888).

12.3   Managing director

The articles such as Table A, Article 72 permit the appointment of a managing director. The appointment of a managing director, however, is not a legal requirement.

The appointment of a managing director will cease if he ceases to be a director. If he has a separate service agreement and is removed as a director, he may of course sue upon this contract, see s 303(5) of the Companies Act 1985. A managing director will be presumed to be an employee of the company unless the opposite is proved – see *Anderson v James Sutherland (Peterhead) Ltd* (1941).

If matters are delegated to the board of directors, this of course means directors who are properly appointed. On occasion, directors may be invalidly appointed and questions arise as to whether those dealing with them may hold the company bound. There are certain rules of law which tend to validate the acts of a director in spite of any irregularities in his appointment in such circumstances.

12.4   Validity of the acts of directors

There is a statutory principle contained in s 285 of the Companies Act 1985 that provides that 'the acts of a director or manager are valid notwithstanding any defect that may afterwards be discovered in his appointment or qualification ...'. It should be noted that s 285 is expressly limited to *initial* defects of appointment or qualification, as is made clear by *Morris v Kanssen* (1946). The principle cannot apply where there has been a fraudulent attempt to appoint a director. It can only apply where there is a *bona fide* attempt to appoint a director which has been unsuccessful.

A quite separate principle is an application of the rule in *Turquand's Case* (1856) which is considered more fully below (at para 12.5). If a person deals with a company through persons who are purporting to act as directors even though they have not been properly appointed, he may be entitled to assume that they are in fact directors and to hold the company bound by their acts, see *Mahony v East Holyford Mining Co* (1875) where the directors who had concluded the transaction had not in fact been appointed.

Furthermore, the outsider may be able to hold the company bound on the basis of holding out or agency by personal bar (estoppel in England). Thus if the company makes it appear that an individual director or person has authority to conclude a particular transaction, an outsider can hold the company bound. A director simply by virtue of holding the office of director has no implied authority as agent of the company to conclude contracts. Yet if the company allows the director to act as if he had such authority, then the company may be personally barred from denying that he has the authority. It is no longer the case that the mere fact that the company's constitution makes it clear that there is no such authority is sufficient to render the authority non-existent. The Companies

Act 1989 amending the Companies Act 1985 abolishes
constructive notice and therefore outsiders have no deemed
knowledge of what is contained in the memorandum and
articles. The question of agency by holding out was discussed
in *Freeman & Lockyer v Buckhurst Park Properties (Mangal)* (1964).
Diplock LJ said that there must have been a representation that
a person had authority and that representation must have been
made by those who had authority within the company. The
other party must have relied on the representation in entering
into the contract. He went on to say that there must be nothing
in the memorandum and articles to countermand that
authority. This last point of Diplock LJ is, of course, no longer
applicable. In *Freeman & Lockyer* itself, the board of directors
had permitted one director to act as if he had been appointed
managing director. In fact he had not been appointed as
managing director but the articles of association made
provision for such an appointment. Accordingly the company
was held liable.

A similar situation arose in Scotland in *Allison v Scotia
Motor and Engineering Co Ltd* (1906) where an individual acted
as managing director before he was formally appointed as
such. It was held that contracts he entered during this period
were, likewise, valid and binding upon the company.

12.5   The rule in
         Turquand's Case

In *Turquand's Case (Royal British Bank v Turquand* (1856)), the
company's articles authorised the directors to borrow money if
this had been sanctioned by ordinary resolution. A resolution
was passed but it did not specify the amount which the
directors could borrow. The directors borrowed money and
the company became insolvent. Turquand was sued as the
liquidator. It was held that the plaintiff's bank was deemed to
be aware that the directors could only borrow up to the
amount of the resolution as the articles were available at
Companies House and therefore there was constructive notice
of the contents of the articles of association. Yet an outsider
had no means of knowing whether an ordinary resolution had
been passed. Ordinary resolutions were not registerable. In the
circumstances the bank was entitled to assume the fact of a
resolution being passed and was not required (indeed not
entitled) to investigate the internal workings of the company.
The rule is sometimes called 'the indoor management rule'.
The rule was applied in Scotland in similar circumstances by
the Inner House in *Gillies v Craigton* (1935).

The rule does not apply in all circumstances. Thus, if the
outsider actually knew or had strong grounds for suspecting
that the act was not authorised, the rule cannot be relied upon,

see *Underwood v Bank of Liverpool & Martins* (1924). Furthermore, if the person dealing with the company is himself one of its directors, then it is reasonable to assume that he will know of the internal operations of the company and may therefore not be able to rely upon the principle, see *Hely-Hutchinson v Brayhead* (1968).

Furthermore, it seems that the principle in *Royal British Bank v Turquand* cannot be relied upon if the document that is presented is a forgery, see *Ruben v Great Fingall Consolidated* (1906).

The principle of indoor management is therefore useful to bind the company to acts of directors (or apparent directors) who are acting beyond their capacity. Those dealing with the company no longer have constructive notice of the articles or memorandum if they should contain restrictions on the capacity of persons to act.

The rule is seemingly restricted to situations where the board as a whole is presumed to have authority rather than individual directors.

The area of agents' authority clearly overlaps with the area of corporate capacity and powers. Section 35A of the Companies Act 1985 will generally afford more protection to an outsider as even knowledge of the act being beyond the authority of the board will not amount to bad faith (s 35A(2)(b)). On the other hand, *Turquand* probably applies where there is not a properly constituted board and so the principle in *Turquand's* case remains of importance.

Powers of Directors

Table A, Article 70 provides for the management of the company's business by the directors and most companies follow this format.

Introduction

It is not generally open to the shareholders in general meeting to take on the functions of the directors. There are certain exceptions to this general rule, however. If the directors are unable to act for some reason such as deadlock or if there are no directors, then the shareholders may act.

If a person acts as director but there is some defect in his initial appointment, nevertheless his acts are to be treated as valid.

Validation of directors' acts

Furthermore, where a person is held out as a director or as having authority to the outside world and this is relied upon where there is nothing to indicate the lack of actual authority, the outsider will be able to hold the company responsible on agency principles.

A further rule, called the indoor management rule or the rule in *Turquand's Case,* provides that if to an outsider the correct procedures appear to have been adhered to, then the outsider can hold the company responsible notwithstanding that there is some *internal* irregularity. An outsider is not bound, indeed not entitled, to enquire into the internal workings of the company.

Chapter 13

Insider Dealing

It was only with the Companies Act 1980 that there was the first legislative intervention in the United Kingdom to combat insider dealing. Other jurisdictions came to this problem much earlier on, for example, the USA in the Securities Exchange Act 1934. Until recently, the relevant UK legislation was contained in the Companies Securities (Insider Dealing) Act 1985 and the Financial Services Act 1986.

New legislation has altered the law on insider dealing to take account of the EC Directive on Insider Dealing (89/592). The new law is contained in Part V of the Criminal Justice Act 1993 and Sched 1 of that Act.

The securities covered by the legislation are set out in Schedule 2. They include shares and gilts. The law for the most part only covers dealings on a regulated market so that the law does not generally extend to unlisted companies. Certain off market deals are caught.

There are two categories of insiders caught by the legislation – primary insiders and secondary insiders or tipees.

Primary insiders are persons who have information as an insider obtained through:

- being a director, employee or shareholder of an issuer of securities; or

- having access to the information by virtue of employment, profession or office.

Secondary insiders are those who have received or obtained information from a person who is an insider either directly or indirectly.

A person is not a secondary insider or tipee merely by virtue of being procured to deal in securities. He must have inside information and must know that it is inside information and he must know that it is from an inside source (s 57).

The legislation prohibits dealing in securities by a person whether by himself or as agent for another person. There is also a prohibition on encouraging or procuring another person to deal and also of disclosing information except in the performance of one's duties or on showing one did not expect the person to act upon the disclosure. Inside information is defined as specific information which is not in the public domain and which is unpublished. It must be information which, if published, would have an effect on the price of the securities (s 56).

The legislation requires that there should be an intention to make a profit or to avoid a loss. The new law, however, tilts the balance towards the prosecution in that it is presumed that persons who deal in securities with the relevant knowledge have the intention to make a profit or avoid a loss. Thus the legislation places the burden on the accused of disproving the intention. There are certain limited defences (s 53 and Sched 1).

There is no civil remedy for insider dealing. The contract itself remains intact. The maximum criminal sanction that applies on indictment is seven years' imprisonment and/or an unlimited fine. On summary conviction the maximum penalty is a fine and/or six months' imprisonment (s 61).

Investigations may be set up under the Financial Services Act 1986 to investigate possible insider dealing (see para 21.5).

13.2   Criticisms

Various criticisms have been made of the UK law on insider dealing.

13.2.1   No civil remedy

The fact that there is no civil remedy is often the subject of criticism. By contrast in the USA, there has been a civil remedy ever since the Securities and Exchange Act whereby the person who has sold shares to an insider (or possibly bought from an insider) is able to sue for the profit made by the other or the loss avoided by the other. There is no civil remedy in the United Kingdom. It is possible that there may be an indirect remedy. Under the Criminal Justice (Scotland) Act 1980 and in England the Powers of the Criminal Courts Act 1973, any victim of a criminal offence may be awarded compensation under the Act. This occurred, for example, in Scotland in *Procurator Fiscal v Bryce* in 1981.

In so far as directors profit from their use of inside information, there may be a remedy available to the company against the directors for breach of duty. It must be borne in mind, however, that insiders are wider than directors and also there may be difficulties with the company suing directors where the directors are in control of the company. In any event as Suter notes (p 122) in *The Regulation of Insider Dealing in Britain* (Butterworths, 1989):

There is no reported decision in Britain on a claim by a company to recover insider dealing profits from an insider. Hence the issue of whether insiders are accountable to their companies for such profits is unresolved.

A second major criticism made of the legislation in the United Kingdom is that there is no institution that has been set up specifically to deal with the matter of insider dealing. There is such an institution in the USA, namely the Securities and Exchange Commission. There have been calls from the Stock Exchange for an insider trading agency. At present most prosecutions are carried out by the Department of Trade on the basis of evidence gathered by the Stock Exchange.

13.2.2   No insider trading agency

A third criticism that is made is that the legislation only applies to quoted companies with one or two minor exceptions. There seems no real reason why the legislation should not apply to non-quoted companies as well. Clearly, the problem is more severe in relation to quoted companies, as in other cases, a person would generally know that he is selling to or buying from an insider. However, it does seem that in circumstances where it can be shown that an insider has acted in contravention of the basic principle that influences the legislation even in a non-quoted company, that person should be subject to some sanctions.

13.2.3   Legislation only applies to quoted companies

A fourth criticism made of the Act is that enforcement is haphazard. There have been few prosecutions and very few convictions. Yet there is still evidence of widespread insider dealing. This is of some significance when it is the case that there is international competition between different stock exchanges and there are few sentences of imprisonment in relation to insider dealing in the United Kingdom. Although the maximum penalty was increased in 1988 from two years' imprisonment to seven years' imprisonment, at that stage there had been very few convictions and there have been very few sentences of imprisonment imposed. This may be contrasted with the United States enforcement where early on Richard Whitney, the Head of the New York Stock Exchange, was despatched for a stay in Sing Sing in 1934.

13.2.4   Enforcement is haphazard

Although the new regime under the 1993 Act goes some way towards making it easier to obtain a conviction for insider dealing (in that it has shifted the burden of proof regarding intention in favour of the prosecution), Scots law still requires corroboration (complimentary evidence from more than one source) to sustain a conviction. Although tried under the 1985 Act, it was this lack of corroboration which allowed the appellant to escape conviction in *MacKie v HMA* (1994).

13.2.5   Problems with proof

Insider Dealing

Legislation on insider dealing was not introduced in the United Kingdom until 1980. The law is now set out in the Criminal Justice Act 1993 which implements the EC Directive on Insider Dealing (89/592).

Criminal sanctions may be applied where an insider deals in securities of a quoted company on the basis of inside information. The law also prohibits secondary insiders (tipees) with insider information from dealing in the securities of quoted companies.

Various criticisms are levelled at the legislation:

- no civil remedy is provided;

- there is no institution specifically charged with investigating insider dealing;

- the legislation does not generally extend to unquoted companies;

- the enforcement of the law on insider dealing is haphazard;

- corroboration may be difficult to obtain.

Chapter 14

Minority Protection

Historically, the rule in *Foss v Harbottle* (1843) has been of the utmost significance in governing when shareholders can take action on behalf of the company in which they hold shares. The facts of the case were as follows:

Certain burghers in Manchester had got together to purchase park land to dedicate to the then heiress to the throne, Princess Victoria. The park opened to great acclamation but difficulties soon followed. It was alleged by some of the company's members that some directors had misapplied company property. The case was heard by Wigwram VC. He held that the action could not proceed as the individual shareholders were not the proper plaintiffs. If a wrong had been committed, the wrong had been committed against the company and the company was therefore the proper plaintiff. The rule in *Foss v Harbottle* has acted like a deadhand on minority protection in British company law. The rule is to some extent justifiable. It has sometimes been justified as preventing a multiplicity of actions and sometimes by the argument that the company can ratify what directors have done and that therefore litigation might well be pointless.

For a Scottish equivalent, see *Orr v Glasgow, Airdrie & Monklands Junction Railway Co* (1860) where it was alleged that the directors had acted in pursuance of competing interests. It was held that the company, rather than independent shareholders, had exclusive title to sue. This decision was followed in *Lee v Crawford* (1890) where a shareholder sought to make a director accountable to the company for company funds allegedly loaned illegally to officials of the company.

The rule, however, does give way to certain exceptions where a minority action may be brought by a member arguing that a wrong has been done to the company.

The principle that the company can ratify what had been done converting an initial wrong into action that was legitimate could not formerly apply to *ultra vires* activities. *Ultra vires* acts could not be ratified, see *Parke v The Daily News* (1962), *Simpson v Westminster Palace Hotel* (1868). This ceased to be the case with the Companies Act 1989. It is now possible for companies to ratify *ultra vires* acts. The Act does, however,

14.1   The rule in
         Foss v Harbottle

14.2   Exceptions to
         the rule

14.2.1   *Ultra vires* acts

provide that shareholders may still restrain companies from acting in an *ultra vires* way before a transaction has been concluded. The exception, therefore, to this extent remains (s 35(2)) – see, also, *Dunn v Banknock Coal Co Ltd* (1901).

14.2.2   Where a special majority is needed

If the company's constitution stipulates that a special majority is needed before a particular course of conduct can be accomplished, then if the company seeks to fly in the face of this provision and not obtain the particular majority, a single shareholder may maintain an action as an exception to *Foss v Harbottle*. This is the basis of the decision in *Edwards v Halliwell* (1950). In fact, that action is a trade union case rather than a company case. The law in this particular is the same in both categories of law. The union was seeking to increase its subscriptions in contravention of the union rule book without obtaining the consent of the union members to the increase. Members of a branch of the union complained of this and were successful. The same principle would operate in company law. The case is an interesting one and the judgment of Jenkins LJ is particularly helpful in setting out lucidly the law in this area.

14.2.3   The personal rights exception

If the company denies a shareholder rights that are set out in the company's constitution, the shareholder can bring an action to enforce the rights that have been negated. Thus, in *Pender v Lushington* (1877), a shareholder was able to enforce his right and that of other shareholders that they should be able to cast their votes and in *Wood v Odessa Waterworks* (1889), a shareholder was able to enforce his right to a dividend in cash rather than a dividend in specie (in the form of property) as provided for under the company's articles.

English law distinguishes between personal and representative actions. A personal action is where the plaintiff seeks a remedy for himself and others in his position. Scots law makes no such distinction – all actions must be brought as personal actions.

14.2.4   Fraud by those in control

This is perhaps the most important of the exceptions. It enables a shareholder to bring an action against the company and the alleged wrongdoer for a fraud perpetrated by somebody in control.

There was some doubt concerning the competency of such an action in Scotland, since Scots law does not distinguish between personal, representative and derivative actions (see below), but an action of this type was allowed to proceed in *Rixon v Edinburgh Northern Tramways Co* (1889) (although the case reached the Lords it ultimately failed on its facts (1893)) and in *Hannay v Muir* (1898).

For a discussion of procedural problems in Scotland, see Allan L MacKenzie, 'The Problem of Enforcement of Directors' Duties in Scotland', 1981 SLT (News) 257 and AA Paterson, 'The Derivative Action in Scotland', 1982 SLT (News) 205.

Fraud can never be ratified so the ratification objection does not arise although a pursuer will have to demonstrate that he has first tried to persuade the company to bring the action (usually by attempting to secure a resolution to this effect in general meeting). In *Brown v Stewart* (1898), a member sought a personal remedy for alleged negligence on the part of the directors. The Inner House held that the pursuer was not entitled to seek a remedy for a wrong done to the company since the directors' actions could be ratified by the company and the pursuer had not shown that he had attempted to raise the matter in general meeting and had been overruled.

In *Cook v Deeks* (1916), a Privy Council case on appeal from Ontario, a shareholder was able to bring an action under this head complaining that directors had diverted corporate opportunities to themselves. The exception does not extend to cases of negligence. In *Oliver's Trustees & Another v WG Walker & Sons (Edinburgh) Ltd* (1948) Lord MacKintosh quoted with approval Lord Davey in the Privy Council decision in *Burland v Earle* (1902) where he said, 'The cases in which the minority can maintain such an action are therefore confined to those in which the acts complained of are of a fraudulent character or beyond the powers of the company'. See also *Pavlides v Jensen* (1956) where the complaint was that the directors had been negligent in selling an asbestos mine in Cyprus at an undervaluation. The exception did not extend either to negligence tantamount to expropriation which was the way that the cause of action was pleaded in *Heyting v Dupont* (1964). A particularly difficult case arose in *Daniels v Daniels* (1978). In this case, a director had purchased property from a company at £4,250 and then re-sold it shortly afterwards for £120,000. The allegation was pleaded as one of negligence. The judge, Templeman J, allowed the action to proceed. This has sometimes been misinterpreted. The case is not authority for the proposition that where there has been gross negligence an action is possible as an exception to *Foss v Harbottle*. The judge specifically stated that:

> To put up with foolish directors is one thing; to put up with directors who are so foolish they make a profit of £115,000 odd at the expense of the company is something entirely different.

Clearly, the decision is exceptional. Templeman J is indicating that there is more to the case than meets the eye.

It has been held to be competent for a minority member to challenge a resolution passed on the basis of insufficient (in terms of content) notice – see *Baillie v Oriental Telephone Co* (1915). It may also be possible to bring an action where the majority's decision is 'irreconcilable with their having proceeded upon any reasonable view of the company's interest' – *per* Lord Kyllachy in *Cameron v Glenmorangie Distillery Co Ltd* (1896).

Another important decision in the area of fraud is that of *Prudential Assurance Co Ltd v Newman Industries Ltd* (1980). The case dealt, *inter alia*, with the question of control. As has already been stated, to succeed in an action based upon this exception to the *Foss v Harbottle* rule, the fraudsters must be in control of the company. The Court of Appeal held that 'control' was more complex an issue than merely an arithmetical assessment of shareholdings of individual members, since often members would vote in accordance with other members out of personal sympathy or apathy. Thus it would require a preliminary hearing in such a case to establish whether the alleged wrongdoers actually were in control, and only once this was established could the issue of fraud be addressed.

English law calls this type of action a *derivative* action. The plaintiff is pursuing the wrongdoer, not for his own direct benefit, but principally for the benefit of the company. The company is brought into the action as a nominal defendant so as to allow the court to award a remedy in its favour. Because the plaintiff seeks a remedy for the company, the court may require the company to pay the plaintiff's legal expenses (known as a *Wallersteiner order* after *Wallersteiner v Moir (No 2)* (1975) where such a costs order was first made). There is no such thing as a derivative action in Scots law, although in Scotland a member may bring an action against the wrongdoer for the benefit of the company. Such an action would proceed as a personal action and again the company must be joined as a co-defender. Scots law does not recognise Wallersteiner costs orders.

In *Barrett v Duckett & Others* (1995), a shareholder (B) sought to bring a derivative action. She was a 50% shareholder in Nightingale Travel Ltd and alleged, *inter alia*, that the other shareholder and sole director (D) was diverting business to another company whose shares were owned by D and his wife. The Court of Appeal, reversing the decision of the court of first instance, held that there was an opportunity to put the company into liquidation which provided an alternative remedy to the derivative action. Furthermore, the Court of Appeal considered that B was not pursuing the *bona fide* interests of the company.

In many ways, minority protection is now the most active area of company law. Until the Companies Act 1980 and s 75 of that Act, now consolidated into the 1985 Act as ss 459–61, minority protection was arguably the most stagnant area.

14.3   The statutory remedy

Section 210 of the Companies Act 1948 which provided relief where a minority had been oppressed was introduced in response to the recommendations of the Cohen Committee in 1945. The section was used very rarely in its 32 years of operation between 1948 and 1980.

It was used successfully in *Scottish CWS v Meyer* (1959) where a shareholder complained that the company's business was diverted away to another company in which the petitioning shareholder had no interest. The petition was successful. In another case, *Re HR Harmer Ltd* (1958), the founding father of a stamp dealing company was ordered not to interfere in the affairs of the company. The petition was presented by his sons. The father, aged 88 at the time of the action, was running the business as if it was his own personal business. He was tyrannical and dictatorial. He defied board resolutions and appointed a private detective to spy on some of his staff whom he wrongly suspected of stealing company assets. The petition was successful.

The old minority remedy section had various drawbacks. These were highlighted by the Jenkins Committee in 1962. The drawbacks were as follows:

14.3.1   Drawbacks of the Companies Act, s 210

- an order could only be made if the facts could be the basis for a winding up order on the just and equitable ground. This meant that the section was very closely allied to the rules relating to winding up;

- a single act was insufficient to justify a petition under s 210. A course of conduct had to be shown to found a petition;

- the petitioner had to show that the conduct was oppressive. This meant 'burdensome, harsh and wrongful' (*Scottish CWS v Meyer* (1959) *per* Viscount Simonds);

- a petition could not be based on omissions or on future conduct;

- it was generally thought that the old minority section could not encompass personal representatives, however, Plowman J in *Re Jermyn Street Turkish Baths Ltd* (1970) took the view that personal representatives could petition.

| 14.3.2 | The new remedy | These shortcomings were all remedied by s 75 of the Companies Act 1980. The link with winding up was swept away. A single act or omission or threatened future conduct can be the basis for a petition. Personal representatives can now sue (see s 459(2) of the Companies Act 1985). Most importantly the new remedy applies in cases of unfair prejudice. This is obviously far easier to demonstrate than oppression which requires a course of deliberate conduct. The section now provides as follows: |

> A member of a company may apply to the court by petition for an order under this part on the ground that the company's affairs are being or have been conducted in a manner which is unfairly prejudicial to the interests of its members generally or of some part of its members (including at least himself) or that any actual or proposed act or omission of the company (including an act or omission on its behalf) is or would be so prejudicial.

| 14.3.3 | Exclusion from management | The most common example of the minority seeking relief is where an undertaking to a member that he would have a say in the management of a company has been breached, usually by his removal from the board of directors. Under the old law, it was essential that the oppression was suffered *qua* member in the narrow sense. This requirement was strictly applied, so that a member complaining of exclusion from management would not have succeeded. For example, in *Elder & Others v Elder & Watson Ltd* (1952), two members brought a petition seeking purchase of their shares by the company since they had been removed from their offices as factory manager and company secretary. Lord President Cooper in the Inner House said, 'the "oppression" required by the section (is) oppression of members in their character as such'. The court accordingly dismissed the petition. The requirement of petitioning *qua* member has now, at least, been more broadly construed so that, for example, a founder member could well argue that a right to participate in the management of the company was a membership right. |

Early on, it seemed that the old rule still applied even under s 459. In *Re a Company (No 004475 of 1982)* (1983), Lord Grantchester QC held that prejudice had to be suffered *qua* member in the narrow sense. However, in an earlier unreported decision, *Re Bovey Hotel Ventures Ltd* (1981, unreported), there had been a successful petition on the basis of exclusion from management. A husband and wife had operated a hotel company. They split up. The erstwhile husband excluded the former wife from participating in the management of the company. She successfully petitioned under s 459 and indeed was able to purchase the husband's shareholding as her remedy.

Another case involving exclusion from management is *Re RA Noble & Sons (Clothing) Ltd* (1983). Here the court accepted that exclusion from management could be the basis of a petition. However, it found that on the facts of the case the petitioner had brought the exclusion on himself by his disinterest. *Re London School of Electronics* (1985) provides a further example of exclusion from management. This case concerned a North London tutorial college where the petitioner complained of his *de facto* dismissal as a director. The other directors argued that the petitioning director, Lytton, had brought the exclusion upon himself by his own conduct. Nourse J held that the petitioner's conduct did not prevent him from bringing the petition. The alleged conduct, if proved, would be a factor in determining what relief should be available to the petitioning shareholder. It might also serve to demonstrate that the prejudice was not unfair.

In *Re a Company (No 002567 of 1982)* (1983), Vinelott J took the view that s 459 would apply in an *Ebrahimi* type situation where a shareholder was wrongly excluded from management in a company. In *Re Bird Precision Bellows Ltd* (1984), the petitioners who were minority shareholders in Bird Precision Bellows Ltd had been removed from the board of directors by the respondents. It was ordered by consent, without any admission of liability on the part of the respondents that they had been responsible for unfairly prejudicial conduct, that the respondents should purchase the petitioners' shares at a price to be determined. Nourse J subsequently held that the exclusion was wrongful.

The pattern is not absolutely uniform. Clearly not every exclusion from management in a small private company is wrongful. In *Teague Petitioner* (1985), the Outer House held that the removal of a director who was also a minority shareholder and the subsequent closure of the business were insufficient grounds to order either a remedy for unfair prejudice or a just and equitable winding up (see para 14.6) petition where there was evidence of neither a close relationship between members as would be found in a quasi partnership company nor of an agreement which entitled the petitioner to participate in the management. In *Coulson, Sanderson & Ward Ltd v Ward* (1986), Slade LJ considered that exclusion from management would not necessarily found a petition under s 459. Furthermore, in *Re XYZ Ltd* (also under the name *Re a Company (No 004377 of 1986)* (1986), it was similarly held that not every exclusion from management in a quasi partnership company would ground a petition. It did not necessarily follow that there was always a legitimate expectation of management in such companies. Whilst it is extremely unlikely that a petition can be presented under s 459 for a public company, still less a quoted company, the door does not seem absolutely closed on this possibility. In *Re Blue Arrow plc* (1987), the court held that although there was generally no room for implying a legitimate expectation of continued employment in a public company, special situations could arise where exclusion from management could be the basis for a petition in respect of a public company.

In *Re Tottenham Hotspur plc* (1994) provides the type of situation where a director may be able to argue successfully that there has been an understanding that there should be a role for him in the management, although Terry Venables the chief executive failed to establish that in this case. He went on to become manager of the England team.

There must, however, be some membership nexus. Thus in *Re JE Cade & Son Ltd* (1992) the petitioning member was seeking to protect his interests as a landowner and failed as protecting such interests was held to be outside of the scope of the remedy.

14.3.4   Other grounds on which petitions have been based

There are various other grounds on which petitions have been based. These might include the following:

- The company failing to purchase the shares of a minority – *Re a Company (No 004475 of 1982)* (1983), before Lord Grantchester QC. This petition was unsuccessful.

- The company changing its business. This was another ground for complaint in *Re a Company (No 004475 of 1982)*, before Lord Grantchester QC. This argument was also unsuccessful. The company had set up as an advertising agency and later diversified to become a wine bar and restaurant.

- A shareholder voting his shares in breach of an undertaking to the government – *Re Carrington Viyella plc* (1983). This was an unsuccessful petition.

- The provision of inadequate information and advice in recommending acceptance of a takeover bid. In *Re a Company (No 008699 of 1985)* (1986), Hoffmann J held that circulars containing inadequate information in a takeover situation may ground a petition.

- Calling a meeting to replace a director of a subsidiary with a nominee of the parent company which at the time was being sued by the subsidiary. This was the basis of a successful petition in *Whyte, Petitioner* (1984).

- Making a rights issue. This was a successful ground in *Re a Company (No 002612 of 1984)* (1985) where Harman J granted an injunction to restrain a rights issue which would have reduced the petitioner's holding from one third to less than 5%, but unsuccessful in *Re a Company (No 007623 of 1984)* (1986) where there had been no refusal by the respondents to buy the petitioner's shares at a fair valuation.

- A proposal to sell property belonging to the company. This was unsuccessful in *Re Gorwyn Holdings* (1985).

- A proposal to sell the company's business substantially undervalued to connected persons. This allegation was not proved and the petition was unsuccessful in *Re Posgate & Denby (Agencies) Ltd* (1987).

- Delay in holding a meeting. This was the basis of a successful petition in *McGuinness v Bremner plc* (1988). This petition was successful notwithstanding that the delay in holding the meeting was not contrary to the provisions of the Companies Act. The loophole has now been closed by para 9 of Sched 19 of the Companies Act 1989 amending s 368 of the Companies Act 1985 and providing that directors must convene a meeting for a date not more than 28 days after the date of the notice convening the meeting which must be sent out no later than 21 days after the requisition.

- Failure to lay accounts. This was a successful ground for the petition in *Re Nuneaton Borough AFC Ltd* (1989).

- Failure to pay dividends. There was previously some doubt as to whether this could be a ground for a petition because of the former requirement that some part of the membership be prejudiced. See *Re a Company (No 00370 of 1987) ex p Glossop* (1988), *Re Sam Weller Ltd* (1990). This difficulty has now been remedied by the amendment in para 11 of Sched 19 of the Companies Act 1989 which provides that the conduct must be unfairly prejudicial to the interest of the company's members generally or some part of the members.

- Deletion of pre-emption rights. It was recognised that this may be a reason for a petition in *Re a Company (No 005685 of 1988) ex p Schwarz* (1989).

- Dilution of voting power. This was a successful ground for the petition in *Re DR Chemicals* (1989).

- Use of company assets for the family and friends of the controller of the company. This was the basis of the successful petition in *Re Elgindata Ltd* (1991).

- The company operating at a loss with the directors taking excessive remuneration. Such a petition failed on the facts in *Re Saul D Harrison & Sons plc* (1995).

- A company purchasing its own shares at too high a price. This was the basis of an unsuccessful petition in *Rutherford, Petitioner* (1994) where the court pointed out that market prices were not necessarily a conclusive indicator of share values, especially where the transaction concerned a particular block of shares which could affect control of the company.

14.4   The section in operation

Only members or personal representatives of members have *locus standi* to present a petition. See *Re a Company (No 007828 of 1985)* (1986).

Previously, there was some doubt as to whether a petition could be brought where all of the members had been unfairly prejudiced, see the *dicta* of Vinelott J in *Re Carrington Viyella plc*. As has been noted above, the amendment in the Companies Act 1989 now puts this matter beyond doubt. Interestingly, the old remedy in s 210 of the Companies Act 1948 was available if all of the members suffered. Relief was granted in *Scottish CWS v Meyer* where all members suffered and it was noted that relief could be granted even if Samson destroys himself as well as the Philistines in a single catastrophe.

In determining if a person can bring a petition, it is not necessary that he comes to court with clean hands. See *Re London School of Electronics*. However, if a petitioner has to some extent brought the conduct upon himself, this may be relevant in determining whether the prejudice is unfair and also in determining what remedy is available to the petitioner.

The question of unfair prejudice is an objective question and does not depend upon the intention of the respondents. See *Re RA Noble & Sons (Clothing) Ltd*.

In *Re Macro (Ipswich) Ltd* (1994), Arden J considered that the question of prejudice was an objective one. If the prejudice was established it then had to be demonstrated that there was unfairness. This was a matter of balancing different interests. The case involved allegations of exclusion from management and corporate mismanagement leading to a loss of value in the petitioner's shareholding. Unfair prejudice was made out.

14.5   Remedies

The court has the power to award whatever relief it considers fit (s 461(1) of the Companies Act 1985).

It may make an order to regulate the company's affairs or to restrict the company from acting in a particular way. It may order the company to do something or it may order civil

- Minority Protection 183

proceedings to be brought in the name of the company. A very common remedy is where the court orders the purchase of the petitioner's shares. On occasion, it may be an order that the respondent sell his shares to the petitioner as in *Re Bovey Hotel Ventures Ltd*. If the court does order the purchase of shares, problems of valuation arise. There is no rule in s 461 regarding share valuation. As Oliver LJ said in *Re Bird Precision Bellows Ltd* (1985):

> It seems to me that the whole framework of the section ... is to confer on the court a very wide discretion to do what is considered fair and equitable in all the circumstances of the case ...

Generally, where a minority shareholding is sold, there is a discount applied as a percentage of the company's value. This rule only applies, however, if a sale is a willing sale, see *dicta* of Nourse J in *Re Bird Precision Bellows Ltd*. On the other hand a discounted valuation might be appropriate if the petitioner brought the exclusion upon himself.

Another moot point is the date of the valuation. Once again, there is no fixed rule to apply. If the petitioner refused a reasonable offer for his shares, the date of valuation may well be the date of the hearing, see *Re a Company (No 002567 of 1982)* (1983).

On the other hand, if a fair offer is not made and the conduct of the majority causes the value of the company's shares to fall, the court may order a valuation at the date the unreasonable conduct began, see *Re OC (Transport) Services Ltd* (1984).

This seems to be the most logical date for valuing the shares.

The old minority remedy was very much a fly-swatter or pea-shooter of a remedy compared to the blunderbuss of the present remedy. It consistently failed to meet the needs of wronged minorities and prompted the Jenkins Committee on Company Law to recommend in 1962 that a broader remedy of unfair prejudice should be introduced (Cmnd 1749, para 205). Under the present remedy, companies must consider carefully the effect that their actions and inactions will have on all of their members. The possibility is now that the pendulum has swung too much in the opposite direction and that from a position of too little protection for shareholders, we have now moved to a position of too much.

A company may be wound up by the court if the court is of the opinion that it is just and equitable that the company should be wound up (s 122(1)(g) of the Insolvency Act 1986). (The

14.6   Just and equitable winding up

procedure on a winding up will be considered in Chapter 23.) Before the advent of ss 459–61 of the Companies Act 1985, just and equitable winding up was sometimes the only possible remedy for a disenchanted minority shareholder. It was this remedy that was sought and obtained in *Ebrahimi v Westbourne Galleries* (1973). The remedy is a sledgehammer remedy. Since the advent of ss 459–61, it has been less common. Indeed, s 125(2) of the Insolvency Act 1986 provides that if the court is of the opinion that there is some other remedy that is available to the petitioners and that they are acting unreasonably in seeking to have the company wound up instead of pursuing that other remedy, then the court should refuse the petition – see *Gammack v Mitchells (Fraserburgh) Ltd* (1983). Yet, in *Virdi v Abbey Leisure Ltd* (1989), the Court of Appeal considered that where a minority shareholder sought a winding up order rather than utilising the mechanism under the articles to have his shares purchased at a fair valuation that the minority was not acting unreasonably. The Court of Appeal took the view, reversing Hoffmann J at first instance, that the minority might legitimately object to the mode of valuation for valuing his shares.

In *Ebrahimi v Westbourne Galleries*, the House of Lords made the point that the categories of conduct where just and equitable winding up might be ordered were not closed. It will be attempted here to classify the cases into certain areas. There is nothing magic in this categorisation:

14.6.1	Exclusion from management

Apart from *Ebrahimi* itself, exclusion from management has featured in other cases. In *Re A&BC Chewing Gum Ltd* (1975), the petitioning shareholder had put up a third of the capital of the company and had been promised a say in the management of the company. The court granted the petitioning shareholder's petition where he had been excluded from management. In *Tay Bok Choon v Tahansan Sdn Bhd* (1987), in similar circumstances a shareholder who had put up a considerable amount of capital and who was excluded from management was held entitled to wind the company up. However, in *Lewis v Haas* (1973) the Outer House held that exclusion from management of itself was insufficient to justify a compulsory winding up order.

14.6.2	Destruction of the substratum of the company

If the main and overriding purpose for which the company has been formed is destroyed so that the company cannot achieve its main objective, then a petition to wind the company up on the just and equitable ground will be successful. In *Re German Date Coffee Co* (1882), the company had been formed to obtain a German patent to manufacture coffee from dates. A request for a patent was refused. It was held that a petition to wind the company up would be successful. It must be that all of the company's main activities are incapable of achievement before such a petition can succeed. In *Re Kitson & Co Ltd* (1946), the company's engineering business had ceased when it was sold. The company had other activities, however, that were still capable of achievement. A petition to wind the company up was therefore not granted.

It is interesting to note that a petition will not succeed merely because a company is making a loss. In order to succeed, it must be demonstrated that the company is incapable of making a profit, see *Re Suburban Hotel Co* (1867).

If there is deadlock within the company and no way of breaking that deadlock by some mechanism in the articles or by the shareholders resolving the problem by appointing a director or removing a director, then a petition will be granted. In *Re Yenidje Tobacco Co Ltd* (1916), the company had two shareholders with an equal number of shares who were each directors. They could not agree on how the company should be managed. There was no provision for breaking the deadlock and a petition to wind the company up on the just and equitable ground was granted.	14.6.3 Deadlock
If a petitioning shareholder can demonstrate a lack of probity and integrity on the part of directors, this will be sufficient ground for winding up the company. In *Re Bleriot Manufacturing Aircraft Co* (1916), the court held that where directors had misappropriated company property, a winding up order could be made. In *Loch v John Blackwood Ltd* (1924), a Privy Council decision on appeal from the Court of Appeal of the West Indies (Barbados), where directors had failed to supply corporate information to shareholders and to hold company meetings and in general ran the company as if it was their own property, a winding up order was granted. Similarly, in *Re Lundie Brothers Ltd* (1965), Plowman J granted a winding up petition in a situation where the directors ran the company as if it was their own business without any account being taken of the interests of shareholders. In addition, the petitioner had been excluded from management.	14.6.4 Lack of probity of the directors
This category overlaps with exclusion from management; indeed, in many of the cases, some of the factors set out in the different areas may be present. In *Re Zinotty Properties Ltd* (1984), it was held that one of the founding shareholders of a business was entitled to assume he would participate in the management. He was excluded from the management. Furthermore, it had been understood that once the company had developed a particular site, the company would be	14.6.5 Breakdown of trust and confidence

dissolved. This did not happen. Some of the company's money was lent to another business in which one of the directors had an interest. The petition brought by the excluded shareholder was successful.

In *Hyndman v RC Hyndman Ltd* (1989), where a shareholder demonstrated that she had been frustrated in attempts to obtain information about the company's affairs over a number of years; that the accounts were not being properly kept; that the directors seemed to be capable of living well above the means that the company could ostensibly afford to pay them and that the substratum of the company appeared to have been dissipated, the court ordered a compulsory winding up on the just and equitable ground on the basis that if the company was allowed to wind up voluntarily it was likely that the petitioning shareholder's interests would be further prejudiced since the directors appeared to have acted fraudulently.

It may thus be seen that the remedy of just and equitable winding up is available in a variety of circumstances although its popularity has decreased since the remedy in ss 459–61 has been on the scene as selling company property in a liquidation generally means obtaining a discounted price for the company's assets which is not in the interests of any of the shareholders.

14.7   Appointment of a judicial factor

In Scotland, the Court of Session, in exercise of its just and equitable jurisdiction (*nobile officium*), is able to appoint a judicial factor to take over the management and administration of an estate where this is necessary to protect against loss or injustice which cannot otherwise be prevented by ordinary legal remedies. A judicial factor may therefore be appointed as a trustee of company property to temporarily manage the company's business until the company is able of itself to protect against further loss or injustice.

Thus, in *Fraser, Petitioner* (1971), where evidence of chaos and dishonesty in a company's management was led, it was held competent to appoint a judicial factor, and in *Weir v Rees* (1991) a judicial factor was appointed pending an election of new directors where a company was left without directors in a power struggle between shareholders, since those left in control of the company could not be trusted to act impartially.

Furthermore, it may be preferable to appoint a judicial factor rather than a provisional liquidator, particularly where an adoption of the latter course would be likely to result in devaluation of the company's assets, since appointment of a judicial factor would allow the company the continue as a going concern – see *McGuinness v Black (No 2)* (1990).

Minority Protection

Historically, the decision in *Foss v Harbottle* has meant that where the company suffers harm the company is the proper pursuer so that shareholders cannot generally sue for wrongs done to the company.

The rule in
Foss v Harbottle

There are certain exceptions:

Exceptions

- where there is an *ultra vires* act;

- where a special majority is needed;

- where personal rights are infringed;

- where fraud has been committed by those in control.

Before ss 459–61 of the Companies Act 1985, the old remedy s 210 of the Companies Act 1948 had certain serious defects:

The statutory remedy

- an order could only be made if a winding up order could have been made on the just and equitable ground;

- a single act was insufficient to found a petition;

- the petitioner had to show that the conduct was oppressive;

- a petition could not be based on omissions or on future conduct;

- probably personal representatives could not present petitions.

Under ss 459–61 all of these defects are remedied. In particular a petitioner needs now to demonstrate unfair prejudice and does not need to show oppression.

The 1985 Act remedy covers a wide range of situations. The courts have interpreted the remedy liberally and it is not necessary for a petitioner to confine his petition to membership matters in the narrow sense and may, for example, in appropriate circumstances complain of exclusion from management. The court has a total discretion as to what remedy to award a successful petitioner although the usual remedy is a purchase of the petitioner's shares.

Just and equitable winding up

'Just and equitable' winding up may not look like a membership remedy at first sight but it is.

A disenchanted member will usually only seek this remedy where all other possible remedies have been exhausted. Just and equitable winding up under s 122(1)(g) of the Insolvency Act 1986 is a sledgehammer remedy and the court should refuse it if there is some other remedy which is appropriate which the petitioner is unreasonable in not seeking.

Just and equitable winding up may be granted in various situations and the categories are not closed. The situations include:

- exclusion from management;

- destruction of the substratum of the company;

- deadlock;

- lack of probity of management;

- breakdown of trust and confidence.

Appointment of a judicial factor

The Court of Session in pursuance of its *nobile officium* function may appoint a judicial factor to act as a temporary trustee of a Scottish company's undertaking so as to prevent further loss or injustice where ordinary legal remedies are inappropriate.

Chapter 15

Company Meetings

There are two types of meetings: annual and extraordinary.

Section 366 of the Companies Act 1985 provides that every company must hold an annual general meeting once in every calendar year and the meeting must be specified as an annual general meeting. The first annual general meeting must be held within 18 months of the company's incorporation (s 366(2)). There can be no more than 15 months between successive annual general meetings. This provision is to prevent companies from going almost two years between annual general meetings which they could otherwise do.

The Companies Act 1989 has amended s 366 by s 366(A) to provide that private companies may dispense with the holding of annual general meetings by unanimous written resolution or unanimous resolution. This only applies to private companies and the members must all be in agreement about this course of action.

If a company fails to hold an annual general meeting the directors' appointments may lapse – see *Alexander Ward & Co v Samyang* (1973).

Repeated failure to hold an annual general meeting is ground for a petition under s 459. This occurred in *Re a Company ex p Shooter* (1990) which concerned a football club which had failed to hold annual general meetings or to lay accounts before the members.

Extraordinary general meetings may be called in various ways. Companies will tend to try to avoid calling these if matters can be postponed until the next annual general meeting but sometimes the need may arise to call a meeting between annual general meetings. The various ways they may be called are set out below:

- **Directors**

  The company's articles may provide for the calling of an extraordinary general meeting by the directors of the company. Article 37 of Table A, for example, makes such provision. This is the normal way in which extraordinary general meetings are called.

15.1   Annual general meetings

15.2   Extraordinary general meetings

- **Request of members**

  Extraordinary general meetings may be called at the request of members. Section 368 of the Act provides that members of the company holding one tenth of the paid up capital of the company with voting rights or in the case of a company without share capital one tenth of the voting rights may requisition a general meeting. It is to be noted that the members are here not calling the meeting directly but are requisitioning the calling of the meeting. The requisition should state the objects of the meeting, be signed by the requisitionists and be left at the company's registered office.

  The directors then have 21 days within which to convene the general meeting and the meeting must be held for a date not more than 28 days after the date of the notice convening the meeting. This latter point remedies a loop-hole in the Act where it was earlier possible under the terms of the Companies Act to send out a notice convening the meeting within 21 days for a date far into the distant future, see *McGuiness v Bremner plc* (1988) and Companies Act 1989, s 145 and Sched 19, para 9.

- **Two or more members holding 10% of the share capital**

  If the articles do not make other provision for the calling of extraordinary general meetings, s 370 of the Companies Act will apply. This states that in the case of companies with a share capital, two or more members holding 10% of the share capital or in the case of a company without share capital 5% of the members may call a meeting. In this instance it is to be noted that the meeting is being called directly by the members themselves. Table A makes contrary provision and it is unusual for s 370 to apply.

- **The court**

  The court has a residual power to order the calling of an extraordinary general meeting. Section 371 provides that if for any reason it is impracticable to call a meeting or to conduct the meeting in the manner prescribed by the articles or the Act, the court may order a meeting to be called and conducted in any manner the court thinks fit. This provision is often used in the case of deadlock where a company perhaps has two members and one member is refusing to attend a meeting, for example, see *Re Sticky Fingers Restaurant Ltd* (1992). In this case, one member of the company had presented a petition under s 459. The other member, Bill Wyman of the Rolling Stones, was allowed to hold a meeting with the quorum fixed at one for the purpose of appointing additional directors provided that any such directors would not act to the prejudice of the other shareholder pending the outcome of the s 459 proceedings. The section was used in a similar way in *Re Whitchurch Insurance Consultants Ltd* (1993) where Mr Rudd wished to remove the other member, Mrs Rudd, as a director. In *Re British Union for the Abolition of Vivisection* (1995), application was made to the court under s 371 to give directions for the calling of a meeting to avoid anticipated disruption. There had been disorder at a previous meeting and what was therefore sought was the convening of a small meeting consisting only of members of the committee, with no other members being entitled to attend in person but to vote by postal means. The application was granted. Under s 371, application is made to the court by a member or members or by a director.

- **Resigning auditors**

  Resigning auditors may requisition a company meeting. Section 392A provides that an auditor may deposit with his notice of resignation a signed requisition calling on the directors to convene an extraordinary general meeting of the company to receive and consider the explanation of his resignation.

- **Serious loss of capital**

  A public company is obliged to call an extraordinary general meeting where there has been a serious loss of capital. Section 142 of the Act provides that where the net assets of a public company are half or less of its share capital, the directors must within 28 days of this fact becoming known to a director convene an extraordinary general meeting for a date not later than 56 days from that date to consider what steps if any should be taken in relation to this situation.

In addition to meetings of the company, meetings may also be held of different classes of shareholders. Such meetings may be necessary, for example, to consider a proposed variation of class rights (see para 6.2). Most of the rules that apply in relation to company meetings also apply in relation to class meetings.

15.3   Class meetings

The Companies Act lays down stringent rules in relation to notices.

15.4   Notice

The period of notice required for meetings varies according to the type of meeting concerned. In the case of the annual general meeting, 21 days' notice is required. In the case of other

15.4.1   Length of notice required

meetings, a period of seven days is required if the company is an unlimited company and 14 days' notice if the company is limited. If a special resolution is to be proposed, then 21 days' notice is required. If an extraordinary resolution is to be proposed, 14 days' notice is required if the company is limited and seven days' notice if it is unlimited. Also, under Table A, if a director is to be appointed, then 21 days' notice is needed. In Scotland, the date of the meeting, although not the date of the service of the notice, may be included in the calculation of the required period of notice – see *Aberdeen Combworks Co Ltd, Petitioners* (1902) and *Neil McLeod & Sons* (1967). This is not, however, the case in England where 'days' notice' means clear days, that is, exclusive of the day of service and of the day of the meeting – see *Re Hector Whaling Ltd* (1936). Under Table A, notice is deemed to be received 48 hours after posting (Article 115). Notice can be served personally or by post (Article 112).

It is possible for meetings to be called on short notice by virtue of s 369(3). In the case of the annual general meeting, the short notice has to be agreed to by all of the members, and in the case of other meetings, it has to be agreed to by 95% (in value of share capital, or if the company has no share capital, 95% in voting rights). This percentage may be reduced to 90% in the case of private companies since the Companies Act 1989 if all of the members agree to this by elective resolution. The waiving of short notice must be done purposefully and cannot be done simply by all of the members turning up to the meeting without realising that there should have been a longer period of notice provided to the members, see *Re Pearce Duff* (1960).

15.4.2   Contents

The notice must set out certain matters. It must clearly set out the date, time and place of the meeting and the nature of the business that is to be transacted. The notice should also state whether the meeting is an annual general meeting or extraordinary general meeting. In the case of companies with a share capital, it is also mandatory that the notice should set out the member's right to appoint a proxy and that that proxy need not be a member.

Under Table A of the Companies Act 1948, certain matters were set out as ordinary business to be transacted at the company's annual general meeting. Such matters did not need to be set out in detail. It was sufficient merely to indicate that the meeting was to transact certain stipulated items of ordinary business. These were:

• the adoption of the accounts;

• the election of directors;

- the declaration of any dividend;

- the appointment of the auditors and the fixing of their remuneration.

Under the Companies Act 1985 Table A, there is no equivalent definition of ordinary business so that ordinary business now needs to be spelt out in detail for those companies adopting Table A under the 1985 Regulations.

In the case of listed companies, there are certain continuing obligations placed upon those companies by the Stock Exchange. Some of these obligations relate to notices of meetings. These obligations include the necessity to place a box for members on the proxy card to tick for or against the specific resolution, which should be numbered. The notice of an annual general meeting for listed companies should also set out where directors' service agreements are kept and state that they are available for inspection there and that they are available for inspection at the annual general meeting itself.

The notice should be fair and reasonable and not be 'tricky' ie it should be plain to those receiving it what is to be transacted at the meeting, see *Baillie v Oriental Telephone & Electric Co* (1915). In *Re Blue Arrow plc* (1987), the question of the sufficiency of a notice was raised under s 459. Vinelott J held that this was an inappropriate mode for challenging the notice and that it was appropriate to challenge it by arguing that the meeting was invalid.

15.4.3 Serving the notice

Section 370(2) of the Companies Act 1985 provides that if a company's articles do not make other provision, then the notice of the meeting shall be served on every member of it in the manner required by Table A (the current Table A). Table A Article 112 provides that it is not necessary to serve a notice on a member outside of the United Kingdom, see *Re Warden & Hotchkiss Ltd* (1945).

Furthermore, Article 39 of the current Table A provides that the accidental omission to give notice does not invalidate the meeting. It is important to realise the effect of this provision. The accidental failure to send notice where there was an oversight did not render the meeting invalid in *Re West Canadian Collieries Ltd* (1962). The error arose here because the dividend payment had been made separately to certain members and their addressograph plates had therefore been kept in a separate place. They were, therefore, omitted when notices were sent out. By contrast, the failure to send notice in *Musselwhite v Musselwhite & Son Ltd* (1962) was quite deliberate. It was considered that the members concerned did not have a right to vote at the meeting as they had agreed to sell their shares. This was a genuine mistake but the failure to send notice was deliberate and therefore the meeting was invalid.

Upon whom should notices be served? Table A, Article 38 provides that notice should be served on members, directors and the company's auditors. Notice should be served even if the person concerned could not have attended the meeting, see *Young v Ladies Imperial Club* (1920).

Table A, Article 116 provides that a notice may be given by the company to the persons entitled to a share in consequence of the death or bankruptcy of a member by sending or delivering it, in any manner authorised by the articles for the giving of notice to a member, addressed to them by name, or by the title of representatives of the deceased, or trustee of the bankrupt or by any like description at the address, if any, within the United Kingdom supplied for that purpose by the persons claiming to be so entitled. Until such an address has been supplied, a notice may be given in any manner in which it might have been given if the death or bankruptcy had not occurred.

Where a member attends a meeting either in person or by proxy, he is deemed to have received notice (Table A, Article 113). If a transferee derives title from somebody else whose name is currently on the register of members and notice is served on that person, that is effective notice to the transferee (Table A, Article 114).

15.4.4 The chairman

Table A provides that the chairman of the board of directors or in his absence some other director nominated by the board of directors shall preside at meetings (Table A, Article 42) (see also s 370(5)). If the chairman or some other nominated director however is not present within 15 minutes from the time appointed for the start of the meeting, the directors present shall elect one of their number to be chairman (Table A, Article 42). If no director is willing to act or if no director is present within 15 minutes of that time, members present who are entitled to vote may elect one of their number to be chairman. It is the function of the director to take the meeting through the agenda and to put matters to the vote as appropriate. The chairman is also responsible for keeping order, see *John v Rees* (1969). If appropriate, the chairman should adjourn the meeting, see Table A, Article 45. When putting matters to the vote, the chairman will first put a matter to a vote on a show of hands (Table A, Article 46). If a poll is properly demanded, the chairman will put the matter to a poll, and, in the event of an equality of votes, will have the casting vote (Table A, Articles 49 and 50). The chairman's statement of the outcome of a vote is conclusive – see *Graham's Morocco Co* (1932).

Section 370(4) provides that unless the company's articles make contrary provision, the quorum for a company meeting shall be two members personally present. This is subject to the qualification now necessary because of implementation of the 12th EC Directive where a private company has only one member, then the quorum for the meeting shall be one (s 370A of the Companies Act 1985). Table A, Article 40 provides that two persons entitled to vote on the business at the general meeting either as member or proxy for a member or as a duly authorised corporate representative shall constitute a quorum. Table A, Article 41 provides that if a quorum is not present within half an hour from the time scheduled for the start of the meeting, or if during a meeting, the quorum ceases to be present, the meeting shall stand adjourned to the same day in the next following week at the same time and place or at such other time and place as the directors may determine.

15.4.5   Quorum

Problems sometimes arise over quorums. The Oxford Concise Dictionary defines a meeting as an assemblage of persons. This implies that there should be more than one person present and that they should be in each other's physical presence. Each of these features tends to cause problems.

At common law, a meeting must be made up of more than one person. In *Sharp v Dawes* (1876), a meeting of a stannary mining company governed under the Stannaries Acts (which governed tin mining companies set up in Cornwall) was called for the purpose of making a call on shares. Only one member, Silversides, turned up at the meeting together with the company secretary who was not a member. Lord Coleridge CJ said in the Court of Appeal '... the word "meeting" *prima facie* means a coming together of more than one person'. The court held that there was no meeting here. Lord Coleridge CJ did acknowledge that on occasion the word 'meeting' could have a different meeting but found there was nothing here to indicate that that was the case.

The same principle applies where one member present has proxies for the other company members, see *Re Sanitary Carbon Company* (1877). The same principle was applied in *Re London Flats Ltd* (1969) where all but one member had left the room when the vote was taken. The court held that there could be no meeting. Plowman J considered that there would need to be special circumstances present to displace the usual rule. In *MJ Shanley Contracting Ltd* (in voluntary liquidation) (1979), the court held there was no meeting where the chairman present at the meeting held a proxy for his wife and had the consent of the other member to voting in favour of voluntary liquidation (although there was no meeting, the decision to put the company into liquidation was upheld on the basis of the assent principle which is discussed below at para 15.5.5). In the Scottish case of *James Prain & Sons Ltd, Petitioners* (1947), the company's articles required a quorum of two persons present in person or by proxy. One person only attended a meeting. In addition to his voting rights as a shareholder, he held another two votes – one as a trustee and another as a proxy. He took the chair, moved a special resolution proposing a reduction in capital in his capacity as shareholder, seconded it in his capacity as proxy and declared it carried. The Court of Session declined to confirm the reduction of capital since no 'meeting' took place.

This decision was distinguished in *Neil McLeod & Sons* (1967) where the quorum specified in the articles was three. It was held that provided at least two persons were physically present (to satisfy the 'meeting' criterion), a person present in more than one capacity could be counted more than once in order to satisfy the 'quorum' criterion.

If the articles require a specific individual to be 'personally present' without further qualification, then that person must be physically present for a meeting to be valid and may not be represented by proxy – see *M Harris Ltd Petitioners* (1956).

This principle that one person cannot constitute a meeting has to give way to certain exceptions.

Sometimes, as has been noted, it is necessary to hold a class meeting, for example, to consider a proposed variation of class rights. It may be that there is only one shareholder of the class in question. In these circumstances, clearly, the quorum for the class meeting cannot be set higher than one, see *East v Bennett Bros* (1911).

This now also applies in relation to private companies which only have one member. As has been noted, since the implementation of the 12th EC Directive on Company Law, private companies may only have one member. In relation to these companies, the quorum for meetings will be one.

The Companies Act recognises two situations where the quorum may be set at one. Under s 367 of the CA 85, the Secretary of State for Trade and Industry may direct an annual general meeting to be held and may fix the quorum at one. He will do so generally where there is deadlock within the company and a member in a two member company is refusing to attend a meeting. In the same way under s 371 of the CA 85, the court may order an extraordinary general meeting to be held and may fix the quorum at one. This would be done in similar circumstances to the exercise of the power under s 367 of the CA 85. In *Re El Sombrero Ltd* (1958), the company had three members. The applicant had 90% of the shares and he wished to remove the other two shareholders as directors. They held 5 % of the shares each. They refused to attend meetings where this was to be proposed. The applicant therefore applied to the court for a meeting to be ordered under s 371 and for the quorum to be fixed at one. This was done. The decision in *Re El Sombrero Ltd* was followed in *Re HR Paul & Son* (1973). In this case, the matter at issue was not the removal of directors but the alteration of the articles where the majority shareholder wished to alter the articles and the minority shareholders were blocking his wishes. In *Re Sticky Fingers Restaurant Ltd* (1992), deadlock in a small private company was again featured. The restaurant was owned jointly by Bill Wyman, of Rolling Stones fame, and one Mr Mitchell. Wyman owned 66 shares and Mitchell owned 34. Wyman sought to remove Mitchell under s 303 but Mitchell refused to attend meetings. Mitchell was also petitioning under s 459 of the Act. Wyman sought an order under s 371 of the Act requiring a meeting to be convened at which the quorum could be fixed at one. The court ordered this, subject to the proviso that any outcome of such a meeting would be stayed until the s 459 matter had been resolved.

A second problem referred to in relation to quorums at meetings is the matter of whether a meeting can be held where members are not in each other's physical presence. This becomes a very real problem in a time of technological change and given the possibility of video and audio link-ups. In *Re Associated Color Laboratories* (1970), a Canadian decision held that it was not possible to hold a meeting by telephone link between California and Vancouver. McDonald J took the view that a meeting meant that the participants were in each other's presence. The decision was, however, reversed by the Canada Business Corporations Act s 109(9). In Britain, *Byng v London Life Association Ltd* (1990) considered the matter of the audio and visual link system of holding meetings. The court held that a meeting may be validly held even though people at the meeting are not together in the same room where there is some audio visual link-up. The decision seems a sensible one.

Special notice has already been considered (at para 10.5).

The Companies Act lays down stringent rules in relation to resolutions.

15.5   Resolutions

15.5.1	Extraordinary resolutions	An extraordinary resolution is one that is passed by a majority of at least 75% of those voting at a general meeting of which notice specifying the intention to propose the resolution as an extraordinary resolution has been given (s 378). A resolution that is proposed as an extraordinary resolution needs 14 days' notice in the case of a limited company and seven days' notice in the case of a unlimited company, subject to the provisions on short notice (at para 15.4.1).
15.5.2	Special resolutions	A resolution is a special resolution if it is passed by a majority of at least 75% of those voting and passed at a general meeting of which notice has been given specifying the intention to propose the resolution as a special resolution – see *Rennie v Crichton's (Strichen) Ltd* (1927). In the case of special resolutions, there must have been at least 21 days' notice whether the company is limited or unlimited, subject to the provisions on short notice (at para 15.4.1).
15.5.3	Ordinary resolutions	Ordinary resolutions are not defined in the Act. An ordinary resolution is a resolution which is passed by a simple majority of those voting. It is used extensively under the Act, for example removing a director under s 303, increasing a company's authorised share capital under s 121, and removing the company's auditors under s 391.
15.5.4	Written resolutions	With the Companies Act 1989, a new procedure has been introduced to allow private companies to act by unanimous written resolution. In the case of such a situation, it is no longer necessary to convene a meeting. The members may agree by signing a document to a particular course of conduct. In fact, it may be a series of linked documents. The date of the passing of the resolution is the date of the last signature (s 381A of the Companies Act 1985). The procedure cannot be used in certain situations. Two examples where it may not be used because of the rights of representation at the company meeting are the removal of directors and the removal of auditors. The company's auditors have certain rights in relation to written resolutions. These are set out in s 381B of the 1985 Act. If the resolution concerns the auditors as auditors, they may within seven days of receiving a copy of the notice of the written resolution require the company to convene a general meeting.
15.5.5	*De facto* resolutions – the assent principle	Quite independently of the Companies Act 1989 reforms, on occasion the courts have been willing to recognise certain acts irrespective of the fact that no proper meeting has been called on the basis of the company's unanimous consent. Thus, in *Re Express Engineering Works Ltd* (1920), where all the members

agreed at a board meeting rather than at a general meeting, the assent principle was applied.

The principle has also been applied in *Parker & Cooper Ltd v Reading* (1926), *Re Bailey Hay & Co Ltd* (1971) and *Cane v Jones* (1980). The position has not been uniform, though, and in some cases the courts have been unwilling to recognise the unanimous assent of members as a substitute for a resolution at a meeting, see *Re Barry Artists Ltd* (1985). In any event, the Companies Act 1989 has made the assent principle of less significance.

Resolutions may be amended at the meeting provided that the amendment is within the general notice of the business that has been sent out to members. This principle does not apply if the resolution has to be set out verbatim. In the case of extraordinary and special resolutions, no amendment can be permitted which alters the substance of the resolution contained in the notice, see *Re Moorgate Mercantile Holdings Ltd* (1980). An amendment to a resolution would be permitted to resolve an ambiguity or to correct an grammatical mistake without the notice usually necessary.

15.5.6   Amendments

If the chairman improperly rejects an amendment and the unamended resolution is then passed, that resolution is then invalid, see *Henderson v Bank of Australasia* (1890).

Where amendments are proposed, the amendment is first put to the vote. If that is passed the amended resolution is then voted upon.

Certain resolutions have to be registered. These are set out in s 380 of the Companies Act 1985. They are as follows:

15.5.7   Registration of resolutions

- special resolution;

- extraordinary resolutions;

- resolutions or agreements of all the members of a company which would have been registerable had they been passed as special resolutions or as extraordinary resolutions;

- resolutions or agreements of a class of members which bind all the members of the class although some have not agreed to;

- a resolution for voluntary winding up;

- a resolution to give, vary, revoke or renew authority to directors to issue shares;

- a resolution conferring, varying, revoking or renewing authority to purchase a company's own shares on the market;

- an elective resolution or a resolution revoking such a resolution (these are discussed at para 15.5.9).

In addition, certain other resolutions are registerable.

- under s 123(3), a resolution increasing the authorised share capital of the company;

- resolutions approving certain acquisitions from the subscribers of the memorandum under s 111(2);

- a resolution treating a meeting called by the Secretary of State as an annual general meeting under s 367(4).

Failure to register such resolutions results in criminal liability. The resolution is not as such invalid, but the company may not be able to rely upon the resolution unless it has been officially notified (see s 42 of the Act).

15.5.8	Circulation of members' resolutions	Section 376 of the Act provides for the circulation of members' resolutions. If a requisition is made by 1/20th of the voting rights of the company or not less than 100 members who hold shares in the company on which on average at least £100 has been paid up, then it is the duty of the company to circulate at the expense of the requisitionists notice of any resolution which may properly be moved at the next annual general meeting and to circulate to members entitled to notice of any general meeting a statement of not more than 1,000 words with respect to the matter referred to in any proposed resolution or the proposed business to be dealt with at that meeting.

This power is not often utilised. The expense must be borne by the member and it provides advance notice to 'the other side' of the case being put by the relevant member.

15.5.9	Elective resolutions	The Companies Act 1989 introduced a new provision whereby private companies may pass an elective resolution dispensing with certain formalities. These formalities are as follows:

- election as to the duration of authority to allot shares. This normally may only subsist for up to five years under s 80 but now by virtue of s 80A a private company may dispense with this time limitation by unanimous resolution;

- election to dispense with the laying of accounts and reports before a general meeting each year. This election is provided for under s 252;

- election to dispense with the holding of an annual general meeting. This election is provided for under s 366A;

- election as to the majority required for authorising short notice of meetings reducing this from 95% to 90% under s 369(4) or s 378(3);

- election to dispense with the annual appointment of auditors. This is provided for under s 386.

An elective resolution must be unanimous. It may be passed at a meeting or it may be agreed to in writing as provided for in relation to written resolutions. This facility is only available to private companies.

The Secretary of State for Trade and Industry has power to add to the list of dispensations under the section by virtue of s 117 of the Companies Act 1989.

Where matters are put to the vote at a general meeting, a vote will be initially conducted on a show of hands. A vote on a show of hands would often be conclusive of the matter. This would be the case, for example, if all members are present and are all voting in the same way. Sometimes, however, a vote on a poll will be necessary. Proxies cannot vote on a show of hands and it may well be that a decision on a show of hands is unrepresentative of the way that votes would split if voting strength were taken into account.

A poll may always be demanded on any matter other than the election of the chairman of the meeting or the adjournment of the meeting. These two matters may be excluded from this general provision by the company's articles (s 373(1)).

A poll may be demanded by any five members present in person or by proxy or by a member or members representing not less than 1/10th of the voting rights at the meeting or by members holding shares in the company with voting rights on which an aggregate sum has been paid up of at least 1/10th of the share capital of shares conferring that right. Articles may provide more generous rights than this; Table A, Article 46 provides that a poll may be demanded by two members. It also provides that a poll may be demanded by the chairman. A vote on a poll may be taken after a vote on a show of hands or it may pre-empt such a vote (Table A, Article 46). Table A, Article 51 also provides that a poll may be demanded on the election of a chairman or on the adjournment of the meeting.

Table A, Article 50 provides in the case of an equality of votes the chairman will have a casting vote.

15.6   Votes

Section 372 of the Act provides that any member of a company who is entitled to attend and vote at a meeting may appoint a person as his proxy and that proxy need not be a member. It

15.7   Proxies

has already been noted that this right must be set out in the notice calling the meeting (s 372(3)).

In the case of a private company, a proxy has a right to speak at the meeting in the same way as the member would have been able to speak.

Any provision in a company's articles requiring delivery of a proxy more than 48 hours before a meeting or adjourned meeting will be void (s 372(5)). A company's articles may be more generous; for example a provision that a proxy may be delivered up to 24 hours before the meeting.

The deposit of proxies as provided for in Table A, Article 62 requires that a proxy instrument must be deposited not less than 48 hours before the holding of the meeting or adjourned meeting or in the case of a poll taken more than 48 hours after it is demanded be deposited not less than 24 hours before the time appointed for the taking of the poll or where the poll is not taken forthwith but is taken not more than 48 hours after it is demanded be delivered at the meeting at which the poll was demanded to the chairman or to the secretary or to any director.

If invitations are sent by a company to appoint a person as proxy, such invitations must be sent to all the members or the company's officers who have knowingly committed proxy invitations to be sent to selected members only are liable to a fine.

Unless the articles provide otherwise, certain limitations apply:

- the rules on proxies only apply to companies limited by shares. In *Re British Union for the Abolition of Vivisection* (1995), proxies were not originally allowed in the company, which was not limited by shares;

- a member of a private company may only appoint one proxy to attend and vote on any one occasion;

- a proxy is not entitled to vote except on a poll ie he may not vote on a show of hands (see Table A, Article 59).

In the absence of a contract, a proxy is not obliged to attend and vote on behalf of a member. If he does attend, the proxy's authority is only to vote as directed by the member.

A proxy may be determined in different ways. It is determined by the death of the member, by express revocation or by the member actually turning up at the meeting. This last point is covered by *Cousins v International Brick Co Ltd* (1931). The company's articles will provide that where a proxy casts a vote, that vote shall be treated as valid notwithstanding the previous determination of the authority of the proxy unless notice of the determination was received by the company at its registered office or such other place at which the instrument of proxy was deposited (Table A, Article 63). However, insanity of the appointer no longer revokes the appointment (Law Reform (Miscellaneous Provisions) (Scotland) Act 1990, s 40).

Table A provides that instruments appointing proxies shall be in writing and should be in the form set out in Table A, Article 60 (a general proxy) or Table A, Article 61 (a two-way proxy giving the appointing member the opportunity to indicate which way the proxy should vote on specific resolutions.

Table A, Article 60 also provides that a proxy instrument may be in a similar form or in any other form which is usual or which the directors may approve of as appropriate.

It is worth noting at this juncture that where companies hold shares in another company, they do not appoint proxies to attend meetings but corporate representatives. Such persons are entitled to exercise the same powers on behalf of the corporation as the corporation could exercise if it were an individual shareholder rather than a corporate shareholder. Table A, Article 63 in relation to the determination of proxy authority also applies in relation to the determination of the authority of a corporate representative.

15.8 Adjournment of the meeting

Table A, Article 45 provides that the chairman, with the consent of the meeting, may adjourn the meeting and shall adjourn the meeting if so directed by the meeting. The chairman may in certain circumstances be obliged to adjourn the meeting. This would be the case, for example, if there is disorder at the meeting, see *John v Rees* (1969). He may need to do so if the room allocated for the meeting is not large enough to accommodate all of those attending or if some audio visual link between different rooms breaks down as in *Byng v London Life Association Ltd* (1990).

15.9 Minutes of the meeting

Section 382 of the 1985 Act requires that every company shall keep minutes of all general meetings as well as board meetings. These minutes if signed by the chairman of the meeting or the chairman of the succeeding meeting will be evidence of the proceedings of that meeting (s 382(2)). Evidence may be adduced to rebut the minutes or to add to them, as in *Re Fireproof Doors Ltd* (1916) where evidence was given that a resolution was passed at a meeting which was not recorded. If the minutes are stated in the articles to be conclusive of matters decided at the meeting, it seems it is no possible to challenge the minutes, *Kerr v John Mottram Ltd* (1940).

Summary of Chapter 15

Company Meetings

Companies must hold annual general meetings (except for private companies which agree unanimously not to do so) and they may hold extraordinary general meetings between annual general meetings.

The Companies Act 1985 and the company's articles set out the rules which companies must follow.

Meetings

The minimum period of notice is 21 days' notice for annual general meetings and for extraordinary general meetings seven days' notice if the company is unlimited, and 14 days' notice if the company is limited. If the extraordinary general meeting involves consideration of a special resolution there must be 21 days' notice. On occasion, short notice may be sufficient (s 369(3) of the Companies Act 1985).

Notices must go to members, directors and the company's auditors.

Notice

The company's articles will generally specify who is to act as chairman. In the event that the articles make no provision the members must act to fill the vacuum and elect one of their number.

The chairman's role is to take the meeting through the agenda, put matters to the vote and keep order.

Chairman

The rules on quorum are generally set out in the company's articles. They must be followed to the letter, although if members are deliberately boycotting meetings then the Secretary of State may seek the calling of an annual general meeting with a lower quorum (s 367(2)) or there may be an application to the court for the holding of an extraordinary general meeting with a lower quorum (s 371(2)).

Quorum

There are several instances where meetings of one have been held to be valid: s 367 – Secretary of State calling an annual general meeting of a company and fixing the quorum at one; s 371 – application to the court to call a meeting and fix the quorum at one; a class meeting where there is only one member of the class – *East v Bennett Bros*; a meeting of a private company which only has one member.

It seems that a meeting is valid even where there is an audio-video link with another room, see *Byng v London Life Association*.

Resolutions

If a special or extraordinary resolution is to be put to the vote at a meeting then it should be set out verbatim in the notice as should any amendment. In practice, ordinary resolutions are also set out verbatim in the notice. Any substantive amendment should also be set out in the notice.

Under the Companies Act 1989, provisions were introduced to permit private companies to resolve matters by unanimous written resolutions without the need for a meeting.

It is also possible for private companies to take advantage of the elective regime and agree to certain courses. This can be done by unanimous resolution or unanimous written resolution.

The provisions are: dispensing with the annual laying of accounts; dispensing with the need to appoint auditors annually; dispensing with the need to hold a general meeting annually; allowing a company to grant a power to issue shares to directors with indefinite duration; providing that an extraordinary general meeting may be held on short notice if 90% of the company's shareholders agree rather than the usual 95%.

Votes

Initially, a vote is taken on a show of hands. This is not conclusive of the matter, however, except in two instances where the articles may state that a vote on a show of hands is decisive – namely, election of the chairman and adjournment of the meeting (s 373(1) of the Companies Act 1985). In every other circumstance, a poll may be demanded by not less than five members or by members representing 10% of the voting rights or by members holding shares in the company conferring a right to vote at the meeting being shares on which an aggregate sum has been paid up equal to not less than 10% of the total sum paid up on all the shares conferring that right.

Where a vote is taken on a poll, the outcome overrides the outcome on a show of hands.

Proxies

A member entitled to attend and vote at a meeting of a company with share capital may appoint somebody else to attend and vote in his place as a proxy. The notice sent to members must set out their right to appoint a proxy.

In a private company, a proxy may speak. Proxies may only vote on a poll. Unless the articles provide otherwise, a member is limited to one proxy in a private company situation.

Adjournment

The chairman of the meeting may adjourn the meeting if it is appropriate to do so – for example, to preserve order – and he must do so if so directed by the company.

Minutes

Companies must cause minutes of general meetings to be kept in a minute book kept for that purpose.

Chapter 16

Accounts, Annual Return, Auditors

Every company is obliged to keep accounting records to explain the company's transactions and such that they disclose at any time the financial position of the company and such that they enable the directors to ensure that any balance sheet and profit and loss account prepared under the Act satisfy the Act's requirements (s 221 of the Companies Act 1985). Private companies must keep records for three years and public companies for six years (s 222 of the Companies Act 1985).

16.1   Accounts

A company must prepare a balance sheet and a profit and loss account (s 226 of the Companies Act 1985). The balance sheet should give a true and fair view of the state of affairs of the company at the end of the financial year and the profit and loss account should give a true and fair view of the profit or loss of the company for the financial year (s 226(2) of the Companies Act 1985). Companies within groups must as well as filing individual company accounts file group accounts for the group as a whole with a consolidated balance sheet and profit and loss account for the group as a whole (s 227 of the Companies Act 1985). (The definition of holding and subsidiary company has already been considered at para 2.2.1.)

Section 241 provides that accounts must be laid before the general meeting and s 242 provides that copies must be delivered to the registrar except for certain unlimited companies.

Every company must attach to the balance sheet and profit and loss account a directors' report (s 234 of the Companies Act 1985 and Sched 7 of the Act). The report should give details of the general nature of the business, changes in its asset values, directors' shareholdings, political and charitable donations, acquisition of its own shares, training matters, policy to the disabled, health and safety matters and employee participation policy.

Small and medium sized companies, defined by turnover, balance sheet total and the number of employees they engage, are entitled to certain filing exemptions in relation to the balance sheet, profit and loss account and directors' report (ss 246–49 of the Companies Act 1985 and Sched 8 of the Act). However, the company's members are entitled to the full information unless the company has passed an elective resolution (see para 15.5.9).

The company's accounts and directors' report should be approved by the board and signed on behalf of the board (s 233, s 234A of the Companies Act 1985). The company's auditors generally must report on the annual accounts and directors' report and the auditors' report should be laid before the company's members and filed with the accounts at the company's registry (the functioning and duties of auditors are considered below at para 16.3.4). The government has exempted private companies with an annual turnover of less than £350,000 from the usual audit requirements by the Companies Act 1985 (Audit Exemption) (Amendment) Regulations 1997 which amended s 249A of the Companies Act 1985.

This exemption does not come into play if members holding 10% or more of the company's capital (or representing 10% or more in number if the company has no share capital) require an audit.

16.2   Annual return

Every company must file an annual return each year with the registrar of companies (s 363 of the Companies Act 1985). This sets out:

- the address of the registered office;

- the type of company and its principal business;

- the name and addresses of directors and the company secretary and certain additional information in respect of directors;

- the place the registers of members and debentureholders are kept;

- the issued share capital;

- a list of members and those ceasing to be members within the year. There are now provisions to ensure that if this information has been given within the last two years then only an update is needed;

- details of any elective resolutions relating to the holding of annual general meetings and laying of accounts (see para 15.5.9).

Since the Companies Act 1989 a new simpler system of 'shuttle return' is employed. The registrar thus sends to the company the information which he has from the last return and the company amends it (if necessary) and returns it.

Every company must appoint auditors except companies which are dormant and private companies which are exempt from the audit requirement (s 384 of the Companies Act 1985).

Auditors are generally appointed at the first general meeting at which accounts are laid and are then appointed annually at successive general meetings at which accounts are laid (s 385 of the Companies Act 1985). The first auditors may be appointed by the directors of the company before the first general meeting of the company and such auditors will then hold office until the conclusion of that meeting (s 385 of the Companies Act 1985).

In the case of private companies which have elected to dispense with the laying of accounts, they must appoint auditors within 28 days of the date when accounts are sent to the company's members. This should be done at general meeting (s 385A of the Companies Act 1985). However, it is possible that private companies may elect additionally to dispense with the annual appointment of auditors. When this occurs, then the auditors are deemed to be reappointed for each succeeding year on the expiry of the time for appointing auditors for that year (s 386 of the Companies Act 1985).

An auditor may be removed by ordinary resolution of the company (s 391 of the Companies Act 1985).

In the case of removal of an auditor, however, special notice must be served (see para 10.5). The auditor is entitled to make written representations which are to be circulated to members of the company. The auditor retains a right to compensation for breach of contract.

An auditor may resign from office by depositing a notice in writing to that effect at the company's registered office (s 392 of the Companies Act 1985). He must at the time of resigning also deposit a statement setting out any circumstances connected with his resignation from office which he considers should be brought to the attention of the company's members or creditors, or a statement that there are no such circumstances. If there are circumstances which the auditor wishes to bring to the attention of the company, the company must within 14 days of the deposit of the statement send copies to the people entitled to copies of the accounts (basically members and debenture holders), or if it considers it contains defamatory matter apply to the court to ask that the matter should not be circulated. Where an auditor does deposit a statement of circumstances which he wishes to bring to the attention of members or creditors, he may deposit a requisition with the statement requiring the company to call an extraordinary general meeting (s 392A of the Companies Act 1985).

16.3   Auditors

16.3.1   Appointment, removal and resignation

The auditor who is removed or who has resigned is still entitled to notice of the general meeting at which it is proposed to fill the vacancy that his ceasing to hold office has created (s 391(4) of the Companies Act 1985 and s 392A(8) of the Companies Act 1985).

16.3.2   Remuneration of auditors

Where auditors are appointed by the general meeting, the remuneration should be decided by the general meeting (s 390A(1) of the Companies Act 1985). If the auditors are appointed by the company's directors, they should fix the remuneration and if by the Secretary of State, where there has been default, he should do so (s 390A(2) of the Companies Act 1985).

16.3.3   Qualification of auditors

Section 289 of the Companies Act 1985 sets out the recognised bodies for the purposes of qualification as a company's auditor. The Companies Act 1989 amended the law to bring British law into line with the 8th EC Company Law Directive on auditors. The Act establishes recognised supervisory bodies for supervising auditors. The recognised bodies in the United Kingdom are:

- The Institute of Chartered Accountants in England and Wales;

- The Institute of Chartered Accountants in Scotland;

- The Chartered Association of Certified Accountants;

- The Association of Authorised Public Accountants;

- The Institute of Chartered Accountants in Ireland.

The Secretary of State may recognise similar qualifications obtained outside of the United Kingdom for these purposes.

An individual or a firm may be appointed as auditor as may a body corporate.

A person is not qualified to act as auditor if he is an officer or servant of the company or a person who is employed by or is a partner of any officer or servant of the company. A person cannot act as auditor if he is an officer or servant of the company's holding or subsidiary companies or an employee or partner of such officer or servant. A person is also disqualified if there exists a close connection such as a close family link eg the company to be audited is controlled by the spouse of the auditor.

16.3.4   Auditors' duties

The auditors should audit the company's accounts (s 236 of the Companies Act 1985).

In conducting the audit, an auditor is now obliged to take a much stricter approach to his client, physically checking the stock, advising of unsatisfactory practices, and scrupulously following up any suspicious circumstances.

His best protection is professional insurance. A clear unequivocal letter of appointment from his client is also desirable. It will remind him of what he has agreed to do.

He should beware of giving *ad hoc* advice and if he does so should stress it is provisional and not to be relied upon. Even here the extent to which he can disclaim liability is limited by the Unfair Contract Terms Act 1977. The Institute's revised Statement on Unlawful Acts or Defaults by Clients of Members provides that:

> A member who acquires knowledge indicating that a client may have been guilty of some default or unlawful act should normally raise the matter with the management of the client at an appropriate level. If his concerns are not satisfactorily resolved, he should consider reporting the matter to non-executive directors or to the client's audit committee where these exist. Where this is not possible or he fails to resolve the matter a member may wish to consider making a report to a third party.

This is, of course, in addition to any statutory or common law obligations placed upon an auditor. An auditor's statutory duties cannot be restricted by the company's articles or by any contract between him and the company (s 310 of the Companies Act 1985). He may, however, be relieved by the court under s 727 of the Act.

An auditor's basic duties have been lucidly and uncontroversially outlined by Lord Denning:

First, the auditor should verify the arithmetical accuracy of the accounts and the proper vouching of entries in the books.

Secondly, the auditor should make checks to test whether the accounts mask errors or even dishonesty.

Thirdly, the auditor should report on whether the accounts give to the shareholders reliable information respecting the true financial position of the company. An auditor must approach his work, *per* Lord Denning in *Fomento (Sterling Area) Ltd v Selsdon Fountain Pen Co Ltd*:

> ... with an inquiring mind – not suspicious of dishonesty ... but suspecting that someone may have made a mistake somewhere and that a check must be made to ensure that there has been none.

The main obligations of an auditor are to audit the accounts of the company and to report to the company on the accounts laid before the company in general meeting during his tenure of office (s 235 of the Companies Act 1985).

These are the basic statements of what an accountant should ensure in auditing a company's balance sheet and profit and loss account but it is proposed to examine these duties in more detail.

Much of the case law is of decidedly Victorian flavour; too much is now at stake in terms of financial amount and prestige for many cases to get beyond the doors of the High Court and one can only speculate on the basis of out of court settlements.

16.3.5   Auditors' liabilities

The starting point of any survey of auditor's liability is the famous *dictum* of Lopes LJ in *Re Kingston Cotton Mill* (1896), that 'an auditor is not bound to be a detective ... he is a watchdog but not a bloodhound'. The auditors in this case had taken on trust a management assessment of the amount of yarn in stock, failing to make a physical check themselves. The assessments were frauds which had been perpetrated by a manager to make the company appear to flourish by exaggerating the quantity and value of cotton and yarn in the company's mills.

The auditors took the entry of the stock-in-trade at the beginning of the year from the last preceding balance sheet, and they took the values of the stock-in-trade at the end of the year from the stock journal.

The book contained a series of accounts under various heads purporting to show the quantities and values of the company's stock-in-trade at the end of each year and a summary of the accounts which was adopted by the auditors.

The auditors always ensured that the summary corresponded with the accounts but they did not enquire into the accuracy of the accounts. The auditors were held not liable; the court concluded they were entitled to accept the certificate of a responsible official. This is a decision that would almost certainly be reversed today. The *dictum* of Lopes LJ, however, still finds approval and has fossilised into an immovable principle of law, though it is now generally accepted that an auditor is a watchdog which must bark loudly and relentlessly at any suspicious circumstance.

At the outset of the audit, an auditor must familiarise himself with the company's memorandum and articles of association, so that he can ensure that payments shown in the accounts have been properly incurred. It will be no defence to assert that he has not read these company documents.

In *Leeds Estate Building and Investment Co v Shepherd* (1887), the terms of the articles had not been carried out, and it was held that it was no excuse that the auditor has not seen them. As a result of this neglect dividends, directors' fees and bonuses were improperly paid and the auditor was therefore held liable for damages.

An auditor is required to investigate suspicious circumstances. In *Re Thomas Gerrard* (1967), Pennycuick J noted that 'the standards of reasonable care and skill are, upon the expert evidence more exacting than those which prevailed in 1896' (*Re Kingston Cotton Mill*). Here, in addition to an overstatement of stock, there had been fraudulent practice in changing invoice dates to make it appear that clients owed money within the accounting period when in fact it was due outside of it and to make it appear that suppliers were not yet owed money for goods when such liability did exist.

In holding Kevans, the auditors, to be liable, Pennycuick J considered that the changed invoice dates should have aroused suspicion:

> I find the conclusion inescapable, alike on the expert evidence and as a matter of business common sense that at this stage (of discovering the altered invoice dates) he ought to have examined the suppliers' statements and where necessary have communicated with the suppliers.

16.3.6   USA experience

In the absence of much British authority, transatlantic experience is instructive for the accounting standards adopted in Britain and the USA are similar.

In the USA, in 1939, there occurred a case of far-reaching significance, *McKesson & Robins*, which involved the most ingenious of frauds. The fraud was engineered by four brothers who were operating under different names and who accomplished a massive deception in the operation of a wholly fictitious crude drug business.

Purchases were claimed to have been made by the McKesson company from Canadian vendors who, it was alleged, sold the goods on to customers. The firms to whom it was alleged that the goods had been sold were real but had done no business of the type claimed. The Canadian vendors were either fictitious or blinds used to support the fictitious transactions. The fraud was supported by fictitious invoicing, advice notes and records of communication. The auditors, Price Waterhouse, failed to discover the fraud. The stocks and debtors of the company were consequently overstated by $23 million.

The US Securities and Exchange Commission was extremely critical of the practice of the auditors, emphasising the need for physical contact with the inventory and the case led to a general change in auditing practice.

The report stated:

It is unusually clear to us that prior to this case many independent public accountants depended entirely too much upon the verification of cash as the basis for the whole auditing programme and hence as underlying proof of the authenticity of all transactions. Where, as here, during the final three years of the audit, physical contact with the operations of a major portion of the business was limited to examinations of supposed documentary evidence of transactions carried on completely off-stage through agents unknown to the auditors ... it appears to us that the reliability of these agents must be established by completely independent methods.

Another notorious US case is also instructive. This is the Salad Oil Swindle case of 1963. De Angelis, an Italian American had built up a massive vegetable oil empire. He was able to negotiate warehouse receipts from American Express to commodity brokers on the basis of his stock.

The stocktaking exercise affords an illustration of the ludicrous acceptance of fiction as fact. De Angelis' employees would climb to the top of each tank to make a depth sounding of the oil which would be shouted down to the American Express man below, who would slavishly take down the figures. While the team moved from one vat to the next the oil would be pumped from one tank to the adjacent one and this process would continue throughout the warehouse.

The case has had a salutary effect on auditing practice in the USA and in England. The importance of a physical stock check is now established. An auditor is unwise to take anything on trust from his client, it is advisable to treat any management statement or assertion with healthy suspicion. Thus, a check should be made of petty cash held (random checks for large firms are probably sufficient). Thus, in *London Oil Storage Co Ltd v Seear Hasluck & Co* (1904), where the auditors failed to check the petty cash which according to the books amounted to £760 but which in fact amounted to £30 they were held liable in damages.

The balance of moneys in the bank should be verified by a bank statement (*Fox v Morrish* (1918)) and similarly certificates of investments held should be examined (*Re City Equitable Fire, Insurance Co Ltd* (1925)).

It may thus be seen that auditing practice has blown the sails of legal practice on a fresh tack so that now the standard expected of an auditor is much higher than at the time of *Re Kingston Cotton Mill*. An auditor might still not be a bloodhound but he must be a watchdog at the very peak of his performance and must never go to sleep on the audit – even with one eye open!

Liability may arise in contract. The auditor will be liable for failing to perform properly what he has undertaken to do. The other party to the contract – the company – is the only person who can sue the auditor under this head of liability.

16.3.7   The auditor's contractual liability

The extent of the auditor's liability will be to pay damages resulting from the breach of contract if the damages are in the contemplation of the parties, for instance if the breach is for failure to detect fraud, damages will be awarded to compensate for further fraud that has been perpetrated after the date when the fraud should have been detected.

An auditor may be liable in negligence to his client or to third parties. Formerly it was the law that there was no duty owed to third parties to exercise care in drawing up accounts. In *Candler v Crane Christmas & Co* (1951), the auditors prepared inaccurate accounts which were relied upon by the plaintiff as the basis of investing money in the company. A majority of the Court of Appeal refused to allow an action in such circumstances.

16.3.8   The auditor's delictual liability

However, in an historic decision in *Hedley Byrne v Heller* (1964), the House of Lords overruled the *Candler* decision. Liability could henceforth arise where an auditor knew or ought to have known that his report would be relied upon and he was negligent in preparing it. Initially, the precise scope of an auditor's liability was not clear. The Institute of Chartered Accountants amongst others took an optimistic view that it was limited to those persons whom the auditor specifically knew would rely upon the audited accounts.

This view was blown sky high by *JEB Fasteners v Marks Bloom & Co (a firm)* (1981), affirmed on other grounds (1983). In 1975, the defendants had audited the accounts of JEB Fasteners. The audited accounts massively overvalued the company's stock. JEB Fasteners had read the negligently audited accounts. Woolf J held that the defendants owed a duty to the plaintiffs. In the event, there was no liability as the judge held that the negligently audited accounts did not induce the purchase. Woolf J relied on his judgment in an earlier unreported English case, *Grover Industrial Holdings Ltd v Newman Harris & Co* (1976) and the judgment of Stocker J in that case, as well as two Commonwealth authorities, the

Canadian case of *Haig v Bamford, Hagan, Wicken & Gibson* (1976) and the New Zealand case of *Scott Group Ltd v McFarlane* (1978). Both resulted in liability being placed on auditors in similar circumstances to JEB Fasteners.

In the later Scottish case of *Twomax Ltd v Dickson, McFarlane and Robinson* (1982), Twomax had acquired a majority stake in a private company, Kintyre Knitwear Ltd. Twomax claimed that in purchasing shares in the company it had relied upon the accounts negligently prepared by the defenders. The court held that the audit was perfunctory and negligent and the auditors were held liable in damages to the pursuers.

In *Caparo Industries plc v Dickman & Others* (1990), the House of Lords considered the position of the liability of an audit firm. The third defendants were the auditors Touche Ross. The first and second defendants were the chairman and chief executive of a company called Fidelity. The contention of the plaintiff Caparo was that it was misled by the fraudulent misrepresentations of the first and second defendants which the third defendants, the auditors, had been negligent in failing to detect and report. The House of Lords considered the possible liability of the auditors. It was held in the circumstances that the auditors did not have liability. The auditors owed a duty to the company and not to individual shareholders.

It is clear post-*Caparo* that liability is restricted to cases where the auditor knows of the user and the use to which he will put the information. Even here an auditor will not be liable in negligence if he reasonably believes that the user will also seek independent advice, compare *James McNaughten Paper Group v Hicks Anderson* (1991) with *Morgan Crucible Co v Hill Samuel Bank Ltd* (1991). See also *Anthony v Wright* (1994) where it was held that a company's auditors do not owe a duty to investors in the company to spot fraud committed by the directors which results in the investment being lost, even where the auditors are aware of a relationship of trust which subsists between the company and its investors.

These cases are concerned with the existence of a duty on the part of the auditors. In *Galoo Ltd v Bright, Grahame and Murray* (1994), the Court of Appeal applied another limiting factor – that of causation. Even where auditors are negligent in the auditing of accounts, if reliance on these accounts is not the predominant cause of the pursuer's loss, the pursuer will not succeed.

16.3.9   The auditor's statutory liability

An auditor may be liable in a winding up for misfeasance or breach of duty to the company (s 212 of the Insolvency

Act 1986). If this were to be so the court will order whatever compensation it thinks fit.

Thus, the class of persons to whom an auditor may be liable is somewhat larger than originally envisaged.

16.3.10   Conclusion

If liability is proved, damages are awarded to compensate the plaintiff for the loss he has sustained by reason of the negligence of the auditor in so far as the losses that they compensate are foreseeable consequences of the auditor's breach of duty.

The possibility of an auditor exempting himself from liability in both contract and delict is now limited to reasonable exemptions (ss 2(2), 2(3) of the Unfair Contract Terms Act 1977), quite apart from the unacceptability of such exemptions from the profession's point of view.

Accounts, Annual Return, Auditors

Accounts

Every company is obliged to keep accounting records. They must be retained for six years if the company is public and three if it is private.

Companies must prepare annual accounts – a balance sheet and profit and loss account and groups must also submit group accounts for the group as a whole. There must also be a directors' report and an auditors' report. The accounts and reports must generally be laid before the company's members and for all except certain unlimited companies they must also be filed at the company's registry. There are certain exemptions in filing information for small and medium sized companies.

Annual return

Every company must file an annual return concerning information about the company's activities, officers, shares and debentures. There is now a simplified 'shuttle return' procedure for updating existing information.

Auditors

All companies except dormant companies and certain exempt private companies must appoint auditors. The auditors have statutory protection if they are to be removed from office. They also have rights to bring matters to the attention of members where they resign.

Auditors must be qualified with a recognised body.

The auditor must adopt a strict approach in conducting the audit. There is a statutory obligation to report to the company on the accounts (s 236 of the Companies Act 1985). There will also be contractual duties owed to the company flowing from the contract concluded between the company and the auditors.

Auditors also owe a duty of care to third parties whom they know are going to rely on the audited accounts for specific purposes without the benefit of other independent advice.

Chapter 17

Company Secretary

One hundred years ago, a company secretary would have found his powers were few. The question of the authority of the company secretary was considered many years ago in *Barnett Hoares & Co v South London Tramways Co* (1887).

In this case, the South London Tramways Co had made an agreement with Messrs Green & Burleigh who were contractors to construct part of the tramline. The company, as is common in building and construction contracts, retained a certain percentage of the amounts for which their engineer had certified completion, since Green & Burleigh were to maintain the line for a period of time. The retention money was payable to the contractors at the end of this period. The contractors had applied to the bankers, Barnett Hoares & Co, for a loan and had given them as security a letter which purported to assign to them to retention money of £2,000 under the contract.

The bankers had then written to the Tramway company's secretary for the confirmation that £2,000 was held and the required confirmation had been given. When Barnett Hoares were not paid back by the contractors, they had claimed the retention money. They then discovered that only £675 was held as retention money, despite the written assurances of the secretary. The issue in the case they brought against the company concerned the authority of the company secretary. Had he had the authority to bind the company?

The outcome in the case was clear and unequivocal: the company secretary had not had the authority to bind the company.

As Lord Esher MR said:

> A secretary is a mere servant; his position is that he is to do what he is told and no person can assume that he has any authority to represent anything at all, nor can anyone assume that statements made by him are necessarily to be accepted as trustworthy without further enquiry ...

This decision is reflected in contemporary Scottish cases – for example, *Niven v Collins Patent Lever Gear Co Ltd* (1900) and *Edington v Dumbar Steam Laundry Co* (1903). However, a company would be personally barred from denying the validity of share certificates signed by the secretary, even without the company's authority, since the secretary is the

17.1 Introduction

proper person to issue share certificates – see *Clavering v Goodwin, Jardine & Co* (1891).

Things have changed. In 1971, the Court of Appeal again considered the role and significance of the company secretary in *Panorama Developments (Guildford) Ltd v Fidelis Furnishing Fabrics Ltd* (1971).

Panorama Developments (Guildford) Ltd ran a car hire business which was called Belgravia Executive Car Rental. The company fleet comprised limousines which included Rolls-Royces and Jaguars. Fidelis Furnishing Fabrics Ltd was a company of good repute, and its managing director was a man of integrity. However, its company secretary R L Bayne was not of the same cloth. He told Panorama that Fidelis wished to hire cars so that he could meet important customers at Heathrow Airport. He claimed that he took these customers to the company's office and the company's factory in Leeds.

This was not true. No customers were met at Heathrow and the company did not have a factory in Leeds. The cars had been used by Bayne personally. Panorama sued Fidelis Fabrics for their hire charges.

As in the earlier *Barnett* case, the defendants argued that they were not bound by the acts of their company secretary, who fulfils a very humble role and has no authority to make any contracts or representations on behalf of the company. However, the Court of Appeal decided that, on the contrary, the company secretary had bound the company. In considering the *Barnett* case, Lord Denning MR said:

> But times have changed. A company secretary is a much more important person nowadays than he was in 1887. He is an officer of the company with extensive duties and responsibilities. This appears not only in the modern Companies Acts, but also by the role which he plays in the day-to-day business of companies. He is no longer a mere clerk. He regularly makes representations on behalf of the company and enters into contracts on its behalf which come within the day-to-day running of the company's business. So much so that he may be regarded as held out as having authority to do such things on behalf of the company. He is certainly entitled to sign contracts connected with the administrative side of a company's affairs, such as employing staff, and ordering cars, and so forth. All such matters now come within the ostensible authority of a company secretary.

Today, then, the company secretary is one of the principal officers of the company and he is the agent through whom much of the company's administrative work is done. Indeed, when making contracts on behalf of the company, it is advisable for the secretary to ensure that he does so as agent of the company to avoid any personal liability.

As an officer, the secretary will be liable to a default fine for contravention along with directors under many provisions of the Companies Acts. The Department of Trade brings many prosecutions for offences under the Companies Acts, especially concerning failures to lodge documents with the registrar of companies.

Although not previously the case in Scotland (see *Scottish Poultry Journal Co* (1896)), the company secretary will now in all probability be an employee, entitled as a 'clerk or servant' to rank as a preferential creditor and as such will be paid off first in a liquidation. However, secretaries who do not give their whole time to the company and perform their duties through a deputy are not within the scope of the provision. This was decided in the case of *Cairney v Back* (1906).

In this case, the company secretary of Consolidated Mines Ltd had to attend directors' meetings, deal with the correspondence and callers and keep the minute book. Mr Justice Walton considered that, if the evidence had stopped there, then the defendant would have been a clerk or servant. However, although the defendant was generally at the office from 12 pm to 2 pm, he had no particular hours of attendance. He also paid a clerk who worked regularly from 10 am to 5 pm. In other words, the general work of the company falling within his purview was really done by the clerk. The defendant did not, therefore, exactly serve the company. Rather, he provided services, attending himself occasionally when required. So he was not an employee.

17.2 Duties of the secretary

As an officer, the secretary owes fiduciary duties to the company and is liable for any secret gain made from the company. An illustration of this principle is *Re Morvah Consols Tin Mining Co* (1876). One James Hammon sold a tin mine in Cornwall to a certain McKay, who set up a company to purchase the mine. McKay became company secretary. Hammon was to be paid partly in cash and partly in shares, and McKay was to receive some shares for setting up the deal. The company knew nothing of this.

Later, the company was wound up by the Stannary Court. (The tin mines of Devon and Cornwall, or Stannaries, were formerly subject to a special legal regime. The jurisdiction is now exercised by the Cornish County Court.) McKay was ordered to pay over the value of the shares to the liquidator because he was in breach of his fiduciary duty.

Any provision in the company's articles, or in any contract between the company and the secretary or otherwise, for exempting any officer from liability for negligence, default, breach of duty or breach of trust is void (s 310 of the Companies Act 1985). However, if it appears to the court in any proceedings that the secretary has acted honestly and reasonably and that in all the circumstances he ought to be excused, the court may relieve him wholly or partly of any liability (s 727 of the Companies Act 1985).

17.3   Responsibilities of the secretary

Formerly, when companies tended to be smaller, their affairs less complex and the legal requirements less onerous, the company secretary was typically a clerk who was employed to perform routine work under orders. Today, the responsibilities of the company secretary would usually include the following:

- The preparation and keeping of minutes of board and general meetings (s 382 of the Companies Act 1985).

- Dealing with share transfers and issuing share and debenture certificates.

- Keeping and maintaining the register of members and debenture holders (s 352 and s 190 of the Companies Act 1985) (in large public companies a professional share registrar often maintains these registers as well as dealing with share transfers).

- Keeping and maintaining the register of directors and secretary (s 288 of the Companies Act 1985).

- The registration of charges and the maintaining of the company's register of charges (s 415 and s 422 of the Companies Act 1985).

- Keeping and maintaining the register of directors' share interests (s 325 of the Companies Act 1985), directors' contracts (s 318 of the Companies Act 1985), and the collation of directors' interests that have to be disclosed (s 232 and Sched 6 of the Companies Act 1985).

- Keeping and maintaining the register of material share interests (s 211 of the Companies Act 1985).

- Sending notices of meetings, copies of accounts, etc.

- Keeping the company's memorandum and articles up to date.

- Preparation and submission of the annual return (ss 363–65 of the Companies Act 1985).

- Filing with the registrar of numerous returns and documents.

- Preparation of the numerous returns required by government departments and official bodies.

- Witnessing documents, that is, signing as witness (together with a director) against the company seal or otherwise.

- Payment of dividends and the preparation of dividend warrants.

Depending on the size of the headquarters staff, the company secretary may also be the chief accounting officer, have charge of staff employment and pension matters, obtain legal advice from solicitors and confer with the auditors. If the company is quoted, he or she may also deal with the Stock Exchange. It is entirely possible that still other responsibilities may be placed upon the secretary by the company's articles.

17.4   Qualifications

Because of the great welter of statutory duties and the increasing responsibilities placed on company secretaries, it was inevitable that a company secretary should have to possess a relevant qualification. Although there are no mandatory qualifications for a company secretary of a private company, there are for a public company. According to s 286 of the Companies Act 1985, it is the duty of directors of a public company to take all reasonable steps to ensure that the secretary or each joint secretary of the company is a person with the requisite knowledge and experience and who:

- was the secretary or the assistant or the deputy secretary of the company on the appointed day; or

- was the secretary of a public company for at least three of the five years immediately preceding the appointment as secretary; or

- is a member of one of the following professional bodies:

  (a) The Institute of Chartered Accountants in England and Wales;

  The Institute of Chartered Accountants of Scotland;

  The Association of Certified Accountants;

  The Institute of Chartered Accountants in Ireland;

  The Institute of Chartered Secretaries and Accountants;

  The Institute of Cost and Management Accountants;

  The Chartered Institute of Public Finance and Accountancy;

  or

  (b) is qualified in the United Kingdom as a barrister, or an advocate or a solicitor; or

(c)   is a person who by virtue of holding or having held any other position or being a member of any other body, appears to the directors to be capable of discharging the functions of a secretary.

It should be noted that the obligation is a continuing one so that, for example, if a person ceases to hold an appropriate qualification, the directors should reconsider his appointment.

It is somewhat ironic that there should be minimum qualifications for the company secretary of a public company but not for directors. Nothing could better illustrate the change in the role of the company secretary and the law's perception of this.

17.5   Conclusion

As the flow of companies legislation has increased, the role of the company secretary has become of increasing importance. The company secretary fills a key post in the corporate environment.

A daunting list of duties and responsibilities awaits the person who is appointed to the position. It has often been said that it is not an honour to be elected to a board of directors but a serious obligation. This is even more true of the post of company secretary where the office has evolved from one of mere service to one of important administration – in many ways eclipsing the directorship in legal significance.

Summary of Chapter 17

Company Secretary

The office of company secretary is of far more significance than one hundred years ago. Today, a company secretary is likely to have many important administrative functions to perform.

Responsibilities include: the preparation and keeping of minutes of board and general meetings (s 382 of the CA 85); dealing with share transfers and issuing share and debenture certificates; keeping and maintaining the register of members and debenture holders (ss 352 and 190 of the CA 85); keeping and maintaining the register of directors and secretary (s 288 of the CA 85); the registration of charges and the maintaining of the company's register of charges (ss 399 and 407 of the CA 85); keeping and maintaining the register of directors' share interests (s 325 of the CA 85), directors' contracts (s 318 of the CA 85), and the collation of directors' interests that have to be disclosed (s 232 and Sched 6 of the CA 85); sending notices of meetings, copies of accounts; keeping the company's memorandum and articles up to date; preparation and submission of the annual return (ss 363–65 of the CA 85); payment of dividends and the preparation of dividend warrants.

Responsibilities

The secretary owes fiduciary duties to the company and is liable for any secret gain made from the company: *Re Morvah Consols Tin Mining Co* (1876). Any provision in the company's articles, or in any contract between the company and the secretary or otherwise, for exempting any officer from liability for negligence, default, breach of duty or breach of trust is void (s 310 of the CA 85).

Duties

In a public company, a company secretary must possess a recognised qualification.

Qualifications

A company secretary may be a director but need not be one.

Chapter 18

Debentures and Securities

A trading company has an implied power to borrow and to grant securities (called 'charges' in England) over any of its assets – see *General Auction Co v Smith* (1891). A company may, however, expressly provide within its memorandum or articles for powers to borrow and to grant securities. These express provisions may limit the company's powers, or the powers of those who act on the company's behalf, but may not allow the company to override provisions contained in the Companies Acts. Any express limitation imposed by the company's constitution is now subject to the provisions of ss 35 and 35A (see 5.10).

Usually, if a company wishes to raise loan capital it will issue debentures. Debentures merely represent a creditor's interest in a company (as, in a similar way, shares represent a member's interest). Under s 744, the term 'debenture' includes 'debenture stock, bonds and any other securities of a company, whether constituting a charge on the assets of the company or not'. A debenture was described in *Levy v Abercorn's Slate and Slab Co* (1887) as 'a document which creates or acknowledges a debt'. In practice, the term 'debenture' is normally used to represent secured borrowing.

18.1 Definition of debentures

Debentures and shares have certain similarities. They are both collectively termed securities. Dealings in debentures on The Stock Exchange are carried out in much the same way as dealings in shares. Prospectus rules are applicable to both shares and debentures in much the same way. There are certain distinctions between shares and debentures, however.

18.2 Debentures compared with shares

The main distinctions are as follows:

- the essential distinction between the two is that a debentureholder is a creditor of the company whereas a shareholder is a member of the company;

- the company is free to purchase its own debentures;

- debentures may be issued at a discount whereas shares cannot, see s 100 of the Companies Act 1985;

- interest on a debenture when due is a debt which can be paid out of capital. There is no automatic right to a dividend and dividends are payable only out of profits.

18.3 Types of debentures

Debentures may be secured or unsecured. Securities may take the form of fixed or floating charges and give the debentureholder rights exercisable over the company's assets. An unsecured debentureholder ranks only as an ordinary creditor if the company winds up.

Debentures may be redeemable or irredeemable. A redeemable debenture may provide that it may be redeemed by the company on a certain date. A redeemed debenture may be re-issued by the company. Irredeemable (or perpetual) debentures specify no date for redemption. Redemption may only be demanded by the holder if the company winds up or if it breaches any conditions attached to the debenture. The company, however, may normally redeem a perpetual debenture at any time. Irredeemable debentures are permitted by s 193 and recognised in Scotland in s 2 of the Redemption of Standard Securities (Scotland) Act 1971 (see also the English case of *Knightsbridge Estates Trust Ltd v Byrne* (1940)).

Convertible debentures (allowing the holder the option of converting the debentures into shares) may be issued if authorised by the articles or by the company in general meeting. However, these may not be issued in order to circumvent the rule that shares must not be issued at a discount – see *Mosely v Koffyfontein Mines Ltd* (1904).

A debenture may be registered (where the lender's particulars are entered in the company's register of debentureholders) or unregistered (a bearer debenture) where it has the status of a negotiable instrument (a freely transferable document providing for payment by the company to the bearer a particular sum on a particular date).

Debentures may be issued singly (for example, to acknowledge or secure a loan from a bank) or in series.

18.4 Ranking of debentures

Debentures rank according to date of issue or in numerical order where more than one debenture is issued on the same day, unless they expressly state otherwise. Thus, if a company wishes to raise loan capital by issuing a number of debentures these must expressly provide for *pari passu* ranking *inter se* or else the holder of debenture number one must be paid in full before the holder of debenture number two receives anything, and so on.

A way around this which confers a number of advantages to all concerned is to issue debenture stock along with a debenture trust deed. The principal creditor in such an arrangement is the trustee and the debenture stock holders will be the beneficiaries of the trust who will automatically rank *pari passu*. The trust deed will set out the terms of the loan, which may be enforced against the company by the trustees. This situation is easier to administer than if the company creates separate direct relationships with each of the individuals supplying funds.

Where there is a debenture trust deed, which there will be if debenture stock has been issued, the trustee acts as the company's creditor. He acts on behalf of all debentureholders. It is his duty to ensure that the terms of the debentures are enforced.

18.5   Debenture trust deeds

Certain conditions are uniform:

- a covenant to repay the amount of the loan at the appropriate time and to pay interest upon the due dates. In default of either of these requirements, the whole loan becomes immediately repayable;

- the creation of a floating charge over some or all of the company's assets;

- the creation of a fixed charge over the company's fixed assets;

- on the happening of certain events, the whole amount of the loan to become immediately repayable, for example, the company ceasing business;

- a covenant to keep the company's property insured;

- a covenant to keep the company's property in good repair;

- the powers and the duties of the debenture trustee will also be set out in the debenture trust deed.

The advantages of a debenture trust deed are clear. It enables the company to deal with the trustee for debenture holders on behalf of all of the debentureholders and thus to act expeditiously. The trustee for debentureholders will be supplied with information by the company on the state of the company's business. The trustee for debentureholders would generally be somebody expert in business and he will thus be able to act with alacrity and with expert knowledge where the debentureholders may lack the appropriate knowledge and would in any event find it difficult to act as promptly as the trustee for debentureholders.

Once it was common to exonerate trustees for debenture holders in advance for any breach of trust by a provision in the trust deed. Now, such provisions are generally void (s 192 of the Companies Act 1985). The court may, however, give relief to a trustee if he has acted honestly and reasonably and ought in fairness to be relieved (s 32 of the Trusts (Scotland) Act 1921 and s 61 of the Trustee Act 1925 in England). Individual debentureholders may also give a release to a trustee for past defaults, as may a meeting of debentureholders for the class of debentureholders by extraordinary resolution (s 192(2) of the Companies Act 1985).

18.6   Charges

The law on charges was amended by Part IV of the Companies Act 1989. In fact the new provisions have not been brought into force. The Department of Trade and Industry has issued a consultative document setting out three possible options for reform. (Company Law Reform: Proposal for the Reform of Part XII of the Companies Act 1985 (November 1994)). The main difficulty with the implementation of Part IV of the Companies Act 1989 was perceived to be that since the new Act only required certain particulars of the charge to be registered the conclusiveness of the registrar's certificate as to the registration of the charge in the instrument would end.

The three options put forward by the DTI are:

• retention of the old law as set out in Part XII of the Companies Act 1985;

• implementation of certain of the reforms of Part IV of the Companies Act 1989 with the introduction of some new reforms but not ending the conclusive certificate of registration;

• introduction of a system of notice filing where there would be registration of secured advances made to companies, retention of title clauses, etc.

The law set out here is as contained in the Companies Act 1985.

Although technically under s 744 of the Companies Act 1985, any form of borrowing by a company is a debenture, in practice the term is used to describe a secured borrowing. The borrowing may be secured in one or both of two different ways. The debenture may be secured by a fixed charge. This is similar to an ordinary mortgage. The charge attaches to the property subject to the charge at the time of its creation. A fixed charge over land is the most common form of fixed charge. The method of creation of a fixed charge over heritable property (land and buildings) in Scotland is by Standard Security under the Conveyancing and Feudal Reform (Scotland) Act 1970 and this must be registered in the Register of Sasines or the Lands Register for Scotland. A fixed charge may be created over other assets, however. A fixed charge over corporeal (tangible) moveable (anything except land or buildings) property will only be effective where the property is *pledged* (physically handed over to the creditor). A fixed charge over incorporeal (intangible) property must be created by an assignation in security which effectively transfers proprietory rights to the creditor pending repayment of the debt. Thus a fixed charge may be created over investments held by the company. It seems, in addition, that a fixed charge may be created over a company's book debts provided that these book debts are paid into a separate bank account, see *Siebe Gorman & Co Ltd v Barclays Bank Ltd* (1979), *Re Keenan Bros Ltd* (1986). In *Re New Bullas Trading Ltd* (1993), Knox J held that a charge over the company's book debts constituted a floating charge. It is also possible to create a floating charge over uncalled capital. However, in England at least, if uncalled capital has been constituted as reserve capital, a floating charge is not competent – *Re Mayfair Property Co, Bartlett v Mayfair Property Co* (1898). In *Re New Bullas Trading Ltd* (1994), the Court of Appeal, reversing Knox J, considered that the parties had created a fixed charge over uncollected book debts as long as they remain uncollected but a floating charge on realisation.

The floating charge is a relatively new phenomenon in Scotland. Although decipherable in English common law at least as far back as the last century, floating charges were only imported into Scotland by the Companies (Floating Charges) (Scotland) Act 1961. Prior to this date, a Scottish company could not create a floating charge over any of its assets, no matter where they were situated, nor could a floating charge created by an English company affect any of its assets which were situated in Scotland – see *Carse v Coppen* (1951).

18.7   A floating charge

Although the 1961 Act permitted the creation of floating charges in Scotland, it did not allow for the appointment of receivers. However, the Companies (Floating Charges and Receivers) (Scotland) Act 1972 replaced the 1961 Act and permitted the appointment of receivers. The relevant statutory provisions are now contained in Part XVIII of the Companies Act 1985 and in the Insolvency Act 1986.

The advantage of creating a floating charge is that it allows a company to raise loan capital on the strength of its assets without registration in the Register of Sasines or in the Lands Register for Scotland (in the case of heritage) or without delivery of the assets to the lender (in the case of moveables). Thus a company may use its assets to generate both loan capital and income. In fact, the company may dispose of existing assets conforming to the description in the charge although if it acquires additional similar assets these may become subject to the floating charge. In this way, the charge is said to 'float' over assets which from time to time form part of the company's property and undertaking.

There is no statutory definition of a floating charge – although s 462 of the Companies Act 1985 goes someway towards achieving this. However, although delivered in an English case, a description by the Lord Chancellor the Earl of Halsbury in the House of Lords in *Re Yorkshire Woolcombers Association Ltd (Illingworth v Houldsworth & Another)* (1904) is helpful:

> In the first place you have that which in a sense I suppose must be an element in the definition of a floating security, that it is something which is to float, not to be put into immediate operation, but such that the company is to be allowed to carry on its business. It contemplates not only that it should carry with it the book debts which were then existing, but it contemplates also the possibility of those book debts being extinguished by payment to the company, and that other book debts should come in and take the place of those that had disappeared. That, my Lords, seems to me to be an essential characteristic of what is properly called a floating security.

The charge continues to float until it attaches (the corresponding English term is crystallise). A floating charge attaches when either the company enters liquidation or when a receiver is appointed. The charge attaches as if it were a fixed security to property as described in the charge belonging to the company at the date of attachment, or which is subsequently acquired by the company if this is specified in the debenture – see *Ross v Taylor* (1985).

Under Scots law, a floating charge will attach to relevant assets comprised in the company's property and undertaking only upon either the appointment of a receiver or the commencement of the winding up of the company (see Chapter 23). It is worth noting that assets may still be regarded as forming part of the property and undertaking of the company if even although the company has contracted to dispose of these assets a real right has not yet been acquired by the purchaser. However, this rule appears to have been significantly eroded by the House of Lords decision in *Sharp v Thomson* (1997) – see para 18.12 below.

In addition to the benefits that the creation of a floating charge conveys from the company's point of view, the creditor also enjoys several advantages. A floating charge holder takes priority over any unsecured creditors (he must be paid in full before unsecured creditors may recover anything) and he may veto a proposed administration order (see Chapter 20). Also, in Scotland, a compulsory winding up may be ordered by the court if a floating chargeholder's security is 'in jeopardy' (s 122(2) of the Insolvency Act 1986).

In England, a floating charge will crystallise if:

- the company goes into liquidation;

- a receiver is appointed either by the court or under the terms of the debenture;

- there is cessation of the company's trade or business, *Re Woodroffes (Musical Instruments) Ltd* (1986);

- an event occurs which by the terms of the debenture causes the floating charge to crystallise.

There is doubt as to whether the happening of an event specified in the debenture would cause automatic crystallisation of the charge or whether the happening of the event merely permits the debentureholders to act to bring about crystallisation. In *Re Manurewa Transport Ltd* (1971), the New Zealand court held that crystallisation could occur automatically on the happening of the specified event. This view was approved *obiter* by Hoffmann J in *Re Brightlife Ltd* (1986) and confirmed by him in *Re Permanent House (Holdings) Ltd* (1989).

The charges that require registration are set out in s 410(4) of the Companies Act 1985. They are:

18.8   Registration of charges

- a security on land or an interest in land other than a charge for rent, ground annual, or other periodical sum payable in respect of land; but including a charge created by a heritable security within the meaning of s 9(8) of the Conveyancing and Feudal Reform (Scotland) Act 1970;

- a security over the uncalled share capital of a company;

- a security over incorporeal moveable property which includes:

  (a) book debts;

  (b) uncalled share capital of the company or calls made but not paid;

  (c) goodwill;

  (d) intellectual property;

- a security over a ship or aircraft or any share in a ship;

- a floating charge.

Section 410(2) of the Companies Act 1985 requires registration of prescribed particulars of most charges within 21 days of their creation. Failure to register the prescribed particulars of a charge renders the charge void. It does not affect the validity of the debt, of course. The charges that involve registration include charges on land, charges created to secure an issue of debentures and floating charges on the undertaking and assets of the company. The obligation to register the prescribed particulars of the charge is an obligation placed upon the company and therefore failure to register a charge constitutes an offence by the company and any officer who is involved. Since the creditor has an interest in registering the prescribed particulars of the charge, it may well be that he will undertake to effect the registration.

The Act requires that the prescribed particulars are delivered to the registrar of companies for registration.

The obligation to register prescribed particulars also extends to the situation where the company acquires a piece of property that is already mortgaged. Failure to register particulars of such a charge, however, does not render the charge invalid but merely results in the liability of the company and any officer in default. Provision is made in s 420 for late delivery of particulars to the registrar after the 21 days time limit has passed. Where prescribed particulars are registered in such a way, it is not void against an administrator or liquidator or any person who for value acquires an interest or right over the charged property unless a relevant event occurs within a specified time.

If at the time of delivery of the particulars, the company is unable to pay its debts as they fall due, or subsequently becomes unable to do so as a result of the transaction involving the charge and insolvency proceedings begin before the end of the relevant period, then the charge is void against the administrator, liquidator or other person. The relevant time period is two years in the case of a floating charge in favour of a connected person, one year in the case of a floating charge in favour of an unconnected person, and six months in any other case.

If the registered particulars of a charge do not contain relevant information and are incomplete, then the charge is void *pro tanto*. Section 420 of the Companies Act 1985 allows amendment, correction or addition to existing particulars by the court. The amended particulars must be signed on behalf of the company and by the lender.

A person taking a charge over a company's property is deemed to have notice of any matter requiring registration and disclosed on the register at the time that his charge is created (see para 5.8 and s 42 of the Companies Act 1985). This area has been unaffected by the statutory erosion of the doctrine of constructive notice (see s 35B of the Companies Act 1985) and appears unlikely to be so (see s 142 of the Companies Act 1989).

The mere registration of a charge does not, however, mean that there is notice of all the terms which apply to that charge, regardless of whether the terms are registered or not. If the particulars that are registered include details, for example, of a negative pledge prohibiting a subsequent charge taking priority over that charge, this will, however, constitute notice and will fix a subsequent chargee with notice of the conditions if registration of such a clause is mandatory – see, for example, *AIB Finance Ltd v Bank of Scotland* (1995) (see para 18.11).

18.9   Constructive notice of charges

Section 419(1) of the Act provides that where a charge has ceased to apply to a company property, then a memorandum to that effect should be delivered to the registrar of companies for registration on the company's file. This memorandum of discharge should be signed on behalf of the company and by the chargee. This minimises the possibility of fraud.

Note that in addition to the requirements of registration at the company's registry, there is a quite separate obligation upon the company to keep a register of charges. This is set out in s 422 of the Companies Act 1985. Failure to enter details of a charge on the company's own register does not have any consequences as to validity of the charge but renders those responsible liable to a fine.

18.10   Discharge of charges

The ranking of floating charges is governed in Scotland by s 464 of the Companies Act 1985 as amended by the Companies Act 1989. As has been noted, a fixed charge applies to the property it covers from the point of creation. A fixed charge will usually take priority over a subsequent fixed charge and over any floating charge no matter when created (s 464(4)). This is, however, subject to s 464(1) which provides that if a floating charge is created prior to a fixed charge and the floating charge contains a negative pledge clause, ie it prohibits the creation of any subsequent charge with priority over that floating charge and this condition is actually registered with the prescribed particulars at the company's registry, then that floating charge will take ahead of a subsequent fixed charge.

18.11   Priorities amongst charges

It is important to note that under s 410(5) of the Companies Act 1985 a floating charge is created at the time of execution whereas a fixed charge is not created until the creditor acquires a real right. Thus, in *AIB Finance v Bank of Scotland* (1993), where both a floating charge and a floating charge over the same assets were executed on the same day (the floating charge containing a negative pledge clause) and the floating charge was registered with the registrar of companies before the standard security creating the fixed charge was entered in the Register of Sasines, the Inner House held that the negative pledge clause allowed the floating charge to take priority over the fixed charge.

Section 464(4) also provides that, unless the ranking of securities is altered under s 464(1), floating charges rank according to the date of registration and where the registrar of companies receives two or more floating charges over the same assets on the same day, these rank *pari passu*.

In England, ranking of charges is a common law matter, and relevant cases include *Re Benjamin Cape & Sons Ltd* (1914) and *Re Automatic Bottle Makers* (1926).

18.12 Special circumstances affecting priorities

In relation to floating charges, six particular situations need to be noted:

- Any person who has effectually executed diligence on the charged property or any part of it takes priority over the floating charge holder (s 463 of the CA 1985 and s 60(1)(b) of the IA 1986). The meaning of 'effectually executed diligence' was examined in *Lord Advocate v Royal Bank of Scotland Ltd* (1977) (distinguished in *Iona Hotels Ltd, Petitioners* (1991)) and in *Armour and Mycroft, Petitioners* (1983).

- A landlord's hypothec (a right in security enjoyed by a landlord over moveable property contained in the landlord's heritable property occupied by the tenant) appears (by virtue of s 464(2) of the CA 1985 and s 179 of the CA 1989) to take priority over a floating charge, irrespective of the terms contained within the charge. In *Grampian Regional Council v Drill Stem (Inspection Services) Ltd (In Receivership)* (1994), it was held by the Sheriff Court that a landlord's hypothec conferred a real right in security upon the landlord over all of the moveable property in leased premises (except for goods in a shop or warehouse left there by the tenant for the purpose of being sold) taking priority over any of the receiver's rights. In addition, any person who had already purchased property from the tenants which was still within the landlord's hypothec (that is, not yet removed by the buyer) could only exercise the rights of an ordinary creditor (that is, the hypothec takes priority). This case falls to be compared with the earlier case of *Cumbernauld Development Corporation v Mustone* (1983).

- Any preferential debts of the company are to be paid out of assets that are subject to a floating charge if there are no other assets free of the charge sufficient to pay off the preferential debts. Preferential debts are examined in detail below at para 23.4.

- A floating charge created after a winding up order is made by a court appears to be void under s 127 of the Insolvency Act 1986 – see *Site Preparations Ltd v Buchan Developments Ltd* (1983).

- Property in which the company does not have a beneficial interest cannot be attached. In *Tay Valley Joinery Ltd v C F Financial Services Ltd* (1987), the pursuer entered into an invoice discounting agreement with the defender, whereby the pursuer sold all of its current and future book debts to the defender. Although there was no formal assignation of these debts and no notification of the defender's interest to each of the pursuer's debtors individually, the pursuer supplied the defender with monthly statements which contained a notice that the included accounts were assigned to the defender. A receiver was subsequently appointed to the pursuer's property and undertaking under the terms of a floating charge. Although the floating charge purported to extend to book debts, the Inner House held that the invoice discounting agreement effectively created a trust over these book debts, the beneficial interest in which was held by the defender, and the book debts were therefore beyond the reach of the receiver. In *Sharp v Thomson* (1997), the defenders had purchased a flat from a company whose property and undertaking was secured by a floating charge. A receiver was appointed under the terms of the floating charge after the defenders had paid for the flat and moved in, but before the disposition transferring title in the flat to the defenders was recorded in the Register of Sasines. Under Scots law, the defenders therefore had not yet acquired a real right in the flat. The Inner House had held that the floating charge accordingly attached to the flat since the company still had a real right in it at the time of the appointment of the receiver. However, this decision was overturned in a landmark ruling by the House of Lords. Although their Lordships expressly rejected that the company held the real right in the flat in trust for the purchasers between the date of the sale and the date of the recording of the disposition, they held that since the company had disposed of the beneficial interest in the flat during this time the floating charge did not attach to it.

- Under s 464(5) of the Companies Act 1985, where a registered floating chargeholder receives intimation of the subsequent registration of another floating charge over (part of) the same property, the first floating charge's priority ranking is restricted to security for:

    (a) the holder's present advances;

    (b) future advances which he may be required to make under the instrument creating the floating charge;

    (c) interest due or to become due on all such advances; and

    (d) any expenses or outlays reasonably incurred by the holder.

Furthermore, a floating charge may be invalid in certain circumstances. Under s 245 of the Insolvency Act 1986, a floating charge which is created in favour of a connected person within the period two years before the onset of insolvency is invalid except to the extent that it is made for good consideration or within 12 months of the onset of insolvency if it is made in favour of an unconnected person. If it is made in favour of an unconnected person, it also needs to be demonstrated that at the time that the charge was created the company was unable to pay its debts. This condition does not apply where the charge was created in favour of a connected person. It is also possible that a fixed or floating charge may be found to be invalid under s 243 of the Insolvency Act 1986 as an unfair preference. If it is made in favour of a connected person, once again the period of time is two years preceding the onset of insolvency. If it is made in favour of an unconnected person, the period is six months ending with the onset of insolvency.

One of the guiding principles behind the insolvency legislation is to achieve equal treatment for like creditors. Therefore, preferring some creditors to others has to be tackled. In *Re M Kushler Ltd* (1943), under a somewhat different provision of the former law, a bank overdraft was paid off to release a director's guarantee. This was challenged successfully and repayment was ordered.

18.12.1   Reservation of title

There are certain additional features which need to be borne in mind in relation to priority of charges (the same features will need to be borne in mind in relation to liquidations). If a company has goods that are let out under a hire purchase agreement or are leased and therefore do not belong to the company, the owner of the goods clearly retains title to them. A similar principle applies where there is a valid reservation of title clause. In *Aluminium Industrie Vaassen BV v Romalpa Aluminium Ltd* (1976), we have a classic exposition of the law in relation to reservation of title. The supplier of aluminium foil in the Netherlands supplied aluminium foil to the company in the United Kingdom. The aluminium foil was supplied on credit terms. The supplier expressly reserved title in the goods until they were paid for. The supplier required the purchaser to store the aluminium foil separately and imposed fiduciary obligations upon the purchaser in relation to the property. Mocatta J held that there was an effective reservation of title. He was upheld unanimously by the Court of Appeal. The relevant clause of the contract of sale provided:

> The ownership of the material to be delivered by [AIV] will only be transferred to [Romalpa] when [it has] met all that is owing to [AIV]. Until the date of payment [Romalpa could be required] to store the material in such a way that it is clearly the property of [AIV].

Three particular features were stressed in the case:

- there must be a clear and unambiguous reservation of the title in the property;

- the goods must not be inextricably linked with other goods and must be capable of being separated from other people's property;

- a fiduciary obligation must be placed on the purchaser by the supplier. In *Romalpa* agency and bailment relationships had been created.

The principles in the *Romalpa* case (interestingly Romalpa was the company suffering from the so-called *Romalpa* clause which was actually a clause in the supplier's terms and conditions) were applied in subsequent cases. In *Borden (UK) Ltd v Scottish Timber Products Ltd* (1979), the supplier of resin reserved title in the resin. This was problematic because although the resin had not been paid for, it was inextricably linked with chipboard. It was held that the supplier of the resin could not effectively reserve title where the resin was mixed with other products and could not be separated out. As Templeman LJ said:

> When the resin was incorporated in the chipboard, the resin ceased to exist, the seller's title to the resin became meaningless and the seller's security vanished. There was

no provision in the contract for the buyers to provide substituted or additional security. The chipboard belongs to the buyers.

In *Re Bond Worth Ltd* (1979), there is an object lesson in how not to create a valid retention of title (or *Romalpa* clause). Acrilan Fibre had been supplied by Monsanto Ltd to Bond Worth. It was to be used in the manufacture of carpets. The sale agreement reserved 'equitable and beneficial ownership' of the fibre. Slade J held that the effect of such a reservation was to create the necessary implication that legal title had not been reserved by the supplier. The effect of this was that the supplier was creating a charge over the property rather than reserving effective title. As such, the charge required registration. It was not registered and was therefore void. Similarly in *Stroud Architectural Systems Ltd v John Laing Construction Ltd* (1994) the plaintiffs supplied glazing units on terms where they reserved the equitable and beneficial ownership in the goods. The was held to create a floating charge. In *Re Peachdart Ltd* (1983), the supplier of leather reserved title in the leather. This leather was used in the manufacture of handbags. Once again, there was an inextricable mixing of the different properties and therefore there could be no valid reservation of title in such circumstances. The provision concerned created a charge and this charge was void for lack of registration. In *Re Clough Mill Ltd* (1984), there was a valid reservation of title in relation to yarn. The Court of Appeal restated the requirements of a valid reservation of title which had been earlier expressed in the *Romalpa* case. In *Chisholm Textiles v Griffiths and Others* (1994), the supplier of cloth to a dress manufacturer sought to reserve title in dresses into which the fabric had been incorporated. The judge held that this created a charge over the manufactured articles which was void for non-registration.

An interesting case on reservation of title is *Hendy Lennox (Industrial Engines) Ltd v Graeme Puttick Ltd* (1984). In this case, the supplier of diesel engines had sought to reserve title in them. The engines were installed into generators. It was contended that there could be no valid reservation where such mixing had taken place. The court held, however, that there was no inextricable linking in such a situation as the engine could be removed from the generator.

In Scotland, it was formerly the position that a retention of title clause could only be effective insofar as it reserved title with the seller until the goods subject to the particular contract were paid for – see, for example, *Archivent Sales and Development Ltd v Strathclyde Regional Council* (1985). It was regarded that an attempt to retain title in goods supplied under one contract until independent contractual obligations owed by the debtor to the supplier were satisfied would be unlawful since this would be an attempt to create a security over moveable property without delivery to the creditor (or creation of a floating charge).

However, in *Armour v Thyssen Edelstahlwerke AG* (1990), the House of Lords permitted a supplier to rely on a reservation of title clause which demanded that payment of sums owed by the buyer to the supplier under separate contracts between the parties be made before ownership of the goods supplied under the contract containing the retention of title clause transferred from the supplier to the buyer. The Court of Session had held that this was an unlawful attempt to circumvent the rule that security over moveable property could only be created by delivery of the property to the creditor. However, the House of Lords overruled the Inner House, pointing out that the retention of title clause did not create a security – it merely stipulated that the right of ownership of the property would remain with the unpaid seller, and that this was permitted by ss 17 and 19 of the Sale of Goods Act 1979.

Another feature which should be watched for in insolvency situations whether involving the enforcement of charges or a liquidation is the situation involving liens. A lien is the situation that exists where a person who has done work for another retains property belonging to that other, for example a car repairer or a watch repairer. In circumstances where a person holds property belonging to the company where that property is subject to a charge (or would otherwise come under the direct control of a liquidator if the company is in liquidation), the holder of the property must be paid off first so that the lien is discharged before the property becomes subject to the control of the receiver or liquidator. Thus, in *George Barker (Transport) Ltd v Eynon* (1974), a transport contractor was held entitled to retain possession of a consignment of meat belonging to the company until it had been paid in respect of money owed to it. Once paid, the lien is released and the property then becomes subject to the control of the receiver (or liquidator). In fact, in *George Barker*, the transport contractors had a specific provision in their contract giving them a lien – a contractual lien. Some liens such as repairers liens arise by operation of law. The transporting company in fact released the meat to the company's receiver without prejudice to any lien that it had.

18.12.2   Liens

Debentures and Securities

Debentures

Technically, a debenture is any form of borrowing by a company but in practice a debenture is a secured borrowing. A debenture may be a single loan eg from a bank or one of an issue of debentures made to the public. An issue of debentures to the public is very similar in many respects to an issue of shares to the public. However, a debenture holder is a lender to the company not a member of the company. Debentures and shares issued to the public are collectively called securities.

Where debentures are issued to the public there must be a debenture trust deed and in other cases of lending there may be. The debenture trustee who is given the task of guarding the debentureholders' interests will act to enforce the security in appropriate situations and will ensure that the terms of the lending are honoured.

Charges

The security given to a company's borrowings may take one of two forms. It may be in the shape of *a fixed charge* which is basically similar to an ordinary mortgage and may be granted over the fixed assets such as land, investments etc. It seems it may also be granted over a company's present and future book debts where these are paid into a separate bank account.

The other type of charge is *a floating charge* which is unique to company law and which a company may grant over its entire assets and undertaking. Unlike a fixed charge, a floating charge is not effective from the date of its creation but rather when it attaches upon the happening of certain events. A floating charge will attach if the company goes into liquidation, or if a receiver is appointed, or, in England if the company ceases business and possibly on the happening of an event specified in the debenture agreement – automatic crystallisation.

Registration of charges

The law in this area is in a state of flux and the DTI is consulting on options for reform. The approach taken in the textbook is to assume that Part XII of the Companies Act 1985 is in force.

Particulars of most but not all charges have to be registered within 21 days of their creation at the companies' registry. Failure to register the prescribed particulars of the charge renders it void against an administrator, liquidator or a person who acquires an interest or right over the charged property.

Late registration is permitted but subject to any rights acquired in the meantime.

In respect of matters required to be placed on the register of charges with the companies' registry, deemed notice still operates.

When a charge is discharged, a memorandum to that effect should be registered with the registrar of companies. The memorandum of discharge should be signed on behalf of the company and by the lender.

Priorities

Fixed charges are generally paid off ahead of later fixed charges and all floating charges. This is subject to the exception that an earlier floating charge which contained a 'negative pledge' provision forbidding later charges taking priority over it will enjoy priority if the restriction is registered.

A first floating charge will generally take priority ahead of a subsequent floating charge unless the first floating charge preserves the possibility of a subsequent limited floating charge taking priority ahead of the earlier one.

Points to note on priorities

In determining priorities in relation to floating charges, certain creditors will take priority ahead of floating chargees. These are creditors who have effectually executed diligence, landlords exercising their hypothec, beneficiaries of property held in trust by the company and preferential creditors.

On occasion floating charges may be held to be invalid where a company goes into liquidation or an administration order is made and fixed or floating charges, if created as unfair preferences (over other creditors), may also be found to be invalid where a company goes into liquidation or an administration order is made.

It is important to watch out for valid reservation of title clauses. If there are such clauses the property concerned does not belong to the company.

Where a person has a valid lien over company property, for example, a repairer's lien over lorries belonging to a company which are with the repairer following work being done on them, then the lien must be released by payment before the receiver or liquidator can take control of the property in question.

Chapter 19

Receivership

In the event of default on the part of a company in satisfying the terms of a debenture, the debentureholder will have one or more remedies available against the company. The availability of remedies depends upon the status of the debentureholder. An unsecured creditor may sue the company for (re)payment or petition for the appointment of a judicial factor (see para 14.7) or possibly for a compulsory winding up (see Chapter 23 below).

A secured debentureholder will have additional remedies as follows:

- the holder of a fixed charge over heritable property may apply to the court for a decree of foreclosure under s 28 of the Conveyancing and Feudal Reform (Scotland) Act 1970;

- the holder of a fixed charge over moveable property may sell or lease the property;

- the holder of a floating charge may petition the court for a compulsory winding up of the company under s 122(2) of the Insolvency Act 1986 (where the relevant security is in jeopardy), or he may appoint a qualified insolvency practitioner as a receiver or he may apply to the court requesting that the court appoint a receiver.

The principal object of receivership is for the debentureholder whose interests are secured by a floating charge over the company's assets to recover what he is owed. A receiver will take over the management of the property to which the floating charge attaches (often, the whole of the company's property and undertaking) with a view to making the most advantageous use of the property for the benefit of the floating chargeholder. Thus, it is sometimes best to continue to run the company (particularly when it has been mismanaged) since the net realisable value of assets disposed of in a liquidation is usually substantially less than their value in any other circumstances.

However, a receiver must pay off certain other creditors from the proceeds of the receivership before the floating chargeholder may be repaid. Once the receiver has completed this task, he returns what is left (if anything) of the charged property to the control of the directors or the liquidator if the company has already entered liquidation.

The law governing receivership has developed independently in Scotland, and is therefore considerably different from the law in England. The Scottish position is governed by ss 50–71 of the Insolvency Act 1986, whilst ss 28–40 of the Insolvency Act 1986 regulate receivership in England.

In spite of this, a receiver appointed in one jurisdiction may exercise his powers in the other jurisdiction under s 72 of the Insolvency Act 1986 – see *Gordon Anderson Plant Ltd v Campsie Construction Ltd* (1977) and *Norfolk House plc (in receivership) v Repsol Petroleum Ltd* (1992).

Receivers were introduced into Scots law by the Companies (Floating Charges and Receivers) (Scotland) Act 1972. The law is now contained in Part III Chapter II of the Insolvency Act 1986 (all statutory references in this chapter will be therefore to the Insolvency Act 1986 unless otherwise indicated). Note that there is no distinction in Scotland between receivers and administrative receivers.

19.1 Appointment

A receiver may be appointed only by a floating chargeholder in Scotland. It is a criminal offence for a body corporate, an undischarged bankrupt or a Scottish firm to act as a receiver (s 51).

A receiver may be appointed on the occurrence of events specified in the instrument creating the floating charge, or, unless the instrument provides otherwise, on the occurrence of any of the following:

- the company fails to pay within 21 days of a demand for payment; or
- two months' interest is in arrears; or
- an order or resolution is made to wind up the company; or
- another receiver is appointed.

A receiver must be appointed in writing unless the appointment is by court order, and notice of the appointment must be sent to the registrar within seven days. The receiver must accept the appointment in writing before the end of the next business day for the appointment to be effective. It is only then that the floating charge attaches to the relevant property then comprised in the company's property and undertaking. The floating charge then becomes a fixed security over that property.

Every receivership must be publicised. Hence, a receiver must inform the company and all known creditors of his appointment within 28 days (s 65) and any party responsible for the issue of a document by the company in the company's name is liable to a fine unless the document also discloses that the company is in receivership (s 64).

The receiver will then require the company's directors or other officers or employees to make a statement of affairs in order to verify the assets and liabilities of the company, details of creditors and securities and the dates when securities were given (s 66).

Section 67 requires the receiver, within three months of his appointment, to send a report to the registrar, to all secured creditors and their trustees and to all unsecured creditors (it is sufficient to inform unsecured creditors that a free copy of the report is available from a specific address). The report should detail:

- the circumstances leading to the receiver's appointment;

- the receiver's disposals and proposed disposals of property;

- the amounts payable to the floating chargeholder and to preferential creditors;

- the amounts available for other creditors; and

- a summary (with the receiver's comments attached) of the statement of affairs obtained under s 66.

However, the report need not disclose any information which would be seriously prejudicial to the carrying out of the receiver's functions. The report should also be laid before a meeting of unsecured creditors (for which at least 14 days' notice is required) and (where a liquidator is appointed more than three months after the receiver's appointment) be copied to the liquidator within seven days of his appointment.

Section 68 provides that creditors attending a s 67 meeting may form their own 'creditors' committee' which may require the receiver to attend before a meeting on at least seven days' notice.

Under s 55, a receiver may exercise any powers specified in the instrument creating the floating charge, supplemented by those specified in Sched 2 of the Insolvency Act 1986. However, these powers are suspended in favour of anyone who has effectually effected diligence affecting the property (see para 18.12) or to anyone with a fixed or floating charge

19.2   The course of the receivership

19.3   Powers of a receiver

ranking in priority or equally with the appointer's floating charge. This section also provides that a third party dealing with the receiver in good faith and for value may assume that the receiver is acting within his powers.

A receiver must obtain the consent of the holder of any prior ranking charge or of anyone who has effectually effected diligence over property to which the floating charge has attached if he wishes to dispose of it. In the event that consent is not forthcoming, s 61 provides that the receiver may apply to the court for authority to dispose of the relevant property free of any charge or encumbrance. The receiver must apply the proceeds of the disposal firstly to satisfy the claim of the relevant secured creditor. Section 61 also provides that the person acquiring the relevant property from the receiver with the authority of the court shall acquire title in the property free of any charge or diligence.

Although a receiver takes over the management of assets subject to the floating charge, the directors of the company in some circumstances may have certain residual powers. Thus, in *Shanks v Central Regional Council* (1987), it was held that directors had the power (and may actually owe a duty to other creditors) to pursue a claim, the subjects of which fell within the charged property subject to the receivership, where the receiver had not pursued the claim himself. The court opined that the residual powers of directors of a Scottish company in receivership were similar to their English counterparts. This case falls to be compared with the earlier case of *Imperial Hotel (Aberdeen) Ltd v Vaux Breweries Ltd* (1978).

Section 56 provides that a receiver appointed under a prior ranking floating charge has powers which exclude any other receiver. Any other receiver's powers are suspended until the prior ranking floating charge ceases to attach to the property charged under the later ranking charge. In such circumstances, a later ranking receiver who has taken into his control property subject to the floating charge will not be obliged to surrender control of any property until he receives an indemnity over his expenses from the receiver appointed under the prior ranking floating charge. Any floating charge suspended in this way does not, however, cease to attach to the charged property.

Section 56 also provides that where floating charges rank *pari passu* the receivers appointed under each are deemed to be joint receivers unless the instruments of appointment provide otherwise. It is also possible for the same receiver to be appointed in respect of more than one floating charge.

A receiver is an agent of the company in relation to property attached by the floating charge (s 57). A receiver is also personally liable on contracts he enters into in pursuance of his functions, but not on contracts entered into before his appointment (nor for rates – see *McKillop & Watters, Petitioners* (1994)). In addition, a receiver incurring personal liability is entitled to be indemnified by the company.

A receiver will not be deemed to have adopted any contract of employment by virtue of anything done or not done within 14 days of his appointment. Any contract entered into by a receiver will remain binding even where the receiver's powers are suspended under s 56 (see above).

19.3.1 Receivers as agents

A receiver's remuneration is to be determined by agreement between the floating chargeholder and the receiver (although it will be paid out of the realisation of the assets subject to the floating charge). However, the Auditor of the Court of Session may fix the receiver's remuneration.

19.3.2 Receiver's remuneration

The priority of payments in a receivership is as follows:

- the holder of any fixed security ranking prior to or *pari passu* with the floating charge;

- creditors who have effectually executed diligence (see para 18.12);

- landlord's hypothec (see para 18.12);

- creditors of the receiver;

- the receiver's expenses and remuneration;

- preferential creditors (see para 23.4);

- the floating chargeholder.

The residue (if any) should be handed over to either any other receiver, any fixed chargeholder of later ranking or the company (or its liquidator).

19.4 Priority of payments in a receivership

When a receiver is appointed at the same time as a liquidator the receiver is entitled to take control of the property to which the floating charge attaches. However, the corollary is that the receiver is principally liable to pay off prior and preferential creditors. In *Manley, Petitioner* (1985), the Outer House held that in such circumstances it was immaterial whether the receiver was appointed before or after the commencement of the winding up. In either case, the liquidator had to surrender property subject to the floating charge to the receiver, who in

19.5 Relationship with a liquidator

turn was obliged to meet the claims of secured and preferential creditors from a realisation of the property before being able to repay the floating chargeholder.

Although a receiver may object to the company entering liquidation (because of the likely devaluation that would be inflicted on charged property), he may find it difficult to prevent this from happening. In *Foxhall & Gyle (Nurseries) Ltd* (1978), although a receiver objected (on the basis that to enter liquidation would result in a les advantageous realisation of assets) to a petition for a compulsory winding up brought by an insubstantial unsecured creditor, the Outer House held that it would only dismiss such a petition if there were compelling reasons for doing so. In this case, the petition was granted. It is worth noting that the petitioning creditor wished to investigate the receiver's valuation (£100,000) of the company's stock – particularly since it had been entered at £700,000 on the company's most recent balance sheet!

19.6 Termination of receivership

Where a receiver has completed his task, he may vacate office. He must give notice within 14 days to the registrar of companies that he is ceasing to act (s 62(5)).

A receiver may also be removed by an order of the court (s 62(1)). Once again the receiver must serve notice under s 62(5). Similarly, a receiver may resign from office. He must give at least seven days' notice to his appointer and the company of his intention to resign. There must also be notice sent to the registrar under s 62(5).

A receiver must also vacate office if he ceases to be a qualified insolvency practitioner (s 62(2)) and also if an administration order is made in respect of the company (s 11(2)). Furthermore, a receivership will terminate upon the death of the receiver (although here under s 62(5) he is not expected to notify the registrar of the termination of his appointment)!

If upon the termination of a receivership before the receivership is completed, no other receiver is appointed within one month (exclusive of any period during which an administration order is in effect), the charge ceases to attach and reverts to floating charge status (s 62(6)).

19.7 Administrative receivers in England

As has already been noted, the law on receivership (although similar in character) is substantially different in England. Thus, in England, a fixed chargeholder may appoint a receiver, and a distinction is made between receivers and administrative receivers. An administrative receiver in England is a receiver or manager of the whole (or substantially the whole) of a company's property (see s 29(2)).

Summary of Chapter 19

Receivership

A receiver may be appointed by the floating chargeholder or by the court where there is default in honouring the terms of a debenture secured by a floating charge. A receiver must be a qualified insolvency practitioner.

The law on receivership is substantially different from England in Scotland, although a receiver appointed under either jurisdiction may exercise powers in the other jurisdiction.

It is the role of the receiver to take control of and to realise the assets subject to the floating charge and to pay off in priority secured creditors, creditors who have effectually executed diligence, landlords exercising their hypothec, the expenses of the receivership, preferential creditors and money owing to floating chargeholders.

A receiver takes priority over a liquidator, but is primarily liable to pay off secured and preferential creditors.

Any surplus should be handed on to any other receiver, or back to the company or its liquidator.

Chapter 20

Voluntary Arrangements and Administration

Part I of the Insolvency Act 1986 (ss 1–7) provides a simple procedure whereby a company which is in financial difficulties may enter into a voluntary arrangement with its creditors. This arrangement may involve either: a composition in satisfaction of its debts, that is, provision for creditors to receive a percentage of what is due to them, or a scheme of arrangement of its affairs.

20.1 Voluntary arrangements

The voluntary arrangement must be supervised by a person, 'the nominee', who must be a qualified insolvency practitioner. The proposal for a voluntary arrangement may be made by the directors of a company or where an administration order is in force by the administrator or where the company is being wound up by the liquidator (s 1 of the Insolvency Act 1986).

If the nominee is not the company's administrator or liquidator, then the proposal should be submitted to him together with a statement of the company's affairs containing particulars of the company's assets, creditors, liabilities and debts. The nominee must then submit a report to the court stating: whether in his opinion meetings of the company and of its creditors should be summoned to consider the proposal, and if in his opinion such meetings should be summoned, the date on which and place at which they should be held (s 2 of the Insolvency Act 1986).

If the nominee is the company's liquidator or administrator, he should summon meetings of the company and of its creditors to consider the proposal (s 3(2) of the Insolvency Act 1986).

The meetings summoned must then determine whether to approve the proposed voluntary arrangement with or without modifications. A meeting may not approve:

- any proposal which affects the right of a secured creditor of the company to enforce his security except with his consent;

- the withdrawal of the priority of a preferential debt over other debts, except with the consent of the creditor;

- the payment of a proportion of preferential debts to a preferential creditor which is a smaller proportion than is to be received by other preferential creditors except with the consent of the creditor.

The proposal must be approved by three quarters in value of the creditors present and voting and by a simple majority of the members, according to the Insolvency Rules.

If the voluntary arrangement is approved, then if the company is being wound up or if an administration order is in force, the court may stay the winding up proceedings or discharge the administration order or it may give such directions as it thinks appropriate to facilitate the implementation of the voluntary arrangement (s 5 of the Insolvency Act 1986). There is a period of 28 days from the date when the nominee reports the results of the meetings' consideration to the court (s 4(6) of the Insolvency Act 1986) for members, creditors and others to object to the court.

On the application of a member, contributory creditor, nominee or, if appropriate, liquidator or administrator, the proposal may be challenged on the ground that it unfairly prejudices the interests of a creditor, member or contributory of the company or that there has been some material irregularity at or in relation to either of the meetings. This section in part echoes s 459 of the Companies Act 1985 (see para 14.3) just like s 27 of the Insolvency Act 1986 in relation to administration (see para 20.4) (s 6 of the Insolvency Act 1986).

Once the proposal for the voluntary arrangement has taken effect, the nominee becomes the supervisor of the composition of the voluntary arrangement. The supervisor may apply for a winding up to be ordered or for an administration order to be made.

If any creditor or some other interested party is dissatisfied with any act, omission or decision of a supervisor, he may apply to the court to give the supervisor directions or to alter the decision etc in question (s 7 of the Insolvency Act 1986).

The voluntary arrangement procedure is a valuable one. It was added to British company law at the behest of the Cork Committee (paras 400–03) which considered that companies, like individuals, should be able to enter into binding arrangements with their creditors.

On 6 April 1995, the government announced proposals for a new form of procedure for dealing with companies in financial trouble (Revised Proposals for a New Company Voluntary Arrangement Procedure). The directors of a company would be given 28 days to put together a rescue plan. During this moratorium the company would be supervised by a licensed insolvency practitioner.

There are safeguards for lenders and creditors. There has to be a reasonable prospect of success in the opinion of the insolvency practitioner before the plan can be put into force. There must be a creditors' meeting within 28 days of the commencement of the moratorium. If more than 75% of the creditors in value support the proposals, it is binding on all creditors. The creditors can reject the entire project. They can also extend it.

Following the report of the Review Committee on Insolvency Law and Practice – the Cork Report (Cmnd 8558, 1982) – a government white paper (A Revised Framework for Insolvency Law (Cmnd 9175, February 1984)) echoing some of its recommendations set out a procedure to facilitate the rehabilitation or reorganisation of a company. This process was the administration process and it was incorporated into the Insolvency Act of 1985 which was in turn consolidated in the Insolvency Act 1986. In essence, the scheme of administration is to make possible the rescue of a company by placing its management in the hands of an administrator. For as long as the administration is in force, it is not possible to commence winding up proceedings or any other process against the company or to enforce any charge, hire purchase or retention of title provision against the company without the leave of the court.

20.2   Administration

The court may make an order on the application of the company or its directors or a creditor or creditors (s 9 of the Insolvency Act 1986) or the supervisor of a voluntary arrangement (s 7(4)(b) of the Insolvency Act 1986) or, in England, in pursuance of an order of the magistrate's court under s 87A of the Magistrates' Courts Act 1980, relating to the enforcement of fines imposed against companies. If the application for an administration order is made by the directors then this application should be the result of a decision at a properly convened board meeting. In *Re Equiticorp International plc* (1989), a properly convened board meeting was held in Hong Kong with some directors physically present and others participating by telephone. Millett J held that the fact that two directors did not attend did not affect the validity of the application. It seems that a decision arrived at by the company directors without a meeting is equally valid, see *Re Instrumentation Electrical Services Ltd* (1988).

20.3   Application

The court must be satisfied that the company is or is likely to become unable to pay its debts and must consider that the making of an order makes one or more of the purposes which will be considered below likely of achievement.

'Inability to pay debts' is determined by s 123 of the Insolvency Act 1986. This provides that inability to pay debts may be demonstrated by one of the following:

- if a creditor is owed a debt exceeding £750 for three weeks after making a written request for payment of that debt;

- execution or process issued on a judgment is returned unsatisfied in whole or in part (in practice the minimum sum owed must exceed £750);

- if it is proved to the satisfaction of the court that the company is unable to pay its debts as they fall due (in practice the same minimum sum applies);

- if the company's assets are worth less than the amount of its liabilities, taking account of contingent and prospective liability (in practice the same minimum sum applies);

- in Scotland a charge for payment on an extract decree or extract registered bond or extract registered protest have expired without payment being made (in practice the same minimum sum applies);

- in Northern Ireland a certificate of unenforceability has been granted in respect of a judgment against the company (in practice the same minimum sum applies).

Before an order may be granted, the court must be satisfied that one or more of the following is likely of achievement (s 8(3)):

- (a) the survival of the company as a going concern in whole or in part;
- (b) the approval of a voluntary arrangement under Part 1 of the Act (see para 20.1);
- (c) the sanctioning of a scheme of arrangement under s 425 of the Companies Act 1985 between the company and such persons as are mentioned in that section (see para 22.5);
- (d) a more advantageous realisation of the company's assets than would be effected on a winding up.

The question as to how one determines whether it is 'likely'. In *Re Consumer and Industrial Press Ltd* (1988), Peter Gibson J took the view that:

> That does not mean that it is merely possible that such purpose will be achieved, the evidence must go further than that to enable the court to hold that the purpose in question will more probably than not be achieved.

However, Hoffmann J refused to follow this line of argument in *In Re Harris Simons Construction Ltd* (1989). He considered that where there was a real prospect that an administration order would achieve one of the purposes in s 9 then an order could be made. This view seems to be the preferred one. It was followed, for example, in *Re Primlaks UK Ltd* (1989) by Vinelott J in considering whether to grant an order in respect of a company trading in Nigeria. He said:

> The question must always be, if there is a real prospect that one or more of the stated purposes would be achieved, is that prospect sufficiently likely in the light of all the other circumstances of the case to justify the making of the order?

The effect of an application for an administration order is set out in s 10 of the Act. Once a petition has been presented for an administration order, none of the following may occur:

- no resolution may be passed or order made to wind up the company;

- no steps can be taken to enforce any security of the company's property or to repossess goods in the company's possession under any hire purchase agreement except with the leave of the court and subject to such terms as it may impose (note that hire purchase agreements are defined to include leasing agreements and retention of title agreements in this part of the Insolvency Act 1986);

- no other proceedings and no execution or other legal process may be commenced or continued and no diligence may be carried out or continued against the company or its property except with the leave of the court and once again subject to such terms as it may impose.

Section 10, however, clearly states that the following do not require leave:

- the presentation of a petition to wind the company up;

- the appointment of an administrative receiver; or

- the carrying out by such a receiver of any of his functions.

Section 11 provides that if the court makes the order, then any petition for winding up the company shall be dismissed and any administrative receiver in place shall vacate office. Whilst an administration order is in force, no resolution to wind the company up can be passed, no administrative receiver may be appointed and no steps may be taken to enforce any security

20.4   Effects of administration

of the company's property or to repossess goods in the company's possession under any hire purchase agreement except with the consent of the administrator or the leave of the court and subject to such terms as the court may impose. Furthermore, no other proceedings and no execution or other legal process may be commenced or continued against the company and no distress may be levied against the company or its property except with the consent of the administrator or the leave of the court and subject to such terms as are considered appropriate.

The question of enforcement of a security arose in *Bristol Airport plc v Powdrill* (1990) where the airport sought to detain aircraft belonging to Paramount Airways Ltd, a company operating under an administration order, for airport charges under s 88 of the Civil Aviation Act 1982. The airport sought leave of the court but was refused.

In *Re Atlantic Computer Systems plc* (1991), the facts were somewhat complex. Finance companies had provided equipment which was leased to the company or let out on HP terms. The company in general then subleased it to others. The Court of Appeal took the view that generally there is no implication that the owner of property suffering loss by reason of the restrictions of s 11 should have some other remedy available. However, in this case the court's discretion was exercised to grant leave to terminate the head leases and to repossess the goods.

In *Scottish Exhibition Centre Ltd v Mirestop Ltd* (1996), landlords sought to enforce an irritancy clause in a lease which provided for termination of the lease by notice upon the appointment of *inter alia* an administrator to manage the affairs of the tenant company. The Outer House held that service of the notice did not amount to a 'legal process' or 'proceedings' in terms of s 10 of the Insolvency Act 1986, and therefore leave of the court was not required to serve the notice.

Whilst the administration is in progress, every invoice, order for goods or business letter which is issued by or on behalf of the company or the administrator being a document on or which the company's name appears shall also contain the administrator's name and a statement that the affairs, business and property of the company are being managed by the administrator.

20.5   Powers of the administrator

The person appointed to administer the company must be a qualified insolvency practitioner (see Chapter 19). He is given wide powers of management to do what is necessary for the management of the affairs, business and property of the company and he has the same powers that are exercised by an administrative receiver and which are set out in Sched 1 of the Insolvency Act 1986. These powers include taking possession of the property, selling and otherwise disposing of it, raising or borrowing money, appointing a solicitor or accountant, bringing or defending legal proceedings, effecting and maintaining insurances, appointing agents, carrying on the business of the company, establishing subsidiaries, granting or accepting surrender of a lease or tenancy and power to do all such things that are incidental to the powers set out in Sched 1.

Section 14(2) also provides that the administrator may remove any director and appoint any person to be a director to fill a vacancy or otherwise. The administrator also has the power to call any meeting of members or creditors of the company.

In relation to charged property, s 15 provides that the administrator may dispose of property which is subject to a charge which as created was a floating charge (s 15(1)). No leave of the court is required. Section 15(2) provides that the administrator may dispose of any property subject to a fixed charge or goods that are in the company's possession under a hire purchase agreement if the effect of the disposal is likely to promote the purpose or one or more of the purposes specified in the administration order on application to the court. The court will authorise the administrator to dispose of that property if it is of the opinion that it would be likely to promote one or more of the purposes set out above (at para 20.3). Where property subject to a floating charge is disposed of, the holder of the security has the same priority in respect of any property directly or indirectly representing the property disposed of as he would have had in relation to the property subject to the floating charge. Thus the interest of the chargee transfers to the proceeds of sale or other property representing the property disposed of (s 15(4) of the Insolvency Act 1986).

In relation to any other form of security or a hire purchase agreement, s 15(5) provides that the court order should specify that the net proceeds of sale of the property and if necessary a supplementary sum to make good any shortfall should be applied towards discharging the sum secured by the security or payable under the hire purchase agreement.

Section 16 provides that in Scotland the rights of the creditor against property subject to a fixed charge or hire purchase agreement, conditional sale agreement, chattel leasing agreement or retention of title agreement are extinguished upon a disposal effected under s 15.

Once an administration order has been made, the administrator must send a notice to the company forthwith and notify the registrar of companies within 14 days of the appointment. He must also within 28 days of the order inform creditors so far as he is aware of their addresses.

The administrator should require a statement of affairs to be made to him by those who have been running the company and in the company's employment (where they will be able to assist in compiling the statement) or involved in the company's formation if this is within one year of the administration order. The statement of affairs should set out the company's assets, debts and liabilities, the names and addresses of its creditors, the securities held by them and the dates the securities were given and any other information that may be prescribed. The statement of affairs should be submitted within 21 days of the notice given to them by the administrator.

The administrator then has three months from the date of the administration order to send to the registrar of companies his proposals for achieving the purpose or purposes set out in the order and laying a copy of the statement before a meeting of the company's creditors summoned on not less than 14 days' notice. The administrator should also send a copy of the statement to all members of the company or publish a notice in the prescribed manner setting out an address to which members should write for copies of the statement to be sent to them free of charge. A copy of the proposals should also be laid before a meeting of creditors summoned to approve the administrator's proposal. The meeting may approve the proposals or modify them but shall not modify them unless the administrator consents to each modification. The administrator should report the result of the meeting to the court and to the registrar of companies.

During the currency of an administration, s 27 of the Insolvency Act 1986 provides that a creditor or member of the company may apply to the court by petition for an order on the ground that the company's affairs, business and property are being or have been managed by the administrator in a manner which is unfairly prejudicial to the interests of its creditors or members generally or some part of them, or that any actual or proposed actual omission of the administrator is or would be so prejudicial.

This remedy obviously mirrors that set out in ss 459–61 of the Companies Act 1985 (see para 14.3). The court may make such order as it thinks appropriate and in particular may make an order:

- to regulate the future management by the administrator of the company;

- to require the administrator to refrain from doing or continuing an act complained of or to do an act which the petitioner has complained he has omitted to do;

- to require the summoning of a meeting of creditors or members;

- to discharge the administration order and make such consequential provision as the court thinks appropriate.

The Insolvency Act makes provision for certain gratuitous alienations (s 242), unfair preferences (s 243), extortionate credit transactions (s 244) and floating charges (s 245) to be invalidated where an administration order has been made. These are considered in more detail below (see para 23.2).

20.6   Fair dealing

Where an administration order is discharged on application by the administrator to the court, the administrator shall within 14 days of the making of the order send a copy of that order to the registrar of companies. The application should be made if it appears to the administrator that the purpose or purposes have been achieved or are incapable of achievement or if he is required to do so by a meeting of the company's creditors which has met to consider discharge of the administration order (s 18 of the Insolvency Act 1986).

20.7   Termination of administration

Summary of Chapter 20

Voluntary Arrangements and Administration

In response to recommendations made by the Cork Committee, Part I of the Insolvency Act 1986 makes provision for companies in financial difficulties to come to voluntary arrangements with their creditors agreeing to pay a percentage of debts that are due. A proposal for a voluntary arrangement may be made by a company's directors, liquidator or administrator. The supervisor charged with implementing the proposal must be a qualified insolvency practitioner.

Voluntary arrangements

Since 1985, it has been possible for the court on the application of a company, its directors or creditors to make an administration order in respect of a company where the company is unable to pay its debts. There then follows a period of intensive care for the company when no enforcement proceedings can be brought against the company and no hire purchase or leasing contract or reservation of title provision can be enforced against it.

Administration

If there is a floating charge in existence, however, the chargeholder can thwart administration by appointing an administrative receiver.

At the end of the administration, the company will hopefully be restored to full health, or there will have been a more advantageous realisation of assets than would have occurred on a winding up or a voluntary arrangement will have been made with creditors or possibly a scheme of arrangement entered into.

Chapter 21

Investigations

Minority remedies have already been considered. On occasion powers are given to the Department of Trade and Industry which buttress the minority remedies which are available. In particular, investigations, or inspections (as they are sometimes called), may be held into companies.

If it believes that there is good reason to do so, the Department of Trade and Industry may require a company to produce documents at such time and place as is specified or it may authorise an officer of the Department or any other competent person to require a company to produce to him any documents which may be specified (s 447 of the Companies Act 1985). The power extends to requiring production of documents from any person who appears to be in possession of documents but without prejudice to any lien that may be held over the documents. The power is reinforced by a power of entry and search of premises set out in s 448 of the Act. Section 450 of the Act provides a punishment for destroying, mutilating or falsifying a document and the offence is punishable by imprisonment and/or a fine. It is usual for an officer of the Department to arrive to inspect documents to prevent destruction of the documents.	**21.1 Production of documents**

In addition to the power to require the production of documents, the Department of Trade and Industry can in certain situations appoint inspectors to investigate the affairs of a company. Very often the investigation is preceded by requiring the production of documents which may then demonstrate that a full-blooded investigation is appropriate. Section 431 of the Act provides that the Secretary of State *may* appoint one or more inspectors to investigate the affairs of a company and to report on them in such manner as he may direct. The appointment may be made in the case of a limited company with share capital on the application of not less than 200 members or members holding one tenth of the issued shares and in the case of a company without share capital on the application of one fifth of the members of the company and in any case an investigation may be held on the application of the company. In general, two joint inspectors are appointed – one is usually a senior solicitor or barrister and the other is usually a senior accountant. For the sake of	**21.2 Investigation of affairs of company**

convenience here, the appointment will be referred to as an appointment of an inspector. The appointment of an inspector to investigate into the affairs of the company is not a judicial proceeding but an administrative one and the decision of the Department of Trade and Industry is final and cannot be challenged provided that the power is exercised *bona fide*, see *Norwest Holst Ltd v Secretary of State for Trade and Industry* (1978). It was stated in this case that an investigation is an administrative act and that the full rules of natural justice did not therefore apply. In the case of such an application, it should be supported by such evidence as the Secretary of State may require to demonstrate that there is good reason for requiring the investigation. The Secretary of State may before appointing an inspector require the applicant or applicants to give security for the costs of the investigation.

Section 432 provides that an investigation must be held into the affairs of a company where it is ordered by the court (s 432(1) of the Companies Act 1985). Furthermore, the Secretary of State *may* order that an investigation should be held if there are circumstances suggesting:

- that the company's affairs are being or have been conducted with intent to defraud creditors or otherwise for a fraudulent or unlawful purpose or in a manner which is unfairly prejudicial to some part of the members; or

- that an actual or proposed act or omission is or would be so prejudicial or that the company was formed for any fraudulent or unlawful purpose (note that the wording of the section was not amended by the Companies Act 1989 when s 459 was amended to permit petitions where all of the members have been prejudiced. The odd result is that it would seem that an investigation cannot be ordered if all of the members are prejudiced);

- that persons connected with the company's formation or management have been guilty of fraud, misfeasance or other misconduct toward the company or its members; or

- the company's members have not been given all the information with respect to the company's affairs which they might reasonably expect (s 432(2) of the Companies Act 1985).

Section 432(2A) provides that inspectors may be appointed under s 432(2) on terms that their report is not for publication. In every other case the Secretary of State may if he thinks appropriate provide that the report is to be published.

Section 442 of the Companies Act 1985 provides that the Secretary of State may order an investigation into the ownership or control of a company to find out who the true owners of the company are if he feels there is good reason to do so. He must order an investigation if an application is made by 200 or more members or by members holding 10% or more of the company's issued shares unless he feels that the investigation is vexatious or that it would be sufficient to carry out an investigation under s 444 (this provides for information being given direct to the Secretary of State without the need for the appointment of inspectors).

If the difficulty in finding out information about any shares appears due to the non-cooperation of persons, then the Secretary of State may make an order that:

- any transfer of the shares will be void;

- voting rights in respect of the shares may not be exercised;

- additional shares may not be issued in respect of those shares;

- sums due on the shares will not be paid except in a liquidation (s 454 of the Companies Act 1985).

An aggrieved person may appeal against such an order (s 456 of the Companies Act 1985).

21.3   Investigation of ownership or control

Section 446 provides that the Secretary of State may appoint an inspector if he feels that there has been a contravention of s 323 or s 324 of the Act. These sections provide for a prohibition on directors dealing in share options (as well as immediate members of their families) (s 323 of the Companies Act 1985) and disclosure by directors of share dealings in their company as well as share dealings of immediate members of their family (s 324 of the Companies Act 1985).

In every case where an inspector is appointed under ss 431, 432, 442 or 446, the inspector may investigate any other company in the group.

21.4   Investigation of directors' share dealings

Section 177 of the Financial Services Act 1986 provides for an inspection to be mounted where it is suspected that there is a breach of the provisions prohibiting insider dealing. The Secretary of State may appoint inspectors to carry out such investigations as are requisite to establish whether or not there has been a contravention of the insider dealing provisions. A prosecution may follow in appropriate circumstances.

21.5   Investigation into insider dealing

21.6   Consequences of inspections

As well as a final report made by the inspector, there may be interim reports. This will particularly be the case if there is a long and complex investigation. Generally speaking, the reports will be published without delay but occasionally there will be a time lag. A delay was challenged unsuccessfully in *R v Secretary of State for Trade (ex p Lonrho plc)* (1989).

Some of the more important consequences of the report or the inspection of documents under the Companies Act may include the following:

- The Secretary of State may petition under s 124(4) of the Insolvency Act 1986 if he considers it is expedient in the public interest to wind the company up on the just and equitable ground. The matter does not have to be considered personally by the Secretary of State but may be considered by an official, see *Re Golden Chemical Products Ltd* (1976). The report will be evidence in the proceedings, see *Re Tower & Holiday Clubs Ltd* (1967). The report itself, however, is open to challenge and other evidence may need to be adduced, see *Re Koscot (Interplanetary) (UK) Ltd* (1972).

- Civil proceedings may be ordered to be brought in the name of the company. Section 438 of the Act provides that the Secretary of State may bring proceedings in the name and on behalf of the company if they ought to be brought in the public interest.

- The Secretary of State if it appears to him that the company's affairs are being or have been conducted in a manner which is unfairly prejudicial to the interests of its members generally or of some part of its members or that an actual or proposed act or omission is or would be so prejudicial may bring a petition on the grounds of unfair prejudice on behalf of members of the company (s 460 of the Companies Act 1985).

- An application may be made for a disqualification order against any person who is or has been a director or shadow director of any company if it appears to the Secretary of State from the report or from information gleaned from documents that have been disclosed that a disqualification order should be made in the public interest. The maximum period for such a disqualification is 15 years (see para 10.6).

If matters come to light during the course of an investigation which suggest that a criminal offence has been committed and those matters are referred to the appropriate prosecuting authority, the Secretary of State can halt the inspection or confine it to specific matters (s 437(1A) of the Companies Act 1985).

The expenses of investigation are borne by the Department of Trade. It may in appropriate cases recover them from persons particularly those convicted as a result of prosecutions consequent upon a report.

21.7   Expenses of investigation

Investigations

The Department of Trade and Industry is given various powers to investigate the affairs, ownership or directors' share dealings within a company. There are also powers to investigate insider dealing.

As a prelude to an investigation, the Department of Trade and Industry may order a company to disclose specified documents to it. This may conclude the matter by revealing what action should be taken or that nothing is amiss or it may be the prelude to a full-blooded investigation. Where inspectors are appointed, one is generally a senior lawyer and one a senior accountant. Their report may be published. The inspection is an administrative proceeding not a judicial one.

As a consequence of the inspection, the Secretary of State may do one or more of the following:

- initiate winding up proceedings on the just and equitable ground;

- initiate civil proceedings in the name of the company;

- petition on the grounds of unfair prejudice;

- apply for a disqualification order against a director or shadow director.

Chapter 22

Takeovers, Reconstructions and Amalgamations

It is important to note that these terms are not specifically legal terms but are often used in business and finance circles to describe particular situations.

The term 'takeover' is generally used to describe the situation where one company acquires the shares of another company (target company). The acquiring or bidding company becomes the holding company of the acquired or target company which therefore becomes a subsidiary. Takeovers may be accomplished by agreement or a takeover bid may be a 'hostile' bid.

22.1   Takeovers

A reconstruction is generally accomplished where the shareholders of the transferring company and the shareholders of this company to which the business has transferred are the same. The people who are carrying on the reconstructed business are thus generally the same as those who carried it on before. Reconstructions may involve an external element such as where a particular company sells its business and assets to another company in exchange for shares in that company; alternatively reconstructions may be internal within a particular group where the capital structure within the group is altered.

22.2   Reconstructions

The term 'amalgamation' is usually used where two companies are brought together. The two companies may become one new company, for example, X plc and Y plc becoming Z plc, or alternatively X plc may be subsumed by Y plc or vice versa. Here clearly there is an overlap with the term 'takeover'.

22.3   Amalgamations

Takeovers are governed by ss 428–30F of the Companies Act 1985 (the original sections having been modified by the Financial Services Act 1986). These sections provide for the compulsory acquisition of shares. If an offer is made to acquire all the shares or all the shares of a class that the offeror does not already hold, then if the offer is accepted by at least 90% in value of shareholders within four months, then within two months of that 90% acceptance the offeror can give notice of his intention to acquire the other 10%.

22.4   Takeovers

The shares must be acquired on precisely the same terms. This may sometimes give an advantage to the 10% who have delayed giving acceptance to the offer. Thus, in *Re Carlton Holdings* (1971), the court ordered that a cash alternative that had been on offer originally must be extended to the non accepting minority. This will on occasion give benefit to those delaying as they will be able to see in which direction the share price moves.

Within six weeks of the service of the notice dissentient shareholders have six weeks to choose from any alternatives that have been on offer.

Section 430C provides that the person upon whom a notice is served (the dissentient) may apply to the court within six weeks of the notice for an order that the offeror shall not be entitled to acquire the shares or to specify different terms for the acquisition. It is very rare for the court to exercise the power to prevent acquisition under the section. One such case, however, was *Re Bugle Press Ltd* (1960) where 90% majority shareholders constructed a takeover scheme in an attempt to oust a minority shareholder with a 10% interest. It was not an economic takeover situation but in reality an attempt to get rid of a difficult dissentient member. The court refused to countenance the use of these sections for such manoeuvres.

There is a corresponding right in the dissentient to be purchased. Section 430A provides for the right of the minority shareholder to be bought out by the offeror.

22.5 Schemes of arrangement

Sections 425–27A of the Companies Act 1985 deal with arrangements and reconstructions. Section 425 provides for a compromise or arrangement to be made between a company and its creditors or any class of them, and between a company and its members or any class of them. The usual situation here is that there is a modification of existing rights and consequently a reorganisation within a group of companies. It may involve, for example, debentureholders giving up rights as debentureholders in exchange for shares in a company. The procedure is as follows:

Application is made to the court by the company or any creditor or member or in the case of a company that is being wound up or where there is an administration order in force, an application may be made by a liquidator or administrator. Upon this application, the court may then order a meeting of the creditors or different classes of creditors or the members or different classes of members to be summoned as the court thinks appropriate. The proposed scheme of compromise or arrangement will then be sent out before each of the meetings. The scheme of arrangement will be sent out with the notice summoning the meeting together with a statement explaining the effect of the compromise or arrangement. If the notice is given by way of advertisement, then the advertisement should state where copies of the statement of compromise or arrangement are available or the statement should be set out in the advertisement.

If a majority in number representing three fourths in value of the creditors or class of creditors or members or class of members consent to the compromise or arrangement, then the matter is reported back to the court. In *Re Hellenic and General Trust Ltd* (1975), the question of what constituted a class was discussed (at para 6.2). Templeman J held that where a wholly owned subsidiary of the offeror held 53% of the shares of the offeree company this constituted those shares a separate class. (Note that this case also considered the extent to which the s 425 procedure could be used instead of the takeover procedure in ss 428–30F for acquisition of shares with the lower level of consent in s 425 being an attraction for the transferee company. Templeman J left the possibility open.)

The court will then consider any minority objections and generally sanction the scheme. The court will be anxious that there has been full and proper disclosure, however.

Thus in *Re Dorman Long & Co* (1934), sanction was not granted where full details of the scheme had not been given as the revaluation of assets did not set out the amount of the revaluation.

Where the court does sanction the scheme, it may make provision for the following:

- the transfer to the transferee company of the undertaking, property or liabilities of the transferor company;

- the allotting or appropriation by the transferee company of shares, debentures, policies or other like interests in that company which are to be appropriated to or for any person;

- the continuation by or against the transferee company of any legal proceedings pending by or against the transferor company;

- the dissolution without winding up of the transferor company;

- provisions to be made for any dissentients;

- any incidental, consequential or supplemental matters as are necessary.

It may be seen that the provisions relating to schemes of compromise and arrangement are costly as they involve two applications to the court. The degree of approval required is less than that required in ss 428–30F as only three quarters majority in value is needed rather than 90% in value.

22.6 Sale of assets in return for shares

Another way of accomplishing a reconstruction is under ss 110 and 111 of the Insolvency Act 1986. This involves the following procedure. The company that is to be transferred is in the course of a voluntary winding up or being proposed for voluntary winding up. The company in voluntary liquidation sells its assets in exchange for shares in the transferee company. The transferee company's shares are then distributed to the former members of the transferor company. Section 111 of the Insolvency Act provides that dissentient members of the transferor company who did not vote in favour of the special resolution placing the company in voluntary liquidation may within seven days by writing to the liquidator require that their interests be purchased for cash.

There is no need to apply to the court here. The main disadvantage for the transferee company is the provision that dissentients may require that their interests be purchased for cash. Indeed, the right of a dissentient member to dispose of his shares for cash is sacrosanct and cannot be excluded by the company's constitution, see *Bisgood v Henderson's Transvaal Estates Ltd* (1908).

22.7 City Code

The City Code on Takeovers and Mergers is a major consideration in this area. As Gower has noted, it is the main body of legislation for quoted companies. The Code is administered by the City Panel on Takeovers and Mergers. It is made up of general principles which are standards which listed companies must follow, detailed rules of which there are 38 which are more specific and set out matters on timing of offers and the degree of information to be given. The City Code is of importance if one or more of the two companies concerned has a Stock Exchange listing. Compliance is crucial as ultimately The Stock Exchange has the power of removing a listing or suspending a listing as a sanction to ensure that the Code is complied with. The membership of the panel is made up of organisations such as the Bank of England, the Confederation of British Industry, The Stock Exchange, the Investment Management and Regulatory Organisation, and the Securities and Futures Authority. The panel publishes reports where it has investigated alleged breaches of the Code.

It should also be noted in this context that there are Stock Exchange rules governing substantial acquisition of shares. These were introduced in the 1980s as a result of dawn raids where takeovers were being accomplished by stealth whereby teams of people acting in concert were each acquiring a small holding of shares then acting together to take over a company. In this context, note should also be made of the concert party provisions in the Companies Act, ss 198–219 of the Companies Act 1985. The provisions apply to public companies. Such companies must keep registers of persons who hold 3% or more of the shares. The rules extend to family and other connected interests, and to require disclosure of concert parties where there is an agreement between parties to act together and acquire shares in a public company. The use of the shares must be restricted and must have been acquired in pursuit of the concert party agreement.

Together, these rules and statutory provisions considerably lessen the prospect of surreptitious acquisition of companies.

Takeovers, Reconstructions and Amalgamations

The Companies Act makes provision for the compulsory acquisition of up to 10% of a target company's shares where the bidding company has acquired 90%. The acquisition of the minority holding would be ordered on the same terms as the majority was acquired. Not only does the majority have a right to acquire the minority but the minority has a corresponding right to be acquired.

Sections 425–27A provide for schemes of arrangement to be made between a company and its creditors or members. These provisions are usually utilised where there is an internal reconstruction. The procedure involves application to the court on two occasions so it can be costly.

A straightforward procedure for merger is presented by the Insolvency Act where a company goes into voluntary liquidation. The liquidator accepts shares from a transferee company in exchange for the assets of the company. The shares are then distributed to the former members of the transferor company. A dissentient in the transferor company can insist on his interest being purchased for cash.

Where there is a takeover involving a quoted company, the City Code on Takeovers and Mergers is of crucial importance. It is extra-statutory but policed by the City Panel on Takeovers and Mergers. The City Code is made up of general principles and detailed rules governing the conduct of takeovers.

There are also Stock Exchange rules governing the substantial acquisition of shares as well as provisions in the Companies Act designed to prevent takeover by stealth.

Chapter 23

Liquidation

It is beyond the scope of this work to give a detailed survey of the law on liquidation. This area of law is a complex one. Not only is the Insolvency Act 1986 devoted in part to the law on liquidation (or winding up), but this is supplemented by detailed insolvency rules governing the practice of insolvency (Insolvency (Scotland) Rules 1986).

The law on winding up was updated by the Insolvency Act 1985 following the Report of the Review Committee on Insolvency Law and Practice (the Cork Report – Cmnd 8558, 1982). The Committee had been appointed as long ago as 1977 with the allotted task of making proposals to reform the law on personal bankruptcy in England and corporate insolvency. This was then consolidated in the Insolvency Act 1986. The law on personal bankruptcy in Scotland is contained in the Bankruptcy (Scotland) Act 1985.

There are essentially two types of winding up. There is compulsory winding up – a winding up by court order, and voluntary winding up – winding up initiated by the members of the company. Voluntary winding up then splits into two types:

23.1   Types of winding up

- members' voluntary winding up which is largely under the control of the members where the directors swear a statutory declaration of solvency; and

- creditors' voluntary winding up which is largely under the control of the creditors as the directors have seen fit not to swear a statutory declaration of solvency.

Section 122(1) of the Insolvency Act 1986 sets out the grounds of compulsory winding up. They are as follows:

23.1.1   Compulsory winding up

A company may be wound up if:

(a) the company has by special resolution resolved that the company be wound up by the court;

(b) that the company is a public company which has registered as such on initial incorporation but has not been issued with a certificate to do business under s 117 of the Companies Act and more than a year has expired since it was so registered;

(c) the company is an old public company within the meaning of the Consequential Provisions Act;

(d) the company has not commenced business within a year of incorporation or suspends business for a year;

(e) the number of members is reduced below two unless it is a private company to which the exemption relating to a membership of one now applies;

(f) the company is unable to pay its debts;

(g) the court is of the opinion that it is just and equitable that the company should be wound up.

In Scotland, s 122(2) provides that a company may be wound up by the court if the security enjoyed by the holder of a floating charge is in jeopardy.

The court clearly has a discretion as to whether or not to grant a petition. This point receives support from s 125 of the Insolvency Act 1986 which provides that the court may dismiss a petition or adjourn the hearing conditionally or unconditionally or make an interim order or any other order that it thinks fit.

Only the last two grounds in s 122(1) are of great importance. The inability to pay debts is 'fleshed out' in s 123 of the Act. This has been covered above (at para 20.4). In considering the various grounds that demonstrate inability to pay debts, the court will take account of any disputed debts and if it feels that there is a *bona fide* dispute concerning a debt, no winding up order will be granted unless it is clear that more than £750 is owed by the company.

In *Re Welsh Brick Industries Ltd* (1946), the Court of Appeal held that a judge was competent to grant a petition on the basis of the evidence before him even though unconditional leave to defend the debt had been given to the company.

Even if it is demonstrated that there is a dispute concerning the debt a winding up petition may be granted if it is established that at least £750 is owing. Thus it was established in *Re Tweeds Garages Ltd* (1962) that the garage owed at least the minimum amount then required by the Act and the petition was granted.

Yet, the existence of a debt of the requisite amount is not sufficient of itself to force a winding up petition. The court has a discretion and will consider the views of contributories and especially of other creditors. In *Re ABC Coupler & Engineering Co Ltd* (1961), a judgment creditor with a debt of in excess of £17,500 petitioned for an order that the company be compulsorily wound up. The petition was not supported by any other creditor and was opposed by a number of them. The company had extensive goodwill and a considerable excess of assets over liabilities. The petition was not granted.

The various grounds on which a petition to wind the company up on the just and equitable ground may be granted have also been considered above (see para 14.6). The petition here is presented by a member or contributory as he is termed in a liquidation situation (see s 124(2) of the Insolvency Act 1986). The presence of the remedy of just and equitable winding up is a clear demonstration of the fact that winding up is available in situations other than where the company is in financial difficulties. The appellation insolvency as applied to the Insolvency Act is in some ways misleading. Indeed, it seems that the contributory whose shares are fully paid must show that he has an interest in the winding up which means that he must demonstrate that assets will be available for distribution. The question was left open in *Re Rica Gold Washing Co* (1879).

In addition, s 124(2) of the Insolvency Act 1986 provides that a contributory may only present a petition if the number of members is reduced below the statutory minimum or he holds shares which were originally allotted to him, or have been transmitted to him on the death of a former holder or he has held the shares for at least six months from the previous 18 months before the commencement of the winding up.

The progress of a compulsory liquidation is that the petition is presented, for example, by a creditor if it is on the ground of inability to pay debts or by a contributory if it is on the ground that it is just and equitable that the company should be wound up.

The Secretary of State for Trade and Industry may also present a petition on grounds (b) or (c) above and also if, following a report made or information received in relation to company investigations or information obtained under s 52 of the Criminal Justice (Scotland) Act 1987 (s 2 of the Criminal Justice Act 1987 in England) in relation to fraud investigations or under s 83 of the Companies Act 1989 in relation to assisting overseas regulatory authorities, he thinks that it is expedient in the public interest that a company should be wound up.

Once the petition has been presented, it is then for the court to decide whether the case has been made out. If it has been made out, the petition may be granted at the court's discretion and an order to wind the company up may be made. The commencement date of the liquidation is the date the petition is presented ie retrospectively the date of the commencement of liquidation is the date of the petition. This is material in many situations as certain acts or transactions may be rendered invalid within certain time limits.

As has been noted, s 125 of the Insolvency Act 1986 provides that on hearing a winding up petition the court can grant the petition or adjourn the hearing conditionally or unconditionally or make an interim order. It should not refuse to grant a winding up petition solely on the ground that the company's assets have been mortgaged equal to or in excess of the company's assets or on the basis that the company has no assets.

Once a winding up petition has been presented, the company or any creditor or contributory can apply to the court for a stay of proceedings where proceedings are pending in the High Court or Court of Appeal in England and in any other case may apply to the court having jurisdiction to wind up the company to restrain further proceedings (s 126 of the Insolvency Act 1986). The actual making of the order operates to stay all proceedings but this provision enables action to be taken to stay proceedings upon presentation of the petition.

Once a winding up petition has been presented, any disposition of the company's property and any transfer of shares or alteration of its status is void unless the court orders otherwise where it has been committed after the commencement of the winding up (s 127 of the Insolvency Act 1986). Since the commencement date of a winding up is the presentation of the petition, this renders void dispositions after the presentation of the petition.

Section 127 includes payments that are made into and out of a company's bank account, see *Re Grays Inn Construction Co Ltd* (1980). The principles on which dispositions may be validated were discussed by the Court of Appeal in *Re Grays Inn Construction Co Ltd*. Buckley LJ said that in general the interests of the unsecured creditors will not be prejudiced in making any validation decision. He went on to say that a disposition carried out in good faith in the course of business at a time when the parties are unaware that a petition has been presented would normally be validated by the court.

Where a winding up order is granted, the court will appoint an interim liquidator (s 138 of the Insolvency Act 1986). In England, the provisional (equivalent of interim) liquidator will be the official receiver (s 136(2)). There is no official receiver in Scotland. The liquidator may require some or all of the company's officers, those involved in its formation within the previous year, those in its employment or previous employment within the last year or those who are officers or in the employment of a company which was within the previous year an officer of the company to provide a statement of affairs setting out the company's assets, debts, liabilities, names and addresses of its creditors, securities held by them and the dates on which the securities were given.

Section 138 of the Insolvency Act 1986 requires the interim liquidator to call separate meetings of creditors and contributories to appoint a permanent liquidator within 28 days of the interim liquidator's appointment. Where, however, the company is insolvent and it appears inappropriate to call a meeting of contributories, this is dispensed with in Scotland. The creditors and the contributories at their respective meetings may nominate a person to be liquidator. The liquidator will be the person nominated by the creditors in the event of any conflict. Usually the interim liquidator will be appointed as permanent liquidator. Yet the contributories may go to court to overturn the decision seeking the appointment of the person nominated by them. The same meetings of creditors and contributories may nominate people to a liquidation committee. The purpose of the liquidation committee will be to liaise with the liquidator during the course of the winding up.

Certain powers of the liquidator in a compulsory winding up can only be exercised with the sanction of the liquidation committee or the court (see s 167(1)(a) of the Insolvency Act 1986). Where there is no liquidation committee, the court may grant the liquidator certain supplementary powers (s 169).

It is the function of the liquidator to realise the company's property for cash during the liquidation. The proceeds should then be distributed to the company's creditors and if there is a surplus to the persons entitled to it, generally the contributories (class rights are again relevant here – see Chapter 6), s 143 of the Insolvency Act 1986.

The liquidator takes into his custody and places under his control all the company's property and things in action (s 144 of the Insolvency Act 1986).

23.1.2   Voluntary liquidation

Voluntary liquidation may commence in the following ways:

1   If a fixed period has been settled for the duration of the company and the fixed period has now passed or if the company is to come to an end, after a certain event, then the company may be wound up by ordinary resolution.

2   If the company resolves to be wound up voluntarily by special resolution.

3   If the company resolves by extraordinary resolution to be wound up on the basis that it cannot by reason of its liabilities continue its business.

(Section 84 of the Insolvency Act 1986.)

Notice of any resolution to wind up should be published in the *Edinburgh Gazette* within 14 days (s 85(1) of the Insolvency Act 1986).

In a voluntary winding up, the winding up commences on the date that the resolution is passed (s 86 of the Insolvency Act 1986).

If the directors of the company or a majority of them swear a statutory declaration of solvency to the effect that the company will be able to pay its debts in full together with interest within the next 12 months, then this represents a statutory declaration of solvency. If such a declaration is made, then the declaration should be delivered to the registrar of companies. Where there is such a declaration, the liquidation proceeds as a members' voluntary winding up as the interests of creditors are supposedly protected by the statutory declaration of solvency that has been sworn. The statutory declaration of solvency should be passed within the five week period immediately before the resolution to wind up (ss 89–90 of the Insolvency Act 1986).

If the winding up proceeds as a members' voluntary winding up, then there will be a general meeting of members or contributories to pass a resolution to wind up and to appoint somebody as liquidator.

If no statutory declaration of solvency is sworn then the liquidation proceeds as a creditors' voluntary winding up. In such a situation, a general meeting of members is needed to resolve to wind up, to nominate a liquidator and to appoint members (up to five) for the liquidation committee.

(Note that a liquidation committee implies a compulsory winding up or a creditors' voluntary winding up. No liquidation committee is appointed in a members' voluntary winding up as it is believed that the interests of creditors are protected by the statutory declaration of solvency. In a compulsory winding up and a creditors' voluntary winding up there *may* be a liquidation committee.)

In the creditors' voluntary winding up, a meeting of creditors will be called to appoint a liquidator and if the creditors so wish to appoint up to five creditors' representatives on to a liquidation committee. In the event of a dispute on the choice of liquidator, the creditors' choice will prevail unless the court orders otherwise (ss 100–01 of the Insolvency Act 1986).

23.2   Fair dealing

Certain matters that should be watched for in relation to a liquidation have already been noted, see invalidity of floating charges (s 245 of the Insolvency Act 1986) and invalidity of unfair preferences (s 243 of the Insolvency Act 1986) (see para 18.12).

There are other provisions in the Insolvency Act concerned with the adjustment of prior transactions (administration and liquidation). These are the so-called fair dealing provisions.

Section 242 of the Insolvency Act 1986 provides that an administrator or liquidator may apply to the court for an order of reduction or for restoration of property to the company's assets or for such other remedy as may be appropriate. This is appropriate where the company has made a gift of its property or has received significantly less consideration for property than its true value.

An order may be made if the transaction is in favour of a connected person, within five years of the onset of insolvency or, if in favour of an unconnected person, within two years of the onset of insolvency. (The onset of insolvency means the date of presentation of a petition to appoint an administrator or the date of commencement of the winding up. Any transaction between the presentation of a petition for administration and the granting of the order is also caught.) (See para 20.7.) There are certain statutory defences available.

Extortionate credit transactions where credit is supplied to the company on terms where the payments are grossly exorbitant or where the terms otherwise grossly contravene ordinary principles of fair dealing are also caught (s 244 of the Insolvency Act 1986). The time limit here is a transaction within the three year period terminating with the date of the administration order or the date when the liquidation commenced (s 244(2) of the Insolvency Act 1986).

The court may order the transaction to be set aside or some part of it. It may vary the terms or order the surrender of money or property or order accounts to be taken. It may order any combination of these.

Another area of law of importance in a liquidation concerns the penalisation of directors and officers for malpractice. Section 212 of the Insolvency Act 1986 provides a summary remedy in winding up where a person who has been an officer, liquidator, administrator or receiver or concerned in the promotion, formation or management of the company has misapplied or retained or become accountable for the company's money or property or been guilty of any misfeasance or breach of any fiduciary or other duty in relation to the company. The court may order repayment of money or restoration of property or such contribution for breach of duty as the court thinks just. It would appear that s 727 of the

23.3   Malpractice

Companies Act 1985 enabling the court to give relief to any officer does not cover liquidators, administrators or receivers (see para 11.9).

A provision of some importance enables the court on the application of the liquidator to declare that any persons knowingly party to the carrying on of the business of a company with intent to defraud creditors or for a fraudulent purpose be ordered to contribute to the company's assets. This is the so-called 'fraudulent trading' section (s 213 of the Insolvency Act 1986). The Cork Committee had recommended that whilst retaining the high standard of proof for criminal proceedings (now s 458 of the Companies Act 1985) a lower standard of proof founded on unreasonable behaviour should become the basis for civil liability. In the event a new provision – s 214 of the Insolvency Act – based on unreasonable behaviour – wrongful trading – supplements rather than replaces s 213 of the Act.

Under s 213, actual deceit on the part of the person carrying on the business must be shown. In *Re Gerald Cooper Chemicals Ltd* (1978), it was said that where the company received forward payment for the supply of indigo knowing that it could not continue to trade because of insolvency and used this to pay off part of a loan, the company was carrying on business fraudulently. The person receiving the money was stated to be liable if he accepted money which he knew full well to have been obtained by the carrying on of a business with intent to defraud creditors.

However, in *Rossleigh Ltd v Carlaw* (1986), the Inner House held that the preference of one creditor (which happened to be a holding company of the insolvent company) to the disadvantage of another did not amount to an 'intent to defraud' the latter creditor. The court held that 'intent to defraud' under the Act required the criminal standard of fraud to be proved. Proof merely of a lack of good faith in concealing the company's insolvency from a creditor was insufficient.

When an order is made on the application of the liquidator the sum which the person is ordered to pay will generally contain a punitive element as well as a compensatory one, see *Re William C Leitch Bros Ltd* (1932), *Re a Company (No 001418 of 1988)* (1991).

Section 214 of the Insolvency Act 1986 extends liability for directors or shadow directors who should know or ought to have concluded that there was no reasonable prospect that the company would avoid going into insolvent liquidation. The section is therefore more limited in catchment than s 213 as s 213 applies to any person knowingly party to the carrying on of the business. Furthermore, s 214 has no corresponding criminal sanction.

The section was considered in *Re Produce Marketing Consortium Ltd (No 2)* (1989). The liquidator of the company sought an order under s 214 of the Insolvency Act 1986 against two directors. The auditors of the company which was in the business of importing fruit had warned the directors of the company's serious financial position. The judge found the directors liable to contribute £75,000. In determining how to decide whether directors ought to have known of the company's position, Knox J had this to say:

> The knowledge to be imputed in testing whether or not directors knew or ought to have concluded that there was no reasonable prospect of the company avoiding insolvent liquidation is not limited to the documentary material actually available at the given time. This appears from s 214(4) which includes a reference to facts which a director of a company not only should know but those which he ought to ascertain, a word which does not appear in s 214(2)(b). In my judgment this indicates that there is to be included by way of factual information not only what was actually there, but what given reasonable diligence and an appropriate level of general knowledge, skill and experience, was ascertainable.

In *Re Purpoint Ltd* (1991), Vinelott J held a director of the company liable under s 214 where it should have been plain to him that the company could not avoid going into insolvent liquidation. The purpose of an order under s 214 is to ensure that any depletion of the company's assets which occurs after a time when there is no reasonable prospect of the company's avoiding an insolvent winding up is made good. The company's business is being conducted at such a time at the risk of creditors.

In *Re Hydrodam (Corby) Ltd* (1994), the extent to which wrongful trading may extend to others was at issue. Liability is imposed under s 214 on shadow directors (s 741(2) defines a shadow director as 'a person in accordance with whose directions or instructions the directors of the company are accustomed to act'. The subsection continues: 'However, a person is not deemed a shadow director by reason only that the directors act on advice given by him in a professional capacity').

Hydrodam was a wholly owned subsidiary of Eagle Trust plc. The liquidator made a claim for wrongful trading against Eagle Trust plc, one of Eagle Trust's subsidiaries, and all of Eagle Trust's directors. Two of Eagle Trust plc's directors applied to have the claim struck out. The company had duly appointed directors, two Channel Island companies. Millett J was prepared to assume that Eagle Trust could be a shadow director. He did not accept, however, that it followed that Eagle Trust's directors were also shadow directors. Although they attended the ultimate holding company's board meetings, they were still not thereby without other factors shadow directors. Millett J held that no case had been made out against either of the defendants.

Previously, it had been thought that banks and substantial creditors ran risks when they gave instructions to companies in financial difficulties. *Re Hydrodam* makes it very clear that cogent evidence will be needed of giving instructions to those people running the company before the shadow directorship is made out.

A person is only liable for wrongful trading if the court is not satisfied that he took every step with a view to minimising the potential loss to the company's creditors as (assuming him to have known that there was no reasonable prospect that the company would avoid going into insolvent liquidation) he ought to have taken. Directors should therefore raise concerns with other board members and urge action, such as discontinuing trading, as is appropriate. This appears to be the only defence available under s 214. Section 727 of the Companies Act 1985 was considered and rejected as a defence in *Re Produce Marketing Consortium Ltd (No 2)* (1989).

As well as the potential liability of directors for matters occurring before the liquidation commences, there are various offences of fraud and deception which may be committed during a liquidation. These include:

- fraud etc in anticipation of a winding up (s 206 of the Insolvency Act 1986);

- past or present officers making gifts or transfers of or charges on company property (s 207 of the Insolvency Act 1986);

- misconduct by past or present officers during the course of the winding up (s 208 of the Insolvency Act 1986);

- falsification, destruction, mutilation etc of the company's books, papers, etc (s 209 of the Insolvency Act 1986);

- material omission from the statement relating to company's affairs (s 210 of the Insolvency Act 1986).

23.4   The conduct of the liquidation

Whilst it is not intended to go into the minutiae of the conduct of the liquidation, it is proposed here to mention one or two miscellaneous facets of the process of liquidation and to consider the priority of payments in a liquidation.

Section 233 of the Insolvency Act implementing a recommendation of the Cork Committee provides that suppliers of gas, water, electricity and telephone services cannot make it a condition of continued supply, where there is an administration, receivership, voluntary arrangement or liquidation, that all moneys owing be paid. The section is a recognition of the dominant bargaining position of such utility suppliers and it prevents them using their 'economic muscle'. The supplier can, however, insist on a personal guarantee in relation to continued supplies.

A liquidator by virtue of common law in Scotland may either adopt or repudiate current company contracts. If the liquidator does not intimate his intention to adopt a contract within a reasonable time after his appointment, he will be deemed to have repudiated it – see *Crown Estate Commissioners v Liquidators of Highland Engineering Ltd* (1975). Where the liquidator repudiates a contract, the company becomes liable in damages for breach of contract.

An equivalent, although substantially different, provision applies in England, which allows the liquidator to disclaim onerous property under s 178 of the Insolvency Act 1986. Onerous property means any unprofitable contract and any other property of the company which is unsaleable or not readily saleable such as a wasting lease. This power must be exercised within 12 months of the commencement of the liquidation. Where it is exercised any person sustaining loss or damage is deemed a creditor and can prove for the extent of the loss or damage in the winding up.

Another matter that may arise in a liquidation situation concerns the re-use of company names. Section 216 of the Insolvency Act 1986 deals with the so-called 'phoenix syndrome' and places certain limitations on the re-use of company names. The section provides that the old name or a similar one cannot be used by the directors or shadow directors for a period of five years from the commencement of the liquidation. In *Thorne v Silverleaf* (1994), the defendant was a director of two companies which had gone into liquidation, Mike Spence (Reading) Ltd and Mike Spence (Motor Sport) Ltd. He had personally guaranteed their overdrafts. The defendant established and became a director of a third company, Mike Spence Classic Cars Ltd. The company dealt in vintage cars. The plaintiff provided the company with finance. The company's financial position deteriorated and the plaintiff complained that the defendant was personally liable for its debts since the company had a name so similar to the two previous companies to suggest an association with them. The court held that this was so and the defendant was held personally liable under s 216 of the Insolvency Act 1986. However, the old name may well have a value and the court can give leave to a director of a failed company to buy-over the old name (see *Re Bonus Breaks Ltd* (1991)).

When the liquidator has realised the company's assets, he is faced with paying off the company's debts. Many features of priority which applied in relation to receivership also apply here (see para 19.4). The order of priority is as follows:

(1) The costs of the liquidation, including the liquidator's remuneration.

(2) Preferential creditors are paid off next.

The categories of preferential debts are set out in Schedule 6 of the Insolvency Act 1986. The categories rank equally and are as follows:

- PAYE contributions due in the 12 months before liquidation commences;

- VAT which is due for the six month period before liquidation;

- car tax due in the 12 month period before liquidation;

- general betting duty, bingo duty and pool betting duty payable in the 12 month period before liquidation;

- NIC contributions which are due for the 12 month period before liquidation;

- any sums owing to occupational and state pension schemes;

- wages due to employees for the four month period before liquidation up to £800 per employee;

- any accrued holiday pay owed to employees.

   Note that any sum advanced by a bank etc for paying salaries and accrued holiday pay which would otherwise have been preferential becomes preferential by subrogation.

(3) Charges secured by floating charges are paid off next.

(4) Ordinary trade creditors who have no security.

(5) Any deferred debts such as dividends which have been declared but not paid.

If there is a surplus of assets (many liquidations are solvent ones) the surplus will be distributed amongst the company's members according to their class rights (see para 6.2).

Any unclaimed assets will vest in the Crown.

If the liquidation is not completed within 12 months after its commencement the liquidator must make returns under s 192 of the Insolvency Act 1986 to the registrar.

23.5   Dissolution

Once the liquidator has completed the ingathering and distribution of the company's assets he will call a meeting in order to lay before it the accounts of the winding up. The following are entitled to receive notice of and attend the meeting:

- in a members' voluntary winding up – the members (s 94);

- in a creditors' voluntary winding up – the members and creditors (s 106); or

- in a compulsory winding up – the creditors (s 146).

The liquidator will obtain his release at the meeting, and will then file with the registrar the final accounts and a return of the meetings. The company will be dissolved at the end of a three month period commencing on the date on which the liquidator's final returns are received by the registrar (ss 201 and 205 of the Insolvency Act 1986).

A dissolution may be declared void by the court under s 651 of the Companies Act 1985 within two years in order to allow the company to complete unfinished business, or within twenty years to allow proceedings to be brought against the company (subject to the Prescription and Limitation (Scotland) Act 1973).

Liquidation

Liquidations (or winding ups) fall into two basic categories: compulsory by court order and voluntary initiated by the members of the company. Voluntary liquidations are of two types: members' voluntary winding up under the control of the members where the directors have sworn a statutory declaration of solvency, and creditors' voluntary winding up. In the latter case, there has been no statutory declaration of solvency and the predominant interest of the creditors is recognised.

In a liquidation, certain prior transactions may be re-opened if they are gratuitous alienations, or if they are extortionate credit agreements or if they constitute unfair preferences. Floating charges made in the run up to a liquidation may also be held to be invalid.

If the company has been trading when it was known that it could not pay its debts, those trading will be civilly and possibly criminally liable. Directors and shadow directors may even be civilly liable where they ought to have known that the company could not survive. There are also various areas of liability for officers during a liquidation such as falsification of a company's books, transferring company property during a liquidation, etc.

The suppliers of utility services – gas, water, electricity and telephone – cannot insist on payment of moneys due as a condition for continued service. During the liquidation the liquidator may adopt or repudiate unperformed company contracts but the other contracting party may then seek damages for breach of contract against the company.

There is a set order for payment of debts – liquidation expenses, preferential debts, floating charges, ordinary debts and the deferred debts. If there is a surplus this should be distributed to members taking account of their class rights.

Chapter 24

Company Law – The Future

It is fitting in conclusion to say a little about the future.
Company law reforms like death, taxes and motorway cones
are always in prospect. Somewhat ironically there are two
opposing movements. It is urged for public and especially
listed companies that there should be more regulation and
control. Sometimes greater statutory control is urged,
sometimes more self regulation. The Cadbury Report which is
considered below comes down in favour of the latter approach.
By contrast for small private companies and particularly for
what are called proprietary companies in jurisdictions like
Australia where the directors and the shareholders are the
same, less legislation, fewer formalities and less control are
urged. Len Sealy in *Company Law and Commercial Reality* (1984)
put his finger on the problem a decade ago:

> So again we see repeated the pattern of development in
> company law reform which has been dominant in our
> domestic legislation all this century: a concentration on the
> regulatory aspects of the subject, a constant stepping up of
> the formalities and a continual tightening up of the rules
> and the sanctions. The burden on business can only grow
> and grow as a result, and the demands made on
> accountants and company secretaries are bound to get
> heavier and heavier. But who is sounding the alarm
> signals? Not the Department of Trade. Not the CBI. Not
> the Law Society or any of the other professional bodies.
> Yet there is surely an urgent need to look ahead and take
> note of the storms that are building up, to anticipate the
> otherwise inevitable crisis, to stir up some concern and
> action and devise the best strategy we can to head off
> what is avoidable, and to cope with what is not.

Since Len Sealy wrote that passage we have of course had
consolidation of the Companies Acts into the Companies Act
1985, the Business Names Act 1985, the Company Securities
(Insider Dealing) Act 1985 and the Companies Consolidation
(Consequential Provisions) Act 1985. We have had the
Insolvency Act 1985 consolidated into the Insolvency Act 1986
and the Company Directors Disqualification Act 1986. We
have had the Financial Services Act 1986, the Companies Act
1989 and the Criminal Justice Act 1993. As well as all this there
have been numerous EC Directives, new Table A Articles and

the new set of Insolvency Rules in 1986. Small businessmen have every right to be confused and overwhelmed.

The Department of Trade and Industry issued a consultative document in November 1994 (*Company Law Review: The Law Applicable to Private Companies*) which considered the possibility of reform of the law relating to private companies. The Law Commission also contributed to the review. The review found that, in general, problematic areas of company law did not rank as a high priority for small businesses compared to their other problems. The study found that major problems faced by small businesses were financial, together with administrative burdens and the lack of advice as to how businesses should be structured and run.

Certain areas of company law were identified as causing problems for small companies – directors' responsibilities, processes for dispute resolution, Table A articles, financial assistance for the acquisition of a company's own shares and shareholders' agreements. Since audit and accounting requirements are being considered separately by the DTI the study did not focus on these.

The study did not find a great clamour for a new incorporated limited liability structure for small businesses although it was felt that a reform of partnership law with a statutory draft partnership agreement would be useful.

24.1 The Cadbury Report

The Cadbury Committee under the chairmanship of Sir Adrian Cadbury was to give it its full name the Committee on the Financial Aspects of Corporate Governance. It was set up in May 1991 by the Financial Reporting Council, the London Stock Exchange and the accountancy profession. It adopted as its terms of reference: to consider the following in relation to financial issues arising from financial reporting and accountability and to make recommendations on good practice:

- the responsibilities of executive and non-executive directors for reviewing and reporting on performance to shareholders and other financially interested parties; and the frequency, clarity and form in which information should be provided;

- the case for audit committees of the board, including their composition and role;

- the principal responsibilities of auditors and the extent and value of the audit;

- the links between shareholders, boards and auditors;

- any other relevant matters.

The Cadbury Report in December 1992 attracted considerable attention. The concern about financial reporting and accountability was no doubt heightened by BCCI, Polly Peck and Maxwell.

The Committee's recommendations are for the most part centred upon the control and reporting functions of boards and the role of auditors. This reflects the Committee's main aim which was to review those aspects of corporate governance related to financial reporting and accountability.

At the core of the Committee's recommendations is a Code of Best Practice which is designed to achieve the necessary high standards of corporate behaviour. The London Stock Exchange is to require all listed companies registered in the United Kingdom, as a continuing obligation of listing, to state whether they are complying with the Code and to give reasons for any points of non-compliance.

The Code is thus directed to *listed* companies. The principles upon which the Code is based are principles of openness, integrity and accountability.

Some of the key recommendations of the Committee are incorporated into the Code. Key recommendations are as follows:

- There should be a clearly defined split of responsibilities at the head of a company to ensure a balance of power and authority between executive and independent non-executive directors.

- There should be a schedule of matters specifically reserved for board decision so that it is clear that the company's control and direction are firmly in its hands.

- There should be an agreed procedure for directors in the furtherance of their duties to take independent professional advice if necessary, at the company's expense.

- Ideally, the posts of Chairman and Chief Executive should be kept separate.

- Executive directors' service contracts should not exceed three years.

- Executive directors' pay should be subject to the recommendations of a remuneration committee made up wholly or mainly of non-executive directors.

- Non-executive directors should be appointed for specified

terms and reappointment should not be automatic.

- Non-executive directors should be selected through a formal process and this should be a matter for the board as a whole.

- The board should establish an audit committee of at least three non-executive directors with written terms of reference.

- The directors should report on the effectiveness of the company's internal controls.

- There should be full disclosure of fees paid to audit firms for non audit work.

24.2   Critique

Various criticisms have been made of the Cadbury Committee report. Some have criticised the lack of statutory teeth. This criticism is rejected by Sir Adrian Cadbury who feels that the report has given companies a checklist and shareholders an agenda to improve the effectiveness of corporate governance in Britain. Yet, some of the recommendations do not 'go the whole hog'. Thus it is urged that *generally* there should be a split of the Chairmanship and post of Chief Executive between different people.

Another criticism levelled at the Cadbury Report is that it fails to address itself to long term solutions of encouraging long term incentives for management and a long term view of investment by investment institutions despite its statement in the opening paragraph of the report that:

> The country's economy depends on the drive and efficiency of its companies.

The governance of companies remains a favourite topic of debate. Boardroom pay has been the focus of attention and the Greenbury Committee set up by the CBI recommended in its report that there should be full disclosure in a comprehensive form of all the earnings for all the directors of a company.

Clearly, the best run companies take account not merely of the short term interests of shareholders but also of employees and the wider community. Indeed even pure self-interest would declare that other interests than those of the shareholders in the narrow sense need to be considered.

24.3   Company law into the next century

Other areas of company law have been more recently examined and proposals have followed. The Law Commission has during 1997 published reports suggesting reform of shareholder remedies and the creation of a statutory corporate killing offence. The DTI has issued a consultation paper on the possibility of the creation of a European Company statute (not itself a novel concept). Corporate Governance has been revisited by the Hampel Committee, whose report was published in January 1998. The Stock Exchange and the DTI are now working to develop the Hampel Report in combination with the Cadbury and Greenbury Reports into a new Code of Practice.

Meanwhile, the DTI has published the consultation paper *Modern Company Law for a Competitive Economy* which recognises that today's company law is built on 'foundations which were put in place by the Victorians in the middle of the last century'. It proposes a new type of core Companies Act which should replace the 1985 Act and 'create a framework of company law which is up to date, competitive and designed for the next century; a framework which facilitates enterprise and promotes transparency and fair dealing'.

Whatever happens, it is clear that the new century will not slow down the development of company law.

Company Law – The Future

Whilst small private companies should have some of the burdens placed upon them alleviated, public companies especially listed ones may need to be subject to greater control and regulation. This may be achieved by statutory means or by self-regulation.

Index